Analog Communications
Volume 2

DBC301825

AM / DSB / SSB

Student Manual
26867-00

Printed in Canada

3 0 2 6 8 6 7 0 0 0 4 1 1 D

Lab-Volt ®

ANALOG COMMUNICATIONS
VOLUME 2

AM / DSB / SSB

by
the Staff
of
Lab-Volt (Quebec) Ltd

Legal Deposit – Second Trimester 1985

ISBN 2-89289-056-X

SECOND EDITION, OCTOBER 1986

Printed in Canada
November 2004

Foreword

As communications equipment and technologies evolve to be more sophisticated and complex, the need for modern up-to-date training programs centered around educationally-designed communications systems becomes more acute. Lab-Volt's Analog Communications Training System provides a realistic approach to resolving the situation.

The Model 8080 Analog Communications Training System is designed to introduce students to the fundamentals of AM and FM communications systems. The training modules have been designed to be as realistic and as near as possible to real systems. The operating frequencies and ranges for AM and FM generators and receivers have been chosen to reflect standard radio broadcasting usage. The physical design of the system emphasizes functionality and the individual modules are stackable. Power is supplied through multi-pin connectors located on the top and bottom panels of the modules. The Power Supply / Dual Audio Amplifier module is double-width and forms the physical base for the other system modules. It also assures efficient overvoltage and short-circuit protection for the system.

In keeping with the hands-on approach to student learning, the courseware consists of a three-volume set of exercise material correlated to the 8080 training system. Volume 1 provides an introduction to the instrumentation modules and also introductory coverage of RF communications fundamentals.

Volume 2 deals with the subject of AM (broadcast AM, DSB, SSB), and contains exercises especially designed to demonstrate the parameters associated with this type of modulation.

Volume 3 treats the topic of angle modulation (FM and PM), and provides detailed coverage of fundamental concepts.

Throughout the student manuals, an attempt is made to relate the subject matter to everyday experience. Also, since signal display in the "frequency domain" is essential to understanding communications systems concepts, emphasis is placed upon spectral analysis of the "energy" content of signals using the Spectrum Analyzer module. Correlation between frequency spectrum observations of signals, and their corresponding "time domain" waveforms is stressed as much as possible.

Because of the flexible nature of the courseware, instructors who wish to cover only the subject matter of AM can readily do so by using Volumes 1 and 2, and a partial 8080 training system. For those classes in which students are already familiar with AM, the topic of FM alone may be pursued. In this case, Volumes 1, 3, and a partial training system may be used.

Acknowledgements

We thank the following people from Laval University for their participation in the development of the Analog Communications Instructional Program: John Ahern, M. Sc. A; Gilles Y. Delisle, Ph. D; Michel Lecours, Ph. D; Marcel Pelletier, Ph. D.

Table of contents

Unit 1   Amplitude Modulation Fundamentals

> Basic concepts and terminology used in AM communications. Using the AM equipment.

Exercise 1-1   An AM Communications System

> Definition of basic concepts. Using the AM / DSB / SSB Generator with the AM / DSB Receiver to demonstrate an AM communications system.

Exercise 1-2   Familiarization with the AM Equipment

> Becoming familiar with the AM / DSB / SSB Generator and the AM / DSB Receiver. Time and frequency domain observations of AM signals.

Exercise 1-3   Frequency Conversion of Baseband Signals

> Demonstrating frequency conversion of baseband signals. The concepts of frequency translation and frequency multiplexing.

Unit 2   The Generation of AM Signals

> The generation and analysis of AM signals. Observation and measurement of the parameters associated with AM signals.

Exercise 2-1   An AM Signal

> Using the AM / DSB / SSB Generator and test instruments to demonstrate the characteristics of an AM signal in the time and frequency domains.

Exercise 2-2   Percentage Modulation

> Definition of percentage modulation and methods used to determine the modulation index of an AM signal. Linear and nonlinear overmodulation.

Exercise 2-3   Carrier and Sideband Power

> Demonstrating how the total RF power is divided between the RF carrier and the AM sidebands. Using the Spectrum Analyzer and the True RMS Voltmeter / Power Meter to determine the power distribution directly. Transmission efficiency.

Introduction

The Lab-Volt® Model 8080 Analog Communications Training System is designed for multi-level training in analog communications. The training system consists of six instrumentation modules and six training modules. The training modules are divided into two groups, AM communications modules and FM communications modules, with the instrumentation modules supporting both groups.

In this volume — Volume 2 AM / DSB / SSB — the subject matter of Amplitude Modulation is examined. Students can quickly set up an operable AM communications system without any prior knowledge of such a system. The major functional blocks are silk-screened on the module front panels, to allow the student to become aware of major system functions and controls. Copies of the front panels are included in Appendix C of the manual.

Most major inputs and outputs to the system functional blocks are readily accessible at the front panel of each module, and it is simply a matter of connecting a BNC cable in order to observe the desired signal.

Also contained within each of the AM communications modules are a large number of test points, which are accessed through the hinged door on top of the module. The test points facilitate troubleshooting for the switch-insertable faults located in each of the modules. More-detailed functional block diagrams, showing the location of module test points, are included in the appendices of the manual.

Each unit of instruction consists of several exercises designed to present material in convenient instructional segments. Principles and concepts are presented first and hands-on procedures augment the written material to involve and better acquaint the student with each module. There is a five-question review section requiring brief written answers at the end of each exercise. Suggested answers for these questions, as well as those found in the exercise procedures are included in the appendices of the manual. Each unit terminates with a ten-question multiple choice test to verify the knowledge gained in the unit.

Performing the Analog Communications Courseware Using the Lab-Volt Data Acquisition and Management System (LVDAM-COM)

The courseware provided with the Analog Communications Training System, Model 8080, consists of a series of laboratory exercises. These exercises have been designed to be performed using Lab-Volt conventional instruments (Frequency Counter, True RMS Voltmeter/ Power Meter, Spectrum Analyzer, and an oscilloscope). The exercises can also be carried out using the Lab-Volt Data Acquisition and Management System (LVDAM-COM), which consists of the Virtual Test Equipment Interface, Model 9407, and the corresponding LVDAM software. When performing the Analog Communications courseware exercises with the LVDAM-COM System, the following guidelines must be taken into account:

- In all module arrangements, the Oscilloscope, the Spectrum Analyzer, the Frequency Counter, and the True RMS Voltmeter/ Power Meter are replaced with the Virtual Test Equipment Interface. Signals applied to the inputs of the Virtual Test Equipment Interface are observed on the computer screen using the LVDAM-COM Virtual instruments.

- Some exercises require setting the Oscilloscope in X-Y mode. With the Oscilloscope of the Virtual Test Equipment Interface, you might have to change the timebase of the X-Y mode to get accurate readings.

- Some exercises require setting the Frequency Counter to either the 10 Hz -10 MHz, or the 10 MHz - 200 MHz frequency range. This frequency range selection is done automatically by the Virtual Test Equipment Interface.

- Some exercises require using the controls in the "Zero adjust" section to adjust the conventional True RMS Voltmeter / Power Meter. This adjustment is obsolete because the True RMS Voltmeter of the Virtual Test Equipment Interface is self adjusting.

- Some exercises suggest re-adjusting the conventional Spectrum Analyzer periodically to correct for central frequency shift caused by VCO drift. In the Spectrum Analyzer of the Virtual Test Equipment Interface, the VCO drift is computer compensated, thus the new Spectrum Analyzer does not require central frequency re-adjustment. The markers have also been eliminated.

- Some exercises require setting the OUTPUT LEVEL knob of the conventional Spectrum Analyzer to the CAL. position. The equivalent setting for the virtual Spectrum Analyzer is to turn the AMPLITUDE ADJUST knob in LVDAM-COM fully counterclockwise.

Finally, it is strongly recommended that you read the User Manual of the Virtual Test Equipment Interface before going further. This manual explains many new useful features that have been added to the Virtual Test Equipment Interface.

Performing the Communications Courseware Using the Latest Versions of the Dual Function Generator and True RMS Voltmeter / Power Meter

A. Dual Function Generator, Model 9402-00 versus Model 9402-10

Completion of the exercises in this manual requires a Lab-Volt Dual Function Generator, Model 9402-**00** or 9402-**10**. These two models provide the same signals, but have different front panel controls. The manipulations in the hands-on exercises of the Communications courseware have been written for the Model 9402-**00** Dual Function Generator. If you perform the exercises using the Model 9402-**10** Dual Function Generator, please take note of the following differences between the front panel controls of these two models of the Dual Function Generator (refer to Figures 1 and 2 which show the front panels of the two models).

1. The display of the Model 9402-**10** Dual Function Generator not only indicates the frequency of the signal produced by channel A or B (as on the Model 9402-**00** Dual Function Generator), but also various settings related to this channel.

2. The A and B channel-selection push buttons on Model 9402-**00** are replaced with a single A/B selection push button on Model 9402-**10**. The A/B selection push button allows selection between channels A and B of the Dual Function Generator. The other channel is selected whenever the A/B button is depressed. The function, frequency range, and attenuator settings of the selected channel are indicated in the display of the Model 9402-**10** Dual Function Generator. When displayed, these settings can be modified using the FUNCTION, FREQUENCY RANGE, and ATTENUATOR push buttons

3. The sine-wave, square-wave, triangle-wave, sawtooth-wave, and pulse FUNCTION selection push buttons of channels A and B on Model 9402-**00** are replaced with a single FUNCTION selection push button on Model 9402-**10**, that is common to both channels. The FUNCTION selection button is used in conjunction with the A/B channel selection push button to select the function of each channel. The function selected is indicated by a symbol in the display of the Model 9402-**10** Dual Function Generator.

4. The 100-Hz, 1-kHz, 10-kHz, and 100-kHz FREQUENCY RANGE selection push buttons of channels A and B on Model 9402-**00** are replaced with a single FREQUENCY RANGE selection push button on Model 9402-**10**, that is common to both channels. The FREQUENCY RANGE selection button is used in conjunction with the A/B channel selection push button to select the frequency range of each channel. The frequency range selected is indicated in the display of the Model 9402-**10** Dual Function Generator.

Performing the Communications Courseware Using the Latest Versions of the Dual Function Generator and True RMS Voltmeter / Power Meter

5. The 0-dB, 20-dB, and 40-dB ATTENUATOR selection push buttons of channels A and B on Model 9402-**00** are replaced with a single ATTENUATOR selection push button on Model 9402-**10**, that is common to both channels. The ATTENUATOR selection button is used in conjunction with the A/B channel selection push button to select the attenuator of each channel. The attenuator selected is indicated in the display of the Model 9402-**10** Dual Function Generator.

6. The control knobs used to set the durations of the pulse signals of channels A and B are referred to as the PULSE DURATION control knobs on the Model 9402-**10** Dual Function Generator.

7. Independent FREQUENCY and OUTPUT LEVEL control knobs for channels A and B are still provided. However, their positions on the front panel have changed.

8. When the frequency is set to 100.00 kHz or more, the display on the Model 9402-**10** Dual Function Generator does not flash as is the case on the Model 9402-**00** Dual Function Generator.

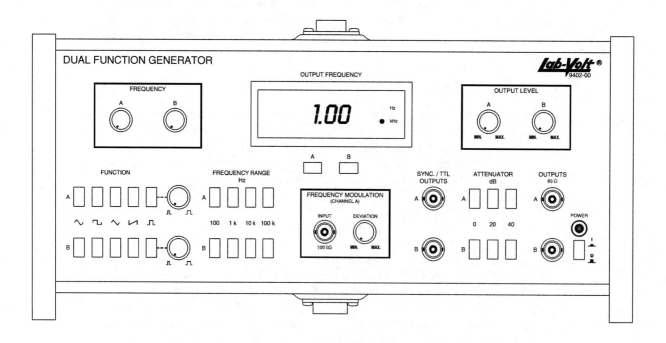

Figure 1. Front panel of the Dual Function Generator, Model 9402-00.

Performing the Communications Courseware
Using the Latest Versions of the Dual Function Generator
and True RMS Voltmeter / Power Meter

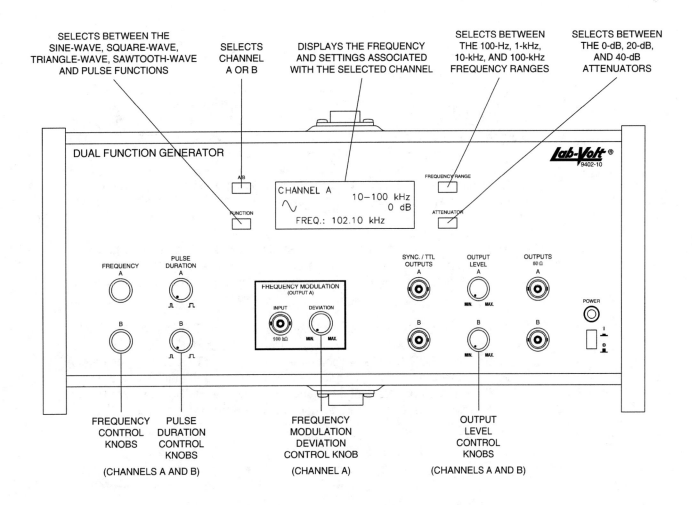

SELECTS BETWEEN THE
SINE-WAVE, SQUARE-WAVE,
TRIANGLE-WAVE, SAWTOOTH-WAVE
AND PULSE FUNCTIONS

SELECTS
CHANNEL
A OR B

DISPLAYS THE FREQUENCY
AND SETTINGS ASSOCIATED
WITH THE SELECTED CHANNEL

SELECTS BETWEEN
THE 100-Hz, 1-kHz,
10-kHz, AND 100-kHz
FREQUENCY RANGES

SELECTS BETWEEN
THE 0-dB, 20-dB,
AND 40-dB
ATTENUATORS

DUAL FUNCTION GENERATOR

A/B

FUNCTION

CHANNEL A
10–100 kHz
0 dB
FREQ.: 102.10 kHz

FREQUENCY RANGE

ATTENUATOR

Lab-Volt ®
9402-10

FREQUENCY
A

PULSE
DURATION
A

B

B

FREQUENCY MODULATION
(OUTPUT A)

INPUT

DEVIATION

100 kΩ

MIN.   MAX.

SYNC. / TTL
OUTPUTS
A

OUTPUT
LEVEL
A

OUTPUTS
50 Ω
A

POWER

MIN.   MAX.

B

B

B

FREQUENCY
CONTROL
KNOBS

PULSE
DURATION
CONTROL
KNOBS

(CHANNELS A AND B)

FREQUENCY
MODULATION
DEVIATION
CONTROL KNOB

(CHANNEL A)

OUTPUT
LEVEL
CONTROL
KNOBS

(CHANNELS A AND B)

Figure 2. Front panel of the Dual Function Generator, Model 9402-10.

Performing the Communications Courseware
Using the Latest Versions of the Dual Function Generator
and True RMS Voltmeter / Power Meter

B. True RMS Voltmeter / Power Meter, Model 9404-00 versus Model 9404-10

Completion of the exercises in this manual requires a Lab-Volt True RMS Voltmeter / Power Meter, Model 9404-**00** or 9404-**10**. These two models are very similar except for a few minor changes. The manipulations in the hands-on exercises of the Communications courseware have been written for the Model 9404-**00** True RMS Voltmeter / Power Meter. If you perform the exercises using the Model 9404-**10** True RMS Voltmeter / Power Meter, please take note of the following differences between these two models of the True RMS Voltmeter / Power Meter (refer to Figures 3 and 4 which show the front panels of the two models).

1. The 100 V (+53 dBm) range on the Model 9404-**00** True RMS Voltmeter / Power Meter is not available on the Model 9404-**10**, True RMS Voltmeter / Power Meter. This range is not required to complete the hand-on exercises in this manual.

2. A ZERO ADJUST knob is provided on the Model 9404-**00** True RMS Voltmeter / Power Meter to manually zero the unit before taking measurements. There is no ZERO ADJUST knob on the Model 9404-**10** True RMS Voltmeter / Power Meter, because zero adjustment is performed automatically by the unit. An LED on the front panel of the Model 9404-**10** True RMS Voltmeter / Power Meter lights up whenever zero adjustment is performed.

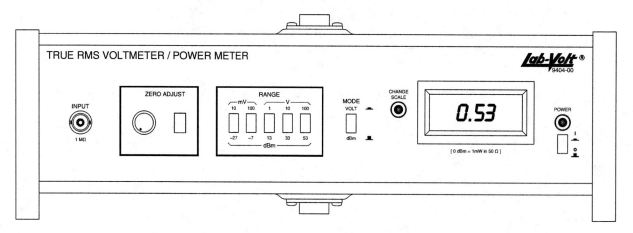

Figure 3. Front Panel of the True RMS Voltmeter / Power Meter, Model 9404-00.

Performing the Communications Courseware
Using the Latest Versions of the Dual Function Generator
and True RMS Voltmeter / Power Meter

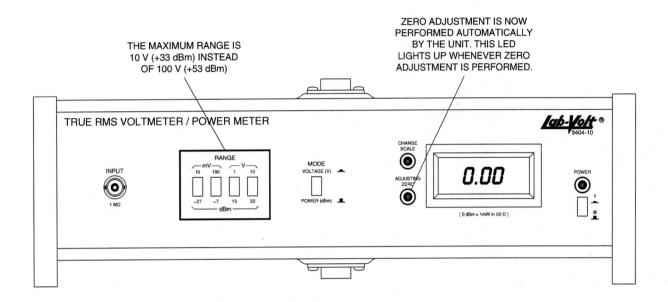

Figure 4. Front Panel of the True RMS Voltmeter / Power Meter, Model 9404-10.

Parts List

The following equipment is required to perform the exercises in the manual.

DESCRIPTION	MODEL
Accessories	8948
Power Supply / Dual Audio Amplifier	9401
Dual Function Generator	9402
Frequency Counter	9403
True RMS Voltmeter / Power Meter	9404
Spectrum Analyzer	9405
RF / Noise Generator	9406
AM / DSB / SSB Generator	9410
AM / DSB Receiver	9411
SSB Receiver	9412

The 8948 Accessories consist of:

QTY	DESCRIPTION	PART NUMBER
1	Folded Dipole	26491
4	BNC T-connector	26851
2	50 Ω Resistive Load (BNC terminated)	26852
1	Stereo Headphones	26853
8	Coaxial Cable BNC/BNC (75 cm)	26854
4	Coaxial Cable BNC/BNC (120 cm)	26854-1
6	Coaxial Cable BNC/BNC (30 cm)	26854-2
2	Telescopic Antenna	27035
2	Wire Antenna	27194

Additional Equipment

The completion of the exercises in this manual require a dual-trace oscilloscope with a bandwidth of 20 MHz (Lab-Volt® Model 797 or equivalent).

Amplitude Modulation Fundamentals

UNIT OBJECTIVE

When you have completed this unit, you will be familiar with basic concepts and terminology used in AM communications.

DISCUSSION OF FUNDAMENTALS

Many of you are familiar with the terms *Amplitude Modulation* (AM) and *Frequency Modulation* (FM). In order to understand AM and FM, auxiliary concepts dealing with **frequency conversion (translation), modulation**, and others are necessary. This unit will provide the background material helpful to understanding these concepts.

The examination of signals in both the time and frequency domains is fundamental. However, it is frequency domain analysis which is more useful in analyzing radio communication signals.

This kind of analysis is accomplished using the Spectrum Analyzer module, and becoming familiar and comfortable with its use and operation is important. The exercises in this unit will permit you to review and practice your skills with this instrument.

As far as theory is concerned, it will be sufficient for the time being to remember that *a pure sine wave is represented by a single, discrete line in the frequency domain*. This discrete line occurs at the frequency of the sine wave as shown in Figure 1-1. As you proceed with the exercises of this volume, you will see that real equipment and signals contain harmonics of the fundamental frequency. When these harmonics are much smaller in amplitude than the fundamental, they can usually be ignored.

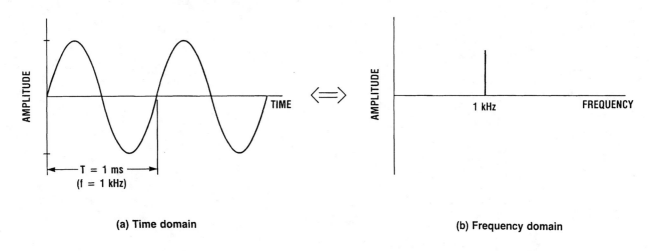

(a) Time domain

(b) Frequency domain

Figure 1-1. Representation of a sine wave in the time and frequency domains.

Amplitude Modulation Fundamentals

NEW TERMS AND WORDS

baseband — the band of frequencies occupied by a message signal.

carrier — a high frequency radio wave which is modulated by a message signal to "carry" information between distant points.

envelope — the curve drawn to enclose the peaks and valleys of an AM waveform. Its shape corresponds to the message signal.

f_c — the symbol used for the RF carrier wave frequency.

f_m — the symbol used for the message signal frequency.

frequency conversion (translation) — the process of displacing the frequency contents of a signal to another place in the frequency spectrum.

frequency spectrum — a range of frequencies in the frequency domain. In spectral analysis, the frequency spectrum of a signal is the set of lines showing the different frequencies present in the signal along with their amplitudes.

message — the term used to identify the information, or intelligence signal; also referred to as the modulating signal.

mixer (multiplier) — a circuit that generates output frequencies equal to the sum and difference of two input frequencies. (This functional element multiplies time domain signals, which corresponds to frequency translation in the frequency domain).

modulation — the process of modifying some characteristic of a carrier wave (amplitude, phase, or frequency), so that it varies in accordance with the message signal.

sidebands — the frequency components generated on each side of the RF carrier wave after it is modulated.

An AM Communications System

EXERCISE OBJECTIVE

When you have completed this exercise, you will be able to demonstrate an AM communications system using the AM / DSB / SSB Generator and the AM / DSB Receiver.

DISCUSSION

If you were asked to define communication, you would probably say that it had to do with the exchange of information. This is essentially what communication is, and it is for this purpose that communications systems exist. A more precise definition of communication would be that it is the transfer of information from one place, or person, to another. A block diagram representation of a basic communications system is shown in Figure 1-2.

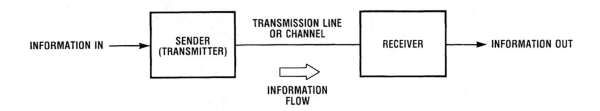

Figure 1-2. A basic communications system.

The essential parts of the system as shown, are the sender or transmitter, the transmission line, and the receiver. The direction of information flow is from sender to receiver, which indicates why the terms transmitter and receiver are used. This system, however, is unidirectional. For a complete communications system to exist, we must have the same equipment operating in the opposite direction. Otherwise, the one who receives the information cannot make his response known to the sender. This is generally taken for granted in the study of communications systems, and not often mentioned.

Now that the concept of a communications system has been defined, let us define electronic communications. It is based on the use of electrical energy to transmit information. Since electrical energy can travel nearly as fast as light, communication is almost instantaneous. The original form of the information (sounds, images) must be converted to electrical signals, which are then transmitted directly over wires, or radiated through the air as electromagnetic radio waves. These signals are picked up by the receiver and reconverted to their original form so that the information can be understood.

An AM Communications System

In order to transmit information using radio waves, a way must be found to add the information to the radio signal. This process is called *modulation*, and the three principal forms of modulation found in analog communications are amplitude modulation, frequency modulation, and phase modulation. It is either the amplitude, the frequency, or the phase of the radio signal that is made to change in accordance with the information signal. The information signal is generally a low frequency audio signal in the case of AM.

EQUIPMENT REQUIRED

DESCRIPTION	MODEL
Accessories	8948
Power Supply / Dual Audio Amplifier	9401
Dual Function Generator	9402
Frequency Counter	9403
AM / DSB / SSB Generator	9410
AM / DSB Receiver	9411
Oscilloscope	—

PROCEDURE

☐ 1. Set up the modules as shown in Figure 1-3. Make sure that all OUTPUT LEVEL and GAIN controls are turned fully counterclockwise to the MIN position, and power up the equipment.

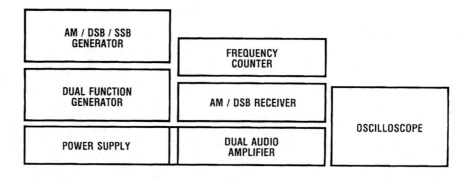

Figure 1-3. Suggested Module Arrangement.

☐ 2. Adjust the channel A controls on the Dual Function Generator as follows:

FUNCTION	: Sine wave
FREQUENCY RANGE	: 10 kHz
OUTPUT FREQUENCY display	: A
FREQUENCY knob	: Adjust for 2 kHz
ATTENUATOR	: 20 dB
OUTPUT LEVEL knob	: ¼ turn cw

An AM Communications System

The low frequency signal now present at OUTPUT A will be used as the input for the AM communications system. What does it represent?

_____

☐ 3. Use a BNC / BNC cable to connect the AM / DSB RF OUTPUT of the AM / DSB / SSB Generator to the Frequency Counter. Turn the CARRIER LEVEL and RF GAIN knobs to MAX. *Make sure that the CARRIER LEVEL knob is pushed in to the LINEAR OVERMODULATION position.*

Note: *The RF GAIN referred to in this exercise is the AM / DSB RF GAIN (amplifier A₂).*

Adjust the RF TUNING control to obtain a radio signal (carrier) frequency of 1000 kHz.

What does the 1000-kHz signal represent?

_____

_____

☐ 4. Adjust the RF GAIN control on the AM / DSB / SSB Generator to one-quarter turn clockwise.

Disconnect the Frequency Counter and connect the AM / DSB RF OUTPUT to the 50 Ω RF INPUT of the AM / DSB Receiver.

Which part of the communications system is represented by the cable connecting the AM / DSB / SSB Generator to the AM / DSB Receiver?

_____

_____

☐ 5. Use a BNC / BNC cable to connect the Frequency Counter to OSC OUTPUT on the receiver. Turn the receiver's RF TUNING knob to obtain a reading of 1455 kHz. You are now "tuned in" to the broadcasting frequency of the transmitter. In a later exercise, you will learn why the RF TUNING control is set at 1455 kHz instead of 1000 kHz.

☐ 6. Depress the SYNC DETECTOR switch on the AM / DSB Receiver, and turn on the AGC (I position).

☐ 7. Now all that is missing from the communications system is an information signal. Use a BNC / BNC cable to connect OUTPUT A of the Dual Function Generator to the AUDIO INPUT of the AM / DSB / SSB Generator.

An AM Communications System

☐ 8. Use a BNC / BNC cable to connect the AUDIO OUTPUT of the receiver to one of the AUDIO INPUTS on the Dual Audio Amplifier. Place the speaker disconnect switch in the off (O) position and plug the headphones into one of the jacks (terminal 5 or 6).

Turn the appropriate GAIN control (A_1 or A_2) clockwise, and adjust for a comfortable listening level.

What do you hear in the headphones?

_____

_____

_____

Note: *If you want to have the sound in both earpieces at the same time, place a BNC T-connector at the input terminal (1 or 2) of the channel you are using. Use a BNC / BNC cable to connect the remaining side of the T-connector to the other AUDIO INPUT. Adjust both A_1 and A_2 GAIN controls to obtain the same listening level in both earpieces.*

☐ 9. Vary the frequency of the audio signal with the FREQUENCY control on the Dual Function Generator.

What happens to the sound you hear in the headphones?

_____

_____

☐ 10. Disconnect the cable between the AM / DSB Receiver and the Dual Audio Amplifier.

Disconnect the Frequency Counter from OSC OUTPUT and connect it to the AUDIO OUTPUT of the receiver. Vary the Channel A FREQUENCY control on the generator and compare the readings on the displays of both modules. What do you observe?

_____

_____

_____

☐ 11. Readjust the frequency of the information signal to 2 kHz and use the oscilloscope to compare the waveforms of the original and recovered signals. Using a BNC T-connector at OUTPUT A of the Dual Function Generator, apply the original information signal to channel 1 of the oscilloscope.

An AM Communications System

Disconnect the Frequency Counter and connect the recovered signal to channel 2. Adjust the oscilloscope controls to display several periods of the waveforms. Set the waveforms one above the other, and sketch both in Figure 1-4.

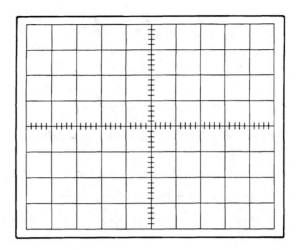

Figure 1-4. Original and recovered information signal waveforms.

How do the waveforms compare?

_____

_____

_____

_____

☐ 12. To verify if you can hear any difference in the sound of both signals, apply each signal to different channels of the Dual Audio Amplifier.

Disconnect channels 1 and 2 of the oscilloscope, and connect each cable to one of the channels of the Dual Audio Amplifier.

Use the headphones and adjust the A_1 and A_2 GAIN controls to obtain the same listening level in both earpieces.

Describe the difference in sound between both signals.

_____

_____

_____

☐ 13. Turn all OUTPUT LEVEL and GAIN controls to the MIN position. Place all power switches in the off (O) position and disconnect all cables.

CONCLUSION

A communications system must be capable of transferring desired information from one location to another. When the received information is reproduced, it must resemble as closely as possible the original information, and all parts of the communications system play a role in this.

REVIEW QUESTIONS

1. What are the principal parts of a communications system?

    _____

    _____

    _____

2. Describe briefly what is meant by electronic communications.

    _____

    _____

    _____

3. What are the three principal forms of modulation used in analog communications?

    _____

    _____

    _____

4. What name is given to the process of adding an information signal to a radio wave?

    ☐ Communication   ☐ Modulation   ☐ Transmission

5. If the original information signal sent over the AM communications system is a 3-kHz sine wave, what signal frequency would you expect to obtain at the audio output of the AM receiver?

    _____

    Why? _____

    _____

Familiarization with the AM Equipment

EXERCISE OBJECTIVE

When you have completed this exercise, you will be familiar with the AM / DSB / SSB Generator and the AM / DSB Receiver, as well as terminology used in amplitude modulation.

DISCUSSION

Modulation is the process of adding information, also called intelligence, to a high frequency radio wave for communication over long distances. This process depends on the type of modulation used, but in general, the amplitude of the information signal is used to vary the amplitude, phase, or frequency of the radio wave. In this manual, the information signal will be referred to as the **message**, which is usually a low frequency audio signal in the 20 Hz to 20 kHz range. The radio frequency (RF) signal is known as the **carrier**, and the frequencies of the message and the RF carrier are symbolized by f_m and f_c respectively.

In amplitude modulation, the amplitude of the carrier wave is made to vary in accordance with the message signal. The waveform of a typical AM signal is shown in Figure 1-5. It represents a high frequency carrier modulated by a sine wave. Notice the dashed curve drawn through the peaks and valleys of the AM waveform. This is called the **envelope** and it is *identical* to the waveform of the *message signal*.

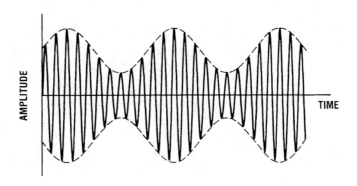

Figure 1-5. A typical AM signal.

Familiarization with the AM Equipment

When the RF carrier wave is amplitude modulated, **sidebands** (or sideband frequencies) are produced. For a 2-kHz tone that modulates a 1000 kHz (1 MHz) carrier, the sideband frequencies are $f_C + f_m = 1\,002\,000$ Hz, and $f_C - f_m = 998\,000$ Hz. Figure 1-6 shows the frequency components of the AM signal.

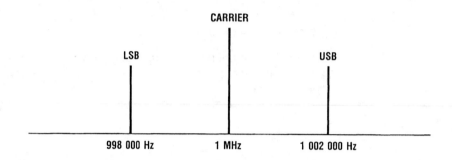

Figure 1-6. Frequency components of an AM signal.

If the transmitted message signal is the human voice, which contains frequencies between 200 Hz and 3 kHz, the sidebands generated on each side of the carrier occupy a range of frequencies equal to the one occupied by the message signal. In this particular case, each sideband is $3000 - 200 = 2800$ Hz wide. The sidebands are known as the *upper sideband* and the *lower sideband* (*USB* and *LSB* respectively). For a 1000 kHz carrier, the LSB ranges from 997 000 to 999 800 Hz, and the USB ranges from 1 000 200 to 1 003 000 Hz. Figure 1-7 shows the sidebands generated in AM voice communications.

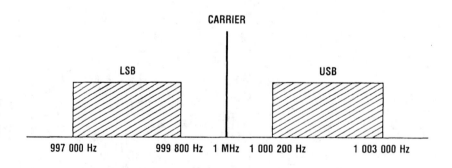

Figure 1-7. AM sidebands generated in voice communications.

Note: *This exercise is relatively long and is divided into two parts – time domain observations and frequency domain observations. Both parts deal essentially with the same phenomena, but they provide different ways of looking at them. If alloted laboratory time is insufficient for completion of the exercise in one session, two consecutive lab periods can be used. In such a case, it is recommended that students review the time-domain-observations section for 10-15 minutes before starting the second section.*

Familiarization with the AM Equipment

EQUIPMENT REQUIRED

DESCRIPTION	MODEL
Accessories	8948
Power Supply / Dual Audio Amplifier	9401
Dual Function Generator	9402
Frequency Counter	9403
Spectrum Analyzer	9405
AM / DSB / SSB Generator	9410
AM / DSB Receiver	9411
Oscilloscope	—

PROCEDURE

Time Domain Observations

☐ 1. Set up the modules as shown in Figure 1-8. Make sure that all OUTPUT LEVEL and GAIN controls are turned fully counterclockwise to the MIN position, and power up the equipment.

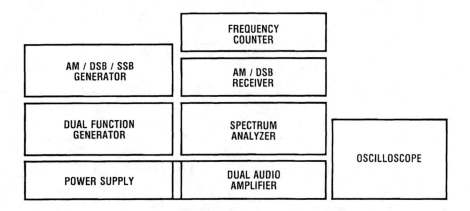

Figure 1-8. Suggested Module Arrangement.

☐ 2. Use a BNC / BNC cable to connect the AM / DSB RF OUTPUT of the AM / DSB / SSB Generator to the oscilloscope. *Make sure that the CARRIER LEVEL knob is pushed in to the LINEAR OVERMODULATION position.* Set the CARRIER LEVEL and the RF GAIN controls to MAX.

Note: *The RF GAIN referred to in this exercise is the AM / DSB RF GAIN (amplifier A_2).*

Familiarization with the AM Equipment

Vary the RF TUNING control and describe its effect on the waveform displayed on the oscilloscope.

_____

_____

_____

☐ 3. Using a BNC T-connector, connect the Frequency Counter to read the frequency of the RF carrier signal at the AM / DSB RF OUTPUT.

What are the upper and lower frequency limits you obtain when you vary the RF TUNING control between its maximum ccw and cw positions.

f_{lower} = _____ kHz f_{upper} = _____ kHz

☐ 4. Adjust the RF TUNING control to obtain a carrier frequency of 1000 kHz. Vary the CARRIER LEVEL control, and then the RF GAIN control between MIN and MAX. Describe the effect the controls have on the waveform displayed on the oscilloscope.

_____

_____

_____

_____

☐ 5. Connect OUTPUT A of the Dual Function Generator to the oscilloscope and select the sine wave function for channel A. Adjust the controls to obtain a 2-kHz signal with a peak-to-peak amplitude of 400 mV.

☐ 6. Inject this 2-kHz message signal at the AUDIO INPUT of the AM / DSB / SSB Generator, and turn the CARRIER LEVEL and RF GAIN controls to MAX. Set the oscilloscope to observe several periods of the message signal. (Remember, the envelope is identical to the waveform of the message signal). Sketch the resulting waveform in Figure 1-9. It should resemble the one shown at the left.

If you have difficulty with synchronization, connect the SYNC / TTL output from Generator A to the EXT TRIG input on the scope and select the EXT TRIG mode.

Familiarization with the AM Equipment

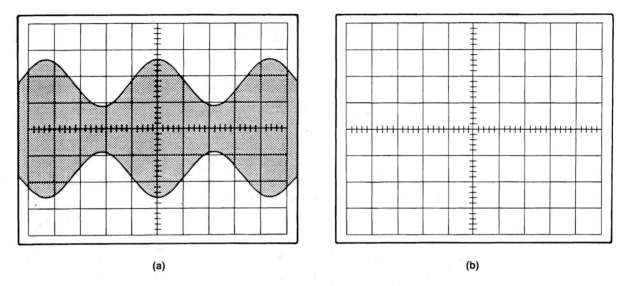

(a)   (b)

Figure 1-9. A 1000-kHz carrier modulated by a 2-kHz sine wave.

☐ 7. Vary the RF GAIN control. Is the effect similar to that obtained in step 4?

☐ Yes   ☐ No

Explain._____

_____

_____

☐ 8. Vary the CARRIER LEVEL control between MIN and MAX and describe what happens.

_____

_____

_____

The changes in the AM waveform are a result of overmodulation, which occurs when the amplitude of the message signal becomes larger than the carrier wave amplitude. This will be covered in a later laboratory exercise.

☐ 9. Return both controls to the MAX position and vary the frequency of the sine wave between 1 kHz and 10 kHz. What change does this cause in the AM waveform?

_____

_____

_____

Familiarization with the AM Equipment

☐ 10. Readjust the frequency of the sine wave to 2 kHz and set the RF GAIN control to one-quarter turn clockwise.

☐ 11. Disconnect the Frequency Counter and connect the AM / DSB RF OUT-PUT of the AM generator to the 50 Ω RF INPUT of the AM / DSB Receiver. Use a BNC / BNC cable to connect the AUDIO OUTPUT of the receiver to one of the AUDIO INPUTS of the Dual Audio Amplifier.

Plug in the headphones and turn the appropriate GAIN control (A_1 or A_2) clockwise for a comfortable listening level. Make sure that the speaker disconnect switch is in the off (O) position.

☐ 12. Connect the Frequency Counter to the local oscillator output (OSC OUTPUT) on the AM receiver. Depress the SYNC DETECTOR switch on the module and turn on the AGC (I position). Turn the receiver's RF TUNING control until the Frequency Counter reads 1455 kHz. You should now be "tuned in to the broadcast", and hear the 2-kHz tone. Fine tune the receiver until the signal is loudest and record the local oscillator frequency (f_{LO}). Note that f_{LO} may have changed slightly, but it should be in the range of 1450-1460 kHz.

$$f_{LO} (f_C = 1000 \text{ kHz}) = \underline{\hspace{1cm}} \text{ kHz}$$

The local oscillator is designed to provide an output frequency equal to the carrier frequency plus the intermediate frequency (IF), or the carrier frequency minus the IF. This depends on the particular receiver, but the incoming RF signal is generally displaced to a lower intermediate frequency and satisfies one or the other of the following relationships:

$$f_{LO} = f_C + f_{IF} \qquad \text{or} \qquad f_{LO} = f_C - f_{IF}$$

In the Analog Communications Training System, *it is the sum of f_C and f_{IF} that is used and f_{IF} is 455 kHz.*

☐ 13. Determine f_{LO} for a carrier frequency of 1510 kHz.

$$f_{LO} (f_C = 1510 \text{ kHz}) = \underline{\hspace{1cm}} \text{ kHz}$$

☐ 14. Disconnect the Frequency Counter from OSC OUTPUT, and connect it to terminal 6 (AM / DSB RF OUTPUT) on the AM generator module in place of the AM receiver.

Temporarily disconnect the AUDIO INPUT signal, and turn the AM generator's RF GAIN to MAX. Adjust the RF TUNING control to obtain a carrier frequency of 1100 kHz.

Familiarization with the AM Equipment

☐ 15. Readjust the RF GAIN to one-quarter turn cw. Reconnect the message signal to the AUDIO INPUT, and the AM / DSB RF OUTPUT to the 50 Ω RF INPUT of the receiver.

Retune the receiver to pick up this new broadcast, and then measure and record the frequency at OSC OUTPUT.

f_{LO} (f_c = 1100 kHz) = _____ kHz

☐ 16. Calculate $f_{LO} - f_c$ for steps 12 and 15.

$f_{LO} - f_c$ (step 12) = _____ kHz

$f_{LO} - f_c$ (step 15) = _____ kHz

Explain the results.

_____

_____

_____

Frequency Domain Observations

In this section of the exercise, you will observe many of the same things seen in the first section. However, when you have learned to correctly interpret the results, you will discover that frequency domain observations are more useful because they provide a clearer picture of what is happening.

☐ 17. If this is the second lab session allocated for the exercise, complete the following connections and adjustments for the AM communications system. If not, go directly to step 18.

    a. Execute Procedure Step 1.
    b. Adjust RF TUNING to obtain f_c = 1100 kHz.
    c. Set CARRIER LEVEL at MAX, and RF GAIN at ¼ turn cw.
    d. Inject 2-kHz sine wave at 400 mV p-p into AUDIO INPUT.
    e. Connect AM / DSB / SSB Generator to AM / DSB Receiver and tune the receiver to obtain 1555 kHz at OSC OUTPUT.

☐ 18. Disconnect channels 1 and 2 of the oscilloscope, and then set up and calibrate the Spectrum Analyzer around 1.1 MHz using the procedure given in Appendix E.

Familiarization with the AM Equipment

☐ 19. Set the Spectrum Analyzer controls to the positions indicated below:

MARKERS	: O
INPUT	: 50 Ω
MAXIMUM INPUT	: 0 dBm
FREQUENCY RANGE	: 0-30 MHz
FREQUENCY SPAN	: 1 MHz / V
OUTPUT SCALE	: LOG
OUTPUT LEVEL	: CAL
MEMory	: A
MODE	: LIVE
PLOTTER	: SCOPE (both switches)

☐ 20. Connect the AM / DSB output of the AM / DSB / SSB Generator to the INPUT of the Spectrum Analyzer. Turn the TUNING controls of the Spectrum Analyzer to position the 1100-kHz broadcast frequency in the center of the oscilloscope screen.

☐ 21. Depress the 200, 50, 10 and 2 kHz / V FREQUENCY SPAN switches successively, and retune the Spectrum Analyzer as necessary to keep the 1100-kHz frequency in the center of the screen. What changes take place in the oscilloscope display as you change the frequency span?

_____

_____

_____

_____

☐ 22. Vary the CARRIER LEVEL control on the AM generator between MIN and MAX. What happens to the carrier displayed on the screen?

_____

_____

_____

☐ 23. Return the CARRIER LEVEL control to the MAX position and vary the RF GAIN control between the MIN and one-half positions. How does the Spectrum Analyzer display change to indicate the different power levels?

_____

_____

_____

Familiarization with the AM Equipment

☐ 24. Return the RF GAIN control to the one-quarter position.

Knowing that each division on the screen represents 2 kHz, and that the sidebands are located at $f_c + f_m$ and $f_c - f_m$, record the values of the sideband frequencies as they appear on the oscilloscope screen.

$f_{USB} =$ _____ kHz $f_{LSB} =$ _____ kHz

How do these values compare with the theoretical values?

_____

_____

_____

☐ 25. Vary the frequency of the message signal between 1 kHz and 10 kHz. What happens on the Spectrum Analyzer display?

_____

_____

_____

☐ 26. Return to the 1 MHz span and vary the AM generator's RF TUNING control over its complete range. According to the Spectrum Analyzer, what is the approximate range of the AM / DSB / SSB Generator?

The approximate range is _____ kHz to _____ kHz.

☐ 27. Readjust the carrier to approximately 1 MHz, and then vary the AM generator's RF GAIN control between MIN and MAX. Do other frequencies, at intervals of 1 MHz, appear?

☐ Yes   ☐ No

These frequencies, which are harmonics of the carrier frequency, are a natural result of frequency mixing and amplification, and their level must be strictly controlled. As you can see, the strongest harmonic of the carrier frequency is about 35 dB below the fundamental – a power ratio of more than 3100, and within acceptable standards for the power involved. Note that these harmonics are undetectable in the time domain, but easily seen in the frequency domain with a Spectrum Analyzer.

☐ 28. Turn all OUTPUT LEVEL and GAIN controls to the MIN position. Place all power switches in the off (O) position and disconnect all cables.

Familiarization with the AM Equipment

CONCLUSION

This exercise has allowed you to become familiar with the concept of amplitude modulation, and to visualize clearly its representation in both the time and frequency domains. Using various tuning and level controls on the equipment, you have demonstrated that frequency domain observations allow us to "see" more clearly the different parts of a communications signal.

REVIEW QUESTIONS

1. What is amplitude modulation?

   _____

   _____

   _____

   _____

2. Sketch an AM waveform in the space below, as well as its representation in the frequency domain. Label clearly the carrier, envelope, USB and LSB.

3. What are the USB and LSB frequencies for a 960-kHz carrier modulated by a 3-kHz sine wave?

   f_{USB} = _____ kHz f_{LSB} = _____ kHz

4. What are the two equations showing the relationships between f_{LO} , f_C , and f_{IF} ?

   _____

   _____

5. Which is more useful for the analysis of communications signals, time domain observations or frequency domain observations? Explain.

   _____

   _____

   _____

Frequency Conversion of Baseband Signals

EXERCISE OBJECTIVE

Upon completion of this exercise, you will be able to demonstrate frequency conversion (translation) of baseband signals using the AM communications modules and the Spectrum Analyzer.

DISCUSSION

If you have already seen telecommunication installations, you will have noticed that there are many kinds of antenna structures. They vary in size from small to very large and yet, they are all used to perform the same function – communication using radio frequency signals. To be effective, the size of an antenna should be at least one-half the wavelength of the radio frequency. This means that a 1000 Hz signal having a wavelength of 300 km, would require an antenna 150 km long – not a very practical size. One way of avoiding this problem is to move (translate) the frequency contents of the message to a higher place in the **frequency spectrum**. Thus, a 1000-Hz signal that is converted to 1000 kHz before transmission only requires an antenna 150 meters long. As a general rule, the higher the radio frequency, the smaller the antenna.

A **mixer (multiplier)** (Figure 1-10 (a)) can be used to perform the process of frequency translation. Figure 1-10 (b) shows the effect of combining two signals through a mixer. The frequency contents of the message signal (f_m) are displaced in the frequency spectrum to a position centered around the RF carrier frequency (f_c). The sidebands are a result of the frequency conversion process, which causes duplication of the frequency contents of the message on each side of the carrier frequency. Mathematically, this corresponds to multiplying the message signal by the carrier signal. Note that in Figure 1-10 (b) the carrier is shown as a dotted line. This is because the theoretical output of a balanced mixer does not contain a carrier component.

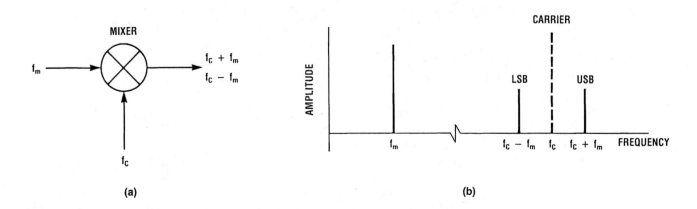

Figure 1-10. Frequency translation of a message signal.

Frequency Conversion of Baseband Signals

If, instead of being a single-frequency tone, the message signal contains a band of frequencies, the mixing of this signal with an RF carrier will translate and duplicate the complete band of frequencies as shown in Figure 1-11 (b).

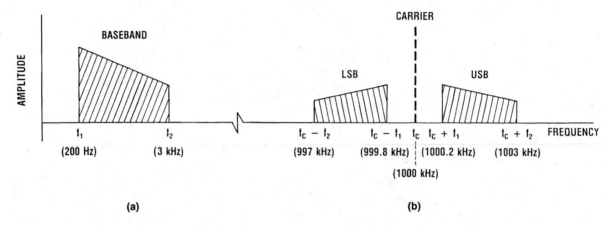

Figure 1-11. Frequency translation of a band of frequencies.

The USB will range from $f_c + f_1$ to $f_c + f_2$, and the LSB from $f_c - f_2$ to $f_c - f_1$. The message signal frequencies are usually called the **baseband**, which is the name given to the signals used to modulate the RF carrier. Note in Figure 1-11 (a) that the baseband is shown to represent a different amplitude level for the frequencies between f_1 and f_2. Also, as shown in Figure 1-11 (b), the LSB is a reversed image of the baseband, while the USB has kept the original image. This will be important when you study SSB (Single Side Band) modulation later in this volume.

Now suppose that another baseband signal is to be transmitted, such as another radio station wishing to transmit news and music. Without moving the baseband signals to different places in the frequency spectrum, it would be impossible to distinguish one from the another. We therefore use another carrier frequency, and translate the second baseband signal so that it is centered around the second carrier frequency. Dividing the spectrum like this to place different stations (or messages) alongside each other, is an example of frequency multiplexing. This allows the transmission and reception of more than one message even if both messages occupy the same baseband. Figure 1-12 shows two baseband signals translated to different places in the frequency spectrum.

EQUIPMENT REQUIRED

DESCRIPTION	MODEL
Accessories	8948
Power Supply / Dual Audio Amplifier	9401
Dual Function Generator	9402
Frequency Counter	9403
Spectrum Analyzer	9405
RF / Noise Generator	9406
AM / DSB / SSB Generator	9410
AM / DSB Receiver	9411
Oscilloscope	—

Frequency Conversion of Baseband Signals

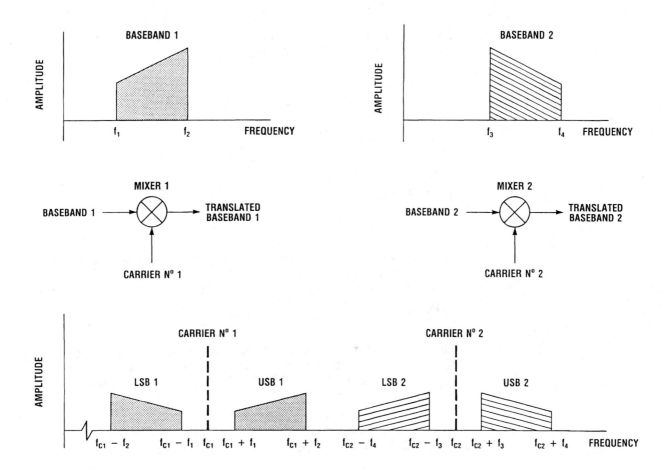

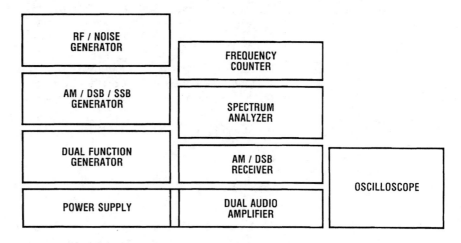

Figure 1-12. Frequency translation of two baseband signals.

PROCEDURE

☐ 1. Set up the modules as shown in Figure 1-13. Make sure that all OUTPUT LEVEL and GAIN controls are turned fully counterclockwise to the MIN position, and power up the equipment.

Figure 1-13. Suggested Module Arrangement.

Frequency Conversion of Baseband Signals

☐ 2. Set up and calibrate the Spectrum Analyzer module around 1.1 MHz, and then set its controls to the following positions:

MARKERS	: O
INPUT	: 50 Ω
MAXIMUM INPUT	: 0 dBm
FREQUENCY RANGE	: 0-30 MHz
FREQUENCY SPAN	: 1 MHz / V
OUTPUT SCALE	: LOG
OUTPUT LEVEL	: CAL
MEMory	: A
MODE	: LIVE
PLOTTER	: SCOPE (both switches)

Note: These settings will be used throughout the rest of this manual as the initial positions for normal use of the Spectrum Analyzer. After setup and calibration of the Spectrum Analyzer, it will be assumed that you have set the controls to these positions.

☐ 3. On the Dual Function Generator module, select the sine wave FUNCTION for both A and B outputs. Depress the 20 dB ATTENUATOR switches for A and B, and adjust their OUTPUT LEVEL controls to one-quarter turn clockwise.

Adjust the FREQUENCY controls to obtain a 2-kHz sine wave for OUTPUT A, and a 3-kHz sine wave for OUTPUT B.

☐ 4. On the AM / DSB / SSB Generator module, set the CARRIER LEVEL and RF GAIN controls to MAX. Make sure that the CARRIER LEVEL knob is pushed in to the LINEAR OVERMODULATION position.

Note: The RF GAIN referred to in this exercise is the AM / DSB RF GAIN (amplifier A_2).

Use the Frequency Counter, and adjust the RF TUNING control to obtain a carrier frequency of 1100 kHz.

☐ 5. Use a BNC / BNC cable to connect OUTPUT A of the Dual Function Generator to the AUDIO INPUT on the AM / DSB / SSB Generator. Set the RF GAIN control to one-quarter turn clockwise.

What will be the LSB and USB frequencies for the transmitted radio signal?

f_{LSB} = _____ kHz f_{USB} = _____ kHz

☐ 6. Connect the AM / DSB output to the Spectrum Analyzer INPUT, and use the TUNING controls on the Spectrum Analyzer to place the 1100-kHz frequency in the center of the screen.

Frequency Conversion of Baseband Signals

Depress the 200, 50, 10 and 2 kHz / V FREQUENCY SPAN switches successively, and retune the Spectrum Analyzer as necessary to keep the 1100-kHz frequency in the center of the screen.

Record the sideband frequencies as displayed on the Spectrum Analyzer.

f_{LSB} = _____ kHz f_{USB} = _____ kHz

Compare with the theoretical values.

_____

_____

☐ 7. Use a BNC T-connector and another BNC / BNC cable to combine the 2-kHz and 3-kHz sine waves from the function generator. Connect this two-tone signal to the AUDIO INPUT of the AM / DSB / SSB Generator. Do you distinguish clearly both messages on the frequency spectrum display?

   ☐ Yes   ☐ No

Would you be able to hear the two different messages individually using an ordinary AM receiver? Explain.

_____

_____

_____

☐ 8. Use Figure 1-14 to sketch this frequency spectrum. *Note that you can freeze the display by placing the MODE switch in the HOLD position. This can be useful for taking precise measurements, or drawing more accurate sketches.*

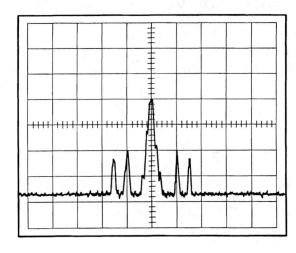

(a) Example Result.   (b) Student's Lab Result.

Figure 1-14. The frequency spectrum for a two-tone signal.

Frequency Conversion of Baseband Signals

☐ 9. Remove the cable connecting the AM / DSB / SSB Generator and the Spectrum Analyzer. Remove also the cable which connects the 3-kHz sine wave (OUTPUT B of the Dual Function Generator) to the BNC T-connector.

☐ 10. Connect the 3-kHz sine wave to the AMPLITUDE MODULATION INPUT on the RF / Noise Generator module. Make sure that the MODULATION control knob on the module is at MIN and then depress the 1-3.2 MHz FREQUENCY RANGE switch. Connect the Frequency Counter to the SYNC OUTPUT and set the RF carrier frequency to 1110 kHz using the FREQUENCY ADJUST knob.

Set the MODULATION and RF OUTPUT LEVEL controls to MAX, and then connect one of the wire antennas to the RF OUTPUT on the module.

☐ 11. Install one of the telescopic antennas at the AM / DSB RF OUTPUT of the AM generator module. Set the RF GAIN control to the MAX position.

☐ 12. Install the second telescopic antenna at the INPUT of the Spectrum Analyzer module, and place the INPUT impedance switch in the 1 MΩ position. Place the wire antenna from the RF / Noise Generator near the telescopic antenna installed on the Spectrum Analyzer.

Note: *Antenna placement is very important. It may even be necessary to wrap the wire antennas around the telescopic antennas. Experiment for best results, especially when placing the antenna in step 13. Also, make sure that the frequency spectra remain separated as in Figure 1-15 (a) by readjusting the carrier frequencies as necessary.*

Successively depress the FREQUENCY SPAN switches and adjust the TUNING controls to observe a frequency spectrum similar to that shown in Figure 1-15. Sketch the spectrum in the space provided. Note that the fine TUNING control must be used with the 10 and 2 kHz spans or the display will shift too quickly and be lost.

Would you be able to hear the two different messages individually using an ordinary AM receiver? Explain.

_____

_____

_____

☐ 13. Install the other wire antenna at the 50 kΩ RF INPUT of the AM / DSB Receiver module. Connect the AUDIO OUTPUT of the receiver to one of the inputs of the Dual Audio Amplifier, and connect the headphones to one of the jacks on this module.

Frequency Conversion of Baseband Signals

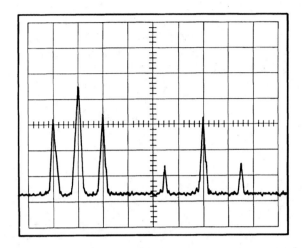

(a) Example Result

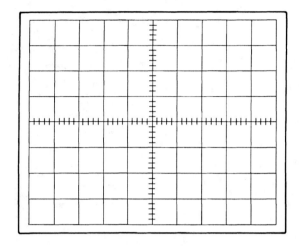

(b) Student's Lab Result

Figure 1-15. Two RF carriers modulated by single tones.

☐ 14. Connect the Frequency Counter to the local OSCillator OUTPUT (terminal 4) on the receiver, and turn the RF TUNING knob to obtain a reading of 1555 kHz. Depress the SYNC DETECTOR switch and turn on the AGC (I position). You should now be "tuned in" to the 2-kHz message at 1100 kHz. What do you hear in the headphones?

_____

_____

_____

☐ 15. Turn the RF TUNING knob on the receiver slightly to the right. What happens to the sound in the headphones?

_____

_____

Explain._____

_____

_____

Frequency Conversion of Baseband Signals

☐ 16. Retune the receiver to the 2-kHz message, and select the 10 kHz / V FREQUENCY SPAN on the Spectrum Analyzer. Vary the FREQUENCY ADJUST control on the RF / Noise Generator module so as to displace the 1110 kHz broadcast towards the 1100 kHz broadcast. Vary the control so that the 1110 kHz broadcast passes through and to the other side of the 1100 kHz broadcast. Do this several times. What kind of changes do you observe in the spectrum and the sound of the 2-kHz message?

_____

_____

_____

_____

_____

☐ 17. Use the 2 kHz / V FREQUENCY SPAN to determine the minimum distance between the carrier frequencies before interference starts. As you vary _very slightly_ the FREQUENCY ADJUST control, you should obtain approximately 8-10 kHz as the minimum distance. Record your result below.

Minimum distance = _____ kHz (approx)

☐ 18. Turn all OUTPUT LEVEL and GAIN controls to the MIN position. Place all power switches in the off (O) position and disconnect all cables.

CONCLUSION

You have seen and demonstrated frequency translation of baseband signals. This concept is fundamental in the design and use of communication systems, as it permits greater flexibility and more efficient use of the radio-frequency spectrum. You have also observed the interference caused by sending two different messages over carrier waves that are too close to each other.

REVIEW QUESTIONS

1. What happens when a message signal is combined with a carrier signal through a mixer?

_____

_____

_____

Frequency Conversion of Baseband Signals

2. What are two reasons for frequency translation?

    _____

    _____

    _____

3. What is meant by the term baseband?

    _____

    _____

    _____

4. A 1500-kHz carrier is modulated by a baseband signal containing frequencies between 500 Hz and 4 kHz. What are the frequency limits for the USB and the LSB?

    The USB ranges from _____ to _____ .

    The LSB ranges from _____ to _____ .

5. Different AM baseband signals can be broadcast at the same time. What essential condition must be respected to allow an ordinary AM receiver to select each baseband signal individually?

    _____

    _____

    _____

    _____

Unit Test

1. Amplitude modulation is

   a. communication with radio signals.
   b. transformation of a message signal.
   c. a process by which message signal information is combined with a carrier signal.
   d. frequency conversion of a carrier signal.

2. The three essential parts of a radio communications system are

   a. the message, the communications line, the receiver.
   b. the transmitter, the receiver, the message.
   c. the audio signal, the RF signal, the antenna.
   d. the transmitter, the communications line, the receiver.

3. The frequency spectrum of an AM signal consists of

   a. three frequency components – the LSB, the carrier, the USB.
   b. only the LSB and the USB.
   c. the carrier and one of the two sidebands.
   d. none of the above.

4. The frequency band used for commercial AM broadcasting in North America is

   a. 1000 kHz to 10 MHz.
   b. 540 kHz to 1600 kHz.
   c. 1.5 to 3.9 MHz.
   d. 5.4 to 16 MHz

5. The envelope of an AM signal is

   a. identical to the message signal waveform.
   b. not an important part of the RF waveform.
   c. dependent on the RF carrier frequency.
   d. independent of the message signal.

6. The Intermediate Frequency (IF) used in ordinary AM receivers is usually

   a. 10.7 MHz.
   b. 3.9 MHz.
   c. 1.6 kHz.
   d. 455 kHz

7. A 1.5-MHz carrier is amplitude-modulated with a 5-kHz sine wave. The sideband frequencies are

   a. 1.45 MHz and 1.55 MHz
   b. 1495 kHz and 1505 kHz.
   c. 995 kHz and 1005 kHz.
   d. 1.49 MHz and 1.51 MHz.

8. The principle of dividing up the frequency spectrum to place different messages and stations side by side is called

   a. time multiplexing.
   b. energy distribution.
   c. spectral analysis.
   d. frequency multiplexing.

9. The frequency spectrum of a sine wave is

   a. a single line located at twice the sine wave frequency.
   b. a single line located at the sine wave frequency.
   c. represented by two lines separated by the frequency of the sine wave.
   d. none of the above.

10. If the radio frequency used for communications is increased,

   a. the antenna size can be decreased.
   b. the antenna size remains the same, but antenna retuning is necessary.
   c. the antenna size must be increased.
   d. it will not effect the size of antenna.

The Generation of AM Signals

UNIT OBJECTIVE

When you have completed this unit, you will be able to use an oscilloscope and a spectrum analyzer to analyze AM signals in the time and frequency domains.

DISCUSSION OF FUNDAMENTALS

Communication by means of radio waves over long distances requires that we perform certain operations or alterations on the electrical signal which carries the information, before it is transmitted. Upon reception, the reverse operations are applied in order to recover the information. In this unit, the generation of amplitude-modulated signals will be studied.

In AM, the amplitude variations of the message signal cause corresponding amplitude variations in the radio wave carrier. This produces a modulation envelope such as you have seen in Unit 1 (Figure 1-5). When the message signal is a sinusoidal tone, the frequency spectrum of the modulated carrier consists of three components – the carrier frequency (f_c), the USB frequency ($f_c + f_m$), and the LSB frequency ($f_c - f_m$). This is shown in Figure 1-6 of Unit 1.

When the message signal is a more complex waveform, such as voice, the frequency spectrum is correspondingly more complex and contains many more frequency components. This means that a wider frequency space (bandwidth) is necessary to transmit the information. Since the frequency spectrum is limited and there are many users, limitations on bandwidth, carrier frequency spacing, and power output have been developed. These limitations are designed to allow diverse groups and individuals to communicate using radio waves without causing interference to each other. Government and regulatory agencies allocate frequencies and ensure adherence to regulations for a variety of civilian and military communications systems.

Commercial AM broadcasting, which is usually in the frequency band from 540 kHz to 1600 kHz, is permitted a 10-kHz bandwidth between stations. AM baseband signals, which include voice and music, are limited from about 100 Hz to 5 kHz. Power limitations vary, depending on the time of day, the season and the distance between stations. In fact, most commercial AM stations are required to lower their power output or modify their radiation pattern after sunset. This is because nighttime favors AM communications – the radio waves travel much further.

NEW TERMS AND WORDS

modulation index (m) — the ratio between the amplitudes of the modulating signal and the unmodulated carrier.

overmodulation — the term used when the modulation index is greater than 1. It occurs when the peak amplitude of the modulating signal is greater than the peak amplitude of the unmodulated carrier.

percentage modulation — the modulation index expressed as a percentage, i.e. $m \times 100\%$.

transmission efficiency (μ) — the fraction of the total AM signal power that is contained in the sidebands. It is usually expressed as a percentage and it is directly related to the modulation index.

An AM Signal

EXERCISE OBJECTIVE

When you have completed this exercise, you will be able to use the AM / DSB / SSB Generator to demonstrate and explain an AM signal in both the time and frequency domains.

DISCUSSION

There are many ways to produce an AM signal, but all of them must allow the amplitude variations of the message signal to be impressed onto the carrier. Figure 2-1 shows a simple modulator that we can use to understand the concept of AM a little better.

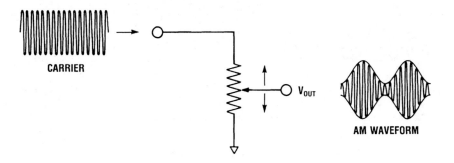

Figure 2-1. A simple modulator.

The input to the potentiometer is a fixed-amplitude high-frequency sine wave (the carrier). The amplitude of V_{OUT} depends on the position of the wiper. If we move the wiper up and down sinusoidally, we obtain the AM waveform shown in the figure. The sinusoidal movement of the wiper (the message) has been impressed onto the carrier.

An AM Signal

The block diagram of Figure 2-2 shows how an AM signal is produced by the AM / DSB / SSB Generator. A dc level (for the carrier level) is added to the message signal. The resulting signal is mixed with the RF carrier to frequency translate the message signal, and is then amplified with the RF amplifier. Figure 2-3 shows the waveforms and frequency spectra for an 1100-kHz carrier modulated by a 10-kHz sine-wave.

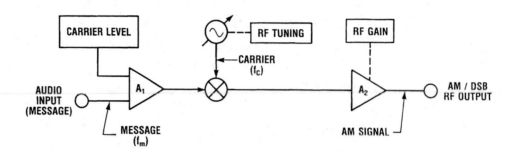

Figure 2-2. Block diagram for generating an AM signal.

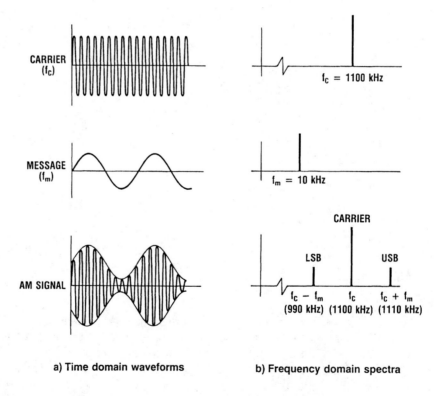

a) Time domain waveforms   b) Frequency domain spectra

Figure 2-3. Waveforms and spectra for the AM signal of Figure 2-2.

Notice that the information (message) has been impressed onto the carrier and that the envelope of the AM signal is an exact copy of the message signal. Also, the envelope varies at the same frequency as the message signal. The effect on the AM signal produced by different message signal amplitudes and frequencies is shown in Figure 2-4.

An AM Signal

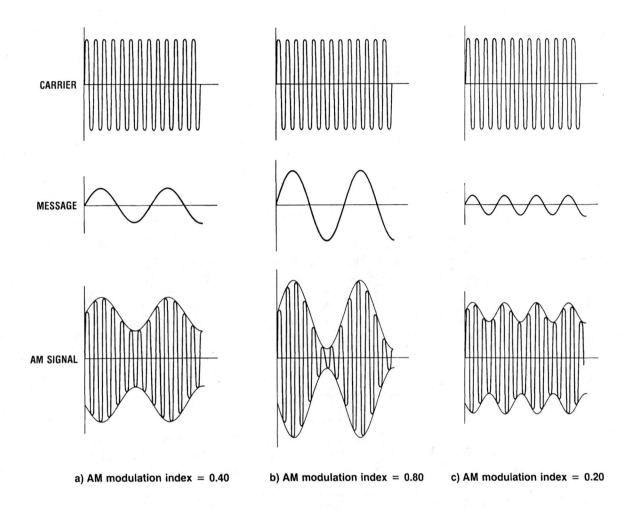

a) AM modulation index = 0.40 b) AM modulation index = 0.80 c) AM modulation index = 0.20

Figure 2-4. AM waveforms for different message signal conditions.

Notice the differences in the three examples. In Figure 2-4 (b), the amplitude of the message signal has been increased with respect to Figure 2-4 (a). The frequency (f_m) has remained the same but the AM envelope shows greater peaks and valleys as a result of the increase in amplitude. This corresponds to a variation in the **modulation index (m)**. In Figure 2-4 (c), the amplitude of the message signal has decreased while the frequency has increased. This results in smaller variations in the peaks and valleys and an increase in their number, as well as a smaller modulation index.

To finish the discussion, a note about terminology. You will find the message signal referred to by many names — the more common being information, intelligence, audio, and modulating signal. The AM signal is often referred to as the modulated signal, or the modulated carrier.

An AM Signal

EQUIPMENT REQUIRED

DESCRIPTION	MODEL
Accessories	8948
Power Supply / Dual Audio Amplifier	9401
Dual Function Generator	9402
Frequency Counter	9403
Spectrum Analyzer	9405
AM / DSB / SSB Generator	9410
Oscilloscope	—

PROCEDURE

☐ 1. Set up the modules as shown in Figure 2-5. Make sure that all OUTPUT LEVEL and GAIN controls are turned fully counterclockwise to the MIN position, and power up the equipment.

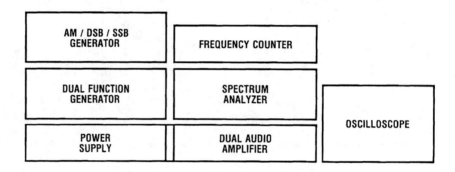

Figure 2-5. Suggested Module Arrangement.

☐ 2. Adjust the channel A controls on the Dual Function Generator as follows:

FUNCTION	: Sine wave
FREQUENCY RANGE	: 100 kHz
OUTPUT FREQUENCY display	: A
FREQUENCY knob	: Adjust for 10 kHz
ATTENUATOR	: 20 dB
OUTPUT LEVEL knob	: ¼ turn cw

The signal now available at OUTPUT A will be used as the modulating signal for the RF carrier. What is another name for the modulating signal?

_____

☐ 3. On the AM / DSB / SSB Generator module, turn the CARRIER LEVEL and RF GAIN (amplifier A_2) controls to the MAX position.

An AM Signal

Adjust the RF TUNING knob on the module to measure a carrier frequency of 1100 kHz at the AM / DSB RF OUTPUT (terminal 6) with the Frequency Counter.

☐ 4. Disconnect the Frequency Counter and connect the AM / DSB output to channel 1 of the oscilloscope. Set the VOLTS / DIV control at .5 V. Describe the waveform displayed on the screen.

_____

_____

_____

☐ 5. Use a BNC T-connector to connect the modulating signal from the Dual Function Generator to both the AUDIO INPUT on the AM / DSB / SSB Generator and channel 2 on the oscilloscope. Set the VOLTS / DIV control at .2 V.

Set the oscilloscope to trigger on the modulating signal and set the TIME / DIV control at 50 μs. Position the modulating signal below the modulated RF waveform. Sketch the waveforms in Figure 2-6.

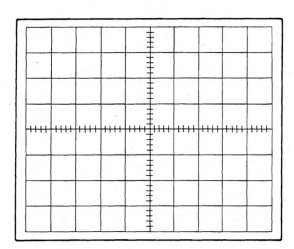

Figure 2-6. Waveforms of the modulating and modulated signals.

☐ 6. Select the square wave FUNCTION for channel A of the Dual Function Generator. Describe the waveform obtained for the AM signal.

_____

_____

_____

An AM Signal

☐ 7. Repeat step 6 for the other FUNCTIONs and describe your observations in each case.

_____

_____

_____

_____

_____

_____

☐ 8. Depress once again the sine wave FUNCTION switch for channel A on the Dual Function Generator. Vary the FREQUENCY control knob for channel A in both directions to confirm that the AM waveform responds to this change in the information signal. Readjust the control to obtain 10 kHz and describe the effect produced by varying the frequency.

_____

_____

_____

☐ 9. Vary the OUTPUT LEVEL control for channel A slightly in both directions, and then return it to the ¼ turn cw position.

How does the AM waveform change to reflect the variation in the amplitude level of the information signal?

_____

_____

_____

☐ 10. In steps 8 and 9 you obtained results similar to those shown in Figure 2-4. Changing the amplitude level of the information signal in step 9 corresponds to a variation of one of the parameters of the AM signal. Which one?

_____

_____

☐ 11. Disconnect channels 1 and 2 of the oscilloscope, and set up and calibrate the Spectrum Analyzer around 1.1 MHz.

An AM Signal

☐ 12. Turn the RF GAIN (amplifier A_2) of the AM / DSB / SSB Generator to the ½ cw position, and connect the AM / DSB output to the INPUT of the Spectrum Analyzer.

Use the Spectrum Analyzer TUNING controls to place the modulated carrier frequency in the center of the screen.

Depress successively the 200, 50, and 10 kHz / V FREQUENCY SPAN switches, and retune the Spectrum Analyzer as necessary to keep the 1100-kHz carrier in the center. Sketch the resulting frequency spectrum in Figure 2-7.

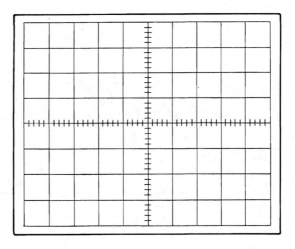

Figure 2-7. The frequency spectrum of an 1100-kHz carrier modulated by a 10-kHz sine wave.

☐ 13. Compare your frequency-spectrum sketch with the one given in Figure 2-3.

_____

_____

_____

☐ 14. Describe the effect produced in the frequency spectrum when the frequency of the modulating signal is varied with the FREQUENCY control knob on the Dual Function Generator.

_____

_____

_____

_____

☐ 15. Describe the effect produced in the frequency spectrum when the amplitude level of the modulating signal is varied with the OUTPUT LEVEL control on the Dual Function Generator.

_____

_____

_____

☐ 16. Varying the modulation index of an AM signal causes what change in the frequency spectrum display of the signal?

_____

_____

☐ 17. Select the square wave FUNCTION on the Dual Function Generator and describe the resulting frequency spectrum. (Select the 50 kHz / V FREQUENCY SPAN on the Spectrum Analyzer for a better view of the spectrum).

_____

_____

_____

☐ 18. Turn all OUTPUT LEVEL and GAIN controls to the MIN position. Place all power switches in the off (O) position and disconnect all cables.

CONCLUSION

You have produced an AM signal and examined the effects caused by varying two major parameters of the modulating signal – frequency and amplitude. You have seen how different message signals affect the AM waveform, and you have been able to look at the effects in both the time and frequency domains. As you have noticed, the message signal information is "carried" by the envelope of the modulated RF signal, and the peaks and valleys of the envelope give an indication of the modulation index.

REVIEW QUESTIONS

1. Based on the results of this exercise, which signal produces a frequency spectrum that could be compared to a complex message signal, the sine wave or the square wave? Explain.

_____

_____

An AM Signal

2. Indicate in a simple sketch how changes in the frequency and in the amplitude of a message signal are reflected in the frequency spectrum of an AM signal.

3. If the modulation index of an AM signal is increased, what effect does this have on the envelope of the AM waveform?

_____

_____

_____

_____

4. What happens to the envelope of the AM signal when the frequency of the modulating signal is increased?

_____

_____

_____

5. When the message signal frequency increases, does the modulation index increase or decrease?

_____

Percentage Modulation

EXERCISE OBJECTIVE

When you have completed this exercise, you will be able to determine the percentage modulation of an AM signal using either an oscilloscope or a spectrum analyzer.

DISCUSSION

As you have seen in Exercise 2-1, increasing or decreasing the amplitude of the message signal causes higher or lower peaks and valleys in the envelope of the AM signal. This corresponds to changing the **percentage modulation** which is the term used when the *modulation index m* is expressed as a percentage. Percentage modulation is equal to *m* multiplied by 100%.

The modulation index is an important parameter in AM. It is defined as the ratio between the amplitudes of the message signal and the unmodulated carrier. The AM modulation index is measured using a single-tone sine wave as the message signal.

$$\text{AM modulation index} = m = \frac{\text{message signal peak amplitude}}{\text{unmodulated carrier peak amplitude}}$$

$$\% \text{ Modulation} = m \times 100\%$$

Figure 2-8 shows how the modulation index is defined and measured. The figure shows a sine wave message signal with a peak amplitude of 200 mV, while the peak amplitude of the unmodulated carrier is 600 mV. The modulation index is therefore 0.2 / 0.6 = ⅓ and the % modulation is ⅓ × 100% = 33⅓%.

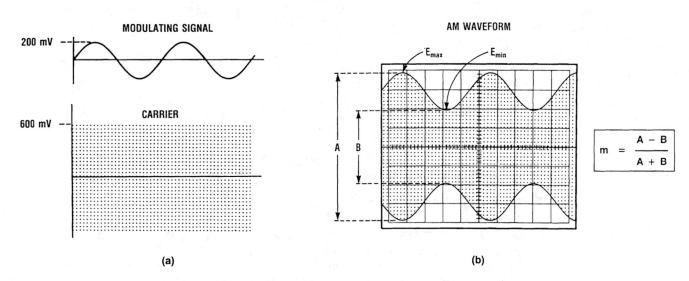

Figure 2-8. The AM modulation index.

Percentage Modulation

Note: *The message signal usually passes through a combination of amplifiers, filters and other circuits at the input of an AM transmitter. This means that the message signal amplitude actually affecting the unmodulated carrier is not the same as the input value, and the modulation index calculated with the input value will be incorrect. In practice the modulation index is determined directly from the AM signal.*

The modulation index can be determined from the AM waveform as shown in Figure 2-8. Measurements of A and B are made with an oscilloscope and we use the equation

$$m = \frac{A - B}{A + B}$$

In this particular case, A = 7.6 divisions and B = 3.8 divisions so that

$$m = \frac{7.6 - 3.8}{7.6 + 3.8} = \frac{3.8}{11.4} = \text{⅓ as before.}$$

Note: *Some books use E_{max} and E_{min}, instead of A and B, in the equation for the modulation index. The same answer will be obtained in both cases because $A = 2E_{max}$ and $B = 2E_{min}$.*

There are two other methods of determining the modulation index of an AM signal. In the first, the oscilloscope is placed in the X-Y mode of operation and the message signal is connected to the X-input. The modulated signal is connected to the Y-input and a trapezoidal pattern, such as shown in Figure 2-9, is obtained.

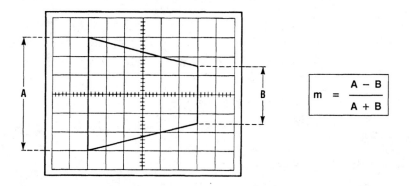

Figure 2-9. The trapezoidal method of determining the modulation index.

Measurements of A and B are then made and the modulation index is calculated using the same equation as before.

In the second method, a spectrum analyzer is used to determine the modulation index. In this method, the difference Δ (pronounced delta) between the carrier power and the sideband power corresponds to a given modulation index. For example, in Figure 2-10, Δ is 7.5 dB. Using the graph of Figure 2-11, we find that this corresponds to a modulation index of 0.84. The modulation index of ⅓ used in previous examples corresponds to a difference Δ of about 15.5 dB.

Percentage Modulation

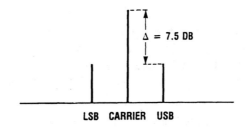

Figure 2-10. Difference between carrier and sideband power in dB.

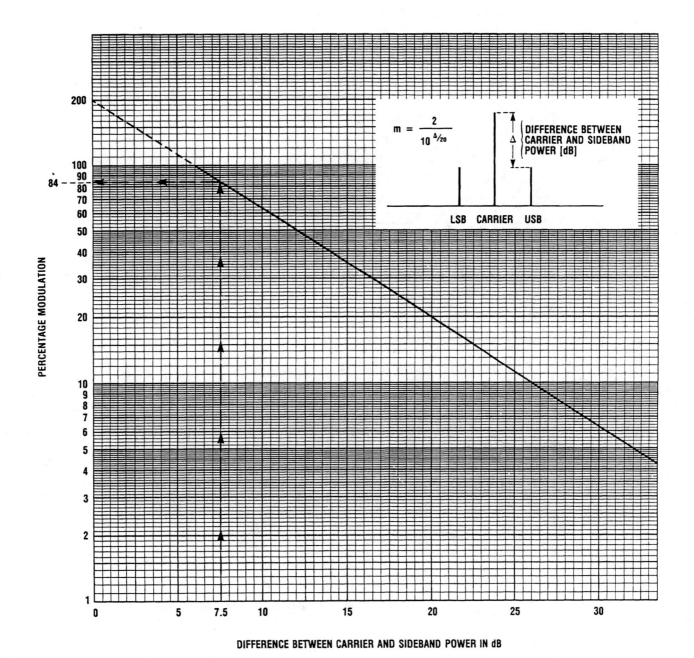

DIFFERENCE BETWEEN CARRIER AND SIDEBAND POWER IN dB

Figure 2-11. Measuring the modulation index with a spectrum analyzer.

Percentage Modulation

Among the methods presented for determining the modulation index, the trapezoidal method is probably the most common. When the modulating signal is voice or music, the modulation index is constantly changing, but the trapezoid pattern provides a uniform display and allows meaningful measurements.

When the peak amplitude of the message signal equals the peak amplitude of the unmodulated carrier, 100% modulation is obtained. Figure 2-12 shows the AM waveforms and trapezoidal patterns for m equal to 0.5 and 1.0. **Overmodulation** (m > 1) occurs when the modulating signal has a peak amplitude greater than that of the unmodulated carrier. As explained in the following text, overmodulation is an undesirable condition in AM communications.

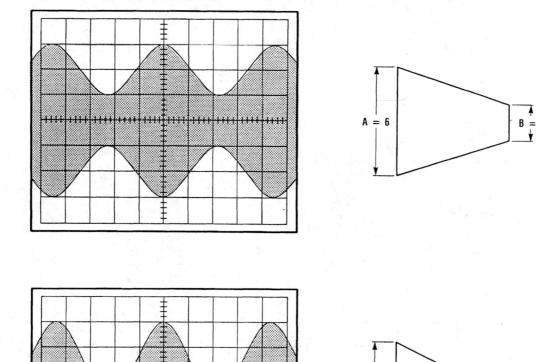

Figure 2-12. AM waveforms and trapezoidal patterns for m = 0.5 and 1.0.

Percentage Modulation

The modulation index is directly related to power and efficiency in AM communications. At 100% modulation each sideband frequency has an amplitude equal to one-half of the carrier amplitude. When overmodulation occurs both sides of the modulation envelope cross over the zero reference line. In commercial AM these extra lobes (see Figure 2-14) of the modulation envelope are clipped and spurious sideband frequencies, called sideband "splatter", are produced. This causes distortion in the receiver and interference with other stations, because frequencies outside the assigned bandwidth of the overmodulating station are produced. Figure 2-13 illustrates overmodulation and shows the extra sideband frequencies which are produced.

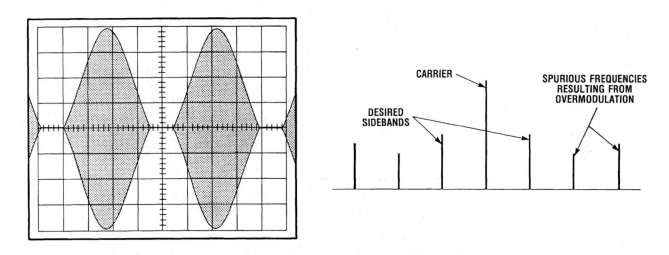

Figure 2-13. Overmodulation produces interference and distortion.

This type of overmodulation is known as non-linear overmodulation because a part of the RF signal is clipped. The other type of overmodulation which occurs is linear overmodulation, in which extra lobes in the RF signal are not clipped when the sides of the modulation envelope cross the zero reference line. Figure 2-14 illustrates linear overmodulation.

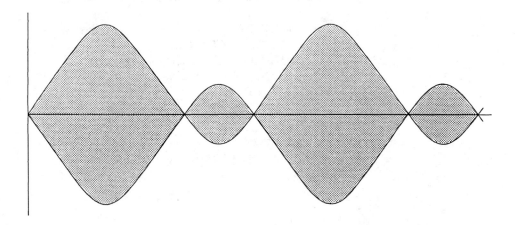

Figure 2-14. The RF waveform obtained with linear overmodulation.

Percentage Modulation

EQUIPMENT REQUIRED

DESCRIPTION	MODEL
Accessories	8948
Power Supply / Dual Audio Amplifier	9401
Dual Function Generator	9402
Frequency Counter	9403
Spectrum Analyzer	9405
AM / DSB / SSB Generator	9410
Oscilloscope	—

PROCEDURE

☐ 1. Set up the modules as shown in Figure 2-15. Make sure that all OUTPUT LEVEL and GAIN controls are turned fully counterclockwise to the MIN position, and power up the equipment.

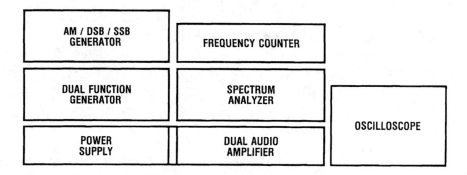

Figure 2-15. Suggested module arrangement.

☐ 2. Adjust the channel A controls on the Dual Function Generator as follows:

FUNCTION	:	Sine wave
FREQUENCY RANGE	:	100 kHz
OUTPUT FREQUENCY display	:	A
FREQUENCY knob	:	Adjust for 10 kHz
ATTENUATOR	:	20 dB
OUTPUT LEVEL knob	:	¼ turn cw

Connect the 10-kHz modulating signal to channel 1 of the oscilloscope, and measure its peak-to-peak amplitude.

$A_m =$ _____ V p-p

☐ 3. On the AM / DSB / SSB Generator, turn the CARRIER LEVEL and RF GAIN (amplifier A_2) controls to the MAX position.

Percentage Modulation

Adjust the RF TUNING control on the module to measure a carrier frequency of 1100 kHz at terminal 6 with the Frequency Counter.

☐ 4. Disconnect the Frequency Counter and connect the AM / DSB output to channel 2 of the oscilloscope. Measure the peak to peak amplitude of the carrier.

$$A_C = \underline{\hspace{2cm}} \text{ V p-p}$$

☐ 5. Using the values obtained in steps 2 and 4, determine the percentage modulation that should be obtained for the AM signal.

$$\% \text{ Mod.} = m \times 100\% = \frac{A_m}{A_C} \times 100\% = \underline{\hspace{1.5cm}} \times 100\% = \underline{\hspace{1.5cm}} \%$$

☐ 6. Use a BNC T-connector and a BNC / BNC cable to connect the modulating signal to the AUDIO INPUT on the AM generator.

Set the oscilloscope controls to obtain the largest usable display and sketch the resulting AM waveform in Figure 2-16.

Measure A and B as shown in Figure 2-8 (b).

$$A = \underline{\hspace{1.5cm}} \qquad B = \underline{\hspace{1.5cm}}$$

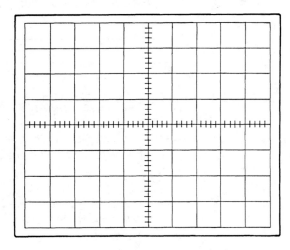

Figure 2-16. The AM signal waveform.

Percentage Modulation

Determine the modulation index and the percentage modulation.

$$m = \frac{A - B}{A + B} = \underline{\hspace{1cm}} \qquad \% \text{ Mod.} = m \times 100\% = \underline{\hspace{1cm}} \%$$

Compare this result with that obtained in step 5. It should be about 2.2 times greater because the modulating signal has undergone signal transformation before affecting the carrier.

_____

_____

☐ 7. Place the oscilloscope in the X-Y mode to obtain a trapezoidal pattern like Figure 2-9. Set the oscilloscope controls to obtain the largest usable display.

Measure A and B as shown in Figure 2-9.

$A = \underline{\hspace{1cm}} \qquad B = \underline{\hspace{1cm}}$

Determine m and the percentage modulation.

$$m = \frac{A - B}{A + B} = \underline{\hspace{1cm}} \qquad \% \text{ Mod.} = m \times 100\% = \underline{\hspace{1cm}} \%$$

Compare the result with that obtained in step 6.

_____

_____

☐ 8. Use the trapezoidal pattern to obtain modulation percentages of 20, 33 and 75% by varying the level of the modulating signal. Record the values of A and B. Note that the equation relating m to A and B can be used to determine the relative values needed for A and B as shown in the example below.

Note: _It may be difficult to obtain the exact values stated above. As long as the value is within 5%, it is acceptable and should be used in place of the values given in the exercise._

Example: To set a modulation index of 50%.

$$\text{Since } \frac{A - B}{A + B} = m, \text{ we have } \frac{A - B}{A + B} = .50 = \frac{1}{2}$$

Percentage Modulation

Cross multiplication gives 2A − 2B = A + B, and solving this equation gives A = 3B. Choosing B = 1 therefore gives A = 3.

$$\text{Verification:} \quad m = \frac{A - B}{A + B} = \frac{3 - 1}{3 + 1} = \frac{2}{4} = .50, \text{ or } 50\%$$

For m = 0.20, A = _____, B = _____ and $\dfrac{A - B}{A + B}$ = _____

For m = 0.33, A = _____, B = _____ and $\dfrac{A - B}{A + B}$ = _____

For m = 0.75, A = _____, B = _____ and $\dfrac{A - B}{A + B}$ = _____

Note: *Once you have adjusted the modulation index at 0.75, do not readjust it until step 14.*

☐ 9. Disconnect channels 1 and 2 of the oscilloscope, and set up and calibrate the Spectrum Analyzer around 1.1 MHz.

☐ 10. Turn the RF GAIN (amplifier A_2) of the AM / DSB / SSB Generator to ½ turn cw and connect the AM / DSB output to the INPUT of the Spectrum Analyzer. *Make sure that the INPUT impedance switch is set at the 50 Ω position.*

☐ 11. Use the TUNING controls on the Spectrum Analyzer to place the 1100-kHz frequency in the center of the screen.

Successively depress the 200, 50 and 10 kHz / V FREQUENCY SPAN switches, and use the TUNING controls to keep the carrier centered in the screen.

☐ 12. Determine Δ, the difference in dB between the carrier and sideband power, as shown in Figure 2-10.

Use Figure 2-11 to determine the percentage modulation.

Δ = _____ and % Mod. = _____

Percentage Modulation

☐ 13. How does this result compare to the value of 75% that you set in step 8?

_____

_____

_____

☐ 14. Vary the amplitude of the modulating signal to obtain two intermediate values between 20 and 70% for the modulation index. Measure and record the values of Δ, and determine the modulation index using Figure 2-11.

$\Delta_1 = $ _____, $m_1 = $ _____

$\Delta_2 = $ _____, $m_2 = $ _____

☐ 15. Turn the Channel A OUTPUT LEVEL control to MAX. You are now overmodulating the AM signal (the modulation index is greater than 1).

Pull the CARRIER LEVEL knob on the AM/DSB/SSB Generator to the NONLINEAR OVERMODULATION position. What happens on the frequency spectrum display? (Select the 50 kHz/V FREQUENCY SPAN on the Spectrum Analyzer for a better view of the spectrum).

_____

_____

_____

☐ 16. Vary the Channel A OUTPUT LEVEL control between MIN and MAX several times, so that the modulation index varies above and below 1. Describe what happens.

_____

_____

_____

☐ 17. Disconnect the Spectrum Analyzer module from the oscilloscope, and connect the AM/DSB output of the AM generator to channel 2. Turn the RF GAIN (amplifier A_2) control to MAX.

Adjust the oscilloscope controls to observe the AM waveform and then repeat step 16. Describe what happens.

_____

_____

_____

Percentage Modulation

☐ 18. Push the CARRIER LEVEL knob in to the LINEAR OVERMODULATION position. Repeat step 16 and compare with the results obtained in step 17.

_____

_____

_____

☐ 19. Connect the modulating signal to channel 1 of the oscilloscope and place the oscilloscope in the X-Y mode to obtain the trapezoidal pattern. Adjust the oscilloscope controls to center the figure.

Vary the modulation index above and below 1 as in step 16. Describe what happens.

_____

_____

_____

☐ 20. Use Figure 2-17 to sketch the trapezoidal pattern obtained when the modulation index is greater than 1. Overmodulate the AM signal so that the small triangle on the right side is clearly visible.

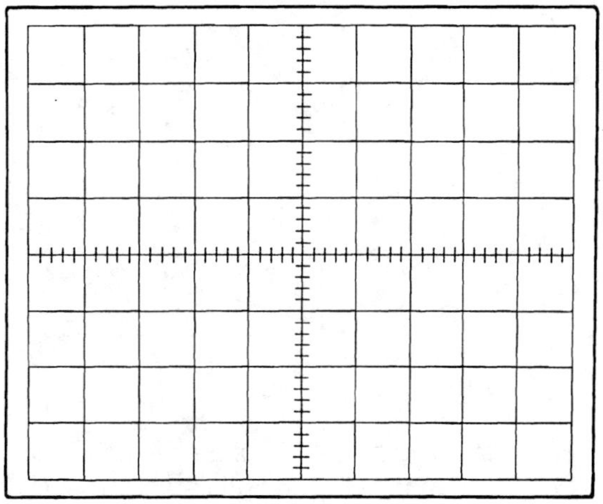

Figure 2-17. Trapezoidal pattern when m > 1.

☐ 21. What happens to the small triangle on the right when the CARRIER LEVEL knob is pulled out to the NONLINEAR OVERMODULATION position?

_____

_____

☐ 22. Turn all OUTPUT LEVEL and GAIN controls to the MIN position. Place all power switches in the off (O) position and disconnect all cables.

CONCLUSION

You have seen that the percentage modulation of an AM signal is directly related to the amplitude of the modulating signal. You have practiced several methods of determining the percentage modulation, and have observed the effect produced by varying the amplitude level of the message. Determining the percentage modulation can be as simple as performing a theoretical calculation based on the amplitudes of the modulating signal and the unmodulated carrier. However, oscilloscope measurements of the AM waveform, or use of the trapezoidal pattern, are the more practical methods used to determine the modulation index.

REVIEW QUESTIONS

1. The following trapezoidal patterns are obtained for different AM signals. Determine the modulation index in each case.

   a.

   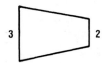

   $$m = \frac{A - B}{A + B} = \underline{\hspace{2cm}}$$

   b.

   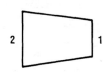

   $$m = \frac{A - B}{A + B} = \underline{\hspace{2cm}}$$

   c.

   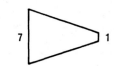

   $$m = \frac{A - B}{A + B} = \underline{\hspace{2cm}}$$

2. The amplitude of a sine-wave message signal is 500 mV p-p, and the amplitude of the unmodulated carrier is 500 mV peak. What is the theoretical modulation index?

   _____

3. What is meant by overmodulation, and why is it undesirable?

   _____

   _____

   _____

Percentage Modulation

4. A technician uses the trapezoidal method to determine the modulation index of an AM signal. The resulting oscilloscope display shows the presence of a small triangle on the right side of the figure. What does this indicate?

_____

_____

_____

5. The frequency spectrum display for an AM signal shows a Δ of 6 dB between the carrier and the sidebands. This means that the modulation index is equal to _____ .

Carrier and Sideband Power

EXERCISE OBJECTIVE

When you have completed this exercise, you will be able to use the modulation index to determine sideband power and transmission efficiency for AM signals.

DISCUSSION

In the previous exercise, you saw that varying the modulation index caused the power level of the sidebands to change, while the carrier power remained constant. Since the useful information contained in the RF signal is located in the sidebands, it is desirable to maximize the sideband power levels. *In AM however, the modulation index must not be greater than 1 or distortion and interference will occur.*

The total power (P_T) in an AM signal is the sum of the carrier power (P_C), and the lower and upper sideband power ($P_{LSB} + P_{USB}$). In equation form, $P_T = P_C + P_{SB}$, where $P_{SB} = P_{LSB} + P_{USB}$. *For AM signals, the upper and lower sideband powers are equal.*

The fraction of the total power that is contained in the sidebands is a measure of the **transmission efficiency (μ)**. In equation form this can be expressed as $\mu = P_{SB} / P_T$.

Since P_{SB} is directly related to the modulation index (m), the ratio P_{SB} / P_T, and the theoretical efficiency, can be determined from the modulation index using the following equation:

$$\mu = \frac{m^2}{2 + m^2} = \frac{P_{SB}}{P_T}$$

The following example illustrates the use of these equations.

An AM station transmits an average carrier power of 40 kW. The modulating signal is a sine wave and m equals 0.707 ($\sqrt{2}/2$). We want to find the total average power output of the station, the average power in each sideband, and the transmission efficiency.

Since we know m, we can find μ. Thus,

$$\mu = \frac{m^2}{2 + m^2} = \frac{(0.707)^2}{2 + (0.707)^2} = \frac{1}{5} = 0.2$$

Therefore, the ratio $(P_{SB} / P_T) = \frac{1}{5}$, or $P_{SB} = 0.2\, P_T$.

The total power can be calculated using $P_T = P_C + P_{SB}$ and substituting the values for P_C and P_{SB}. This gives

$$P_T = 40 + 0.2\, P_T$$

$$0.8\, P_T = 40$$

$$P_T = 40/0.8 = 50 \text{ kW}$$

Carrier and Sideband Power

The total sideband power P_{SB} is the difference between the total power P_T and the carrier power P_C, and is equal to 10 kW (50 − 40 = 10 kW). Since the upper and lower sideband powers are equal for AM signals, each sideband contains 5 kW.

Figure 2-18 can be used to find the transmission efficiency directly, once the modulation index is known. Since m ⩽ 1 for AM, the maximum efficiency that can be obtained is $33^1/_3$%. You can verify this by substituting m = 1 into the equation relating μ and m.

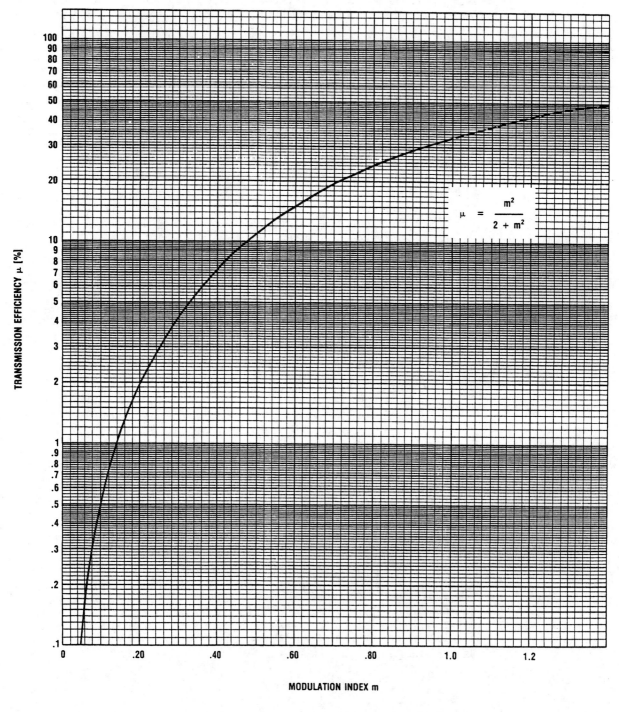

$$\mu = \frac{m^2}{2 + m^2}$$

Figure 2-18. Graph of transmission efficiency vs the modulation index.

Carrier and Sideband Power

Because of the limitation on the modulation index, AM communication is not very efficient as far as power utilization is concerned. At maximum efficiency, two-thirds of the output power is "wasted" on the carrier which contains no intelligence. This however, is offset by the fact that a large audience is reached and relatively simple receivers can be used to demodulate AM signals. The more efficient AM methods of Double Side Band (DSB) and Single Side Band (SSB) will be covered in Units 4 and 5, and you will discover that the carrier power can be greatly reduced to increase efficiency.

EQUIPMENT REQUIRED

DESCRIPTION	MODEL
Accessories	8948
Power Supply / Dual Audio Amplifier	9401
Dual Function Generator	9402
Frequency Counter	9403
True RMS Voltmeter / Power Meter	9404
Spectrum Analyzer	9405
AM / DSB / SSB Generator	9410
Oscilloscope	—

PROCEDURE

☐ 1. Set up the modules as shown in Figure 2-19. Make sure that all OUTPUT LEVEL and GAIN controls are turned fully counterclockwise to the MIN position, and power up the equipment.

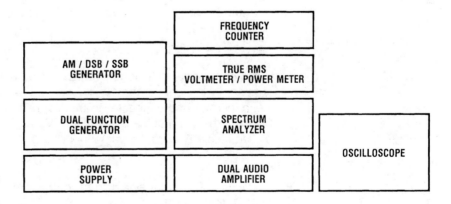

Figure 2-19. Suggested Module Arrangement.

Carrier and Sideband Power

☐ 2. Adjust the channel A controls on the Dual Function Generator as follows:

      FUNCTION   : Sine wave
      FREQUENCY RANGE   : 100 kHz
      OUTPUT FREQUENCY display : A
      FREQUENCY knob   : Adjust for 10 kHz
      ATTENUATOR   : 20 dB
      OUTPUT LEVEL knob   : ¼ turn cw

☐ 3. On the AM / DSB / SSB Generator, turn the CARRIER LEVEL control to MAX and set the RF GAIN (amplifier A_2) control to ½ turn cw.

Adjust the RF TUNING control on the module to measure a carrier frequency of 1100 kHz at terminal 6 with the Frequency Counter.

☐ 4. Disconnect the Frequency Counter and connect the AM / DSB output of the AM / DSB / SSB Generator to channel 2 of the oscilloscope.

☐ 5. Use a BNC T-connector to connect the 10-kHz sine wave to both channel 1 of the oscilloscope and the AUDIO INPUT on the AM / DSB / SSB Generator.

☐ 6. Place the oscilloscope in the X-Y mode to use the trapezoidal method of measuring the modulation index.

☐ 7. Set the modulation index at 0.50 by adjusting the OUTPUT LEVEL control (channel A) on the Dual Function Generator to obtain the desired values of A and B. Use the actual values obtained (see the note following step 8 in Exercise 2-2).

☐ 8. When the modulation index has been adjusted at the proper value, temporarily disconnect the 10-kHz signal from the AUDIO INPUT on the AM generator and connect it to the True RMS Voltmeter / Power Meter. Measure the value of the rms voltage (V_{AUDIO}) corresponding to the modulation index. Record the value in Table 2-1.

☐ 9. Disconnect the audio signal from the voltmeter and reconnect it to the AUDIO INPUT of the AM generator. Readjust the amplitude level of the modulating signal to obtain a modulation index of 0.75 and repeat step 8.

☐ 10. Repeat step 9 for a modulation index of 1.00.

☐ 11. Disconnect both channels of the oscilloscope, and set up and calibrate the Spectrum Analyzer around 1.1 MHz.

Carrier and Sideband Power

			TRUE RMS VOLTMETER RESULTS					SPECTRUM ANALYZER RESULTS							
m	μ	P_{SB}/P_T*	V_{AUDIO}	P_C (unmodulated)		P_{AM} (modulated)		$P_T = P_C + P_{SB}$**		P_C		P_{LSB}		P_{USB}	
—	$m^2/2 + m^2$	%	V_{rms}	dBm	mW	dBm	mW	dBm	mW	dBm	mW	dBm	mW	dBm	mW
.50															
.75															
1.00															
1	2	3	4	5	6	7	8	9	10	11	12	13	14	15	16

$$* \ \frac{P_{SB}}{P_T} = \frac{P_{AM} - P_C}{P_{AM}} \ \text{(in mW) from columns 6 and 8}$$

** $P_T = P_C + P_{LSB} + P_{USB}$ (in mW) from columns 12, 14 and 16.

Table 2-1. Power measurements for different values of m.

☐ 12. Place a BNC T-connector at the AM/DSB output of the AM generator, and use a short BNC/BNC cable to connect the output to the INPUT of the True RMS Voltmeter/Power Meter. Use another BNC/BNC cable to connect the other side of the T-connector to the INPUT of the Spectrum Analyzer. *Make sure that the INPUT impedance switch is in the 50 Ω position.*

☐ 13. Use the TUNING controls to place the carrier frequency in the center of the screen, and successively depress the 200, 50 and 10 kHz/V FREQUENCY SPAN switches. Adjust the TUNING controls as necessary to keep the carrier centered in the screen.

☐ 14. Make sure that the AUDIO INPUT signal for the AM generator is disconnected, and adjust the RF GAIN (amplifier A_2) control to read a value of −10 dBm for P_C (unmodulated). Ensure that the MODE switch on the True RMS Voltmeter/Power Meter is in the dBm position. Record the value of P_C (unmodulated) in Table 2-1 and *DO NOT READJUST the RF GAIN control until the end of the Exercise.*

☐ 15. Verify that the modulation index is still equal to 1.00 by measuring the voltage of the 10-kHz signal with the True RMS Voltmeter/Power Meter. If necessary, readjust the voltage to the value previously recorded in Table 2-1 to obtain m = 1.00.

☐ 16. When the modulation index has been adjusted at the proper value, reconnect the 10-kHz signal to the AUDIO INPUT of the AM generator. Use the True RMS Voltmeter/Power Meter to measure the dBm value of the AM signal at the output of the AM generator. Record the value of P_{AM} (modulated) in Table 2-1.

☐ 17. Using the Spectrum Analyzer TUNING controls to displace the frequency spectrum as necessary, measure the values of P_C, P_{LSB} and P_{USB} as they appear on the Spectrum Analyzer. Record the results in Table 2-1. *Make sure that the OUTPUT LEVEL control is in the CAL position.*

☐ 18. Use the True RMS Voltmeter / Power Meter and the values of V_{AUDIO} previously recorded in Table 2-1 to set m = 0.75, and repeat steps 16 and 17. Do the same thing for m = 0.50.

☐ 19. Use Figure 2-20 to convert the dBm values of Table 2-1 to mW. An example of converting −27 dBm to 0.01 V and 0.002 mW is shown on the figure.

☐ 20. Complete Table 2-1.

☐ 21. Compare the theoretical and measured values of the transmission efficiency μ for the three cases (columns 2 and 3 of Table 2-1).

_____

_____

_____

_____

☐ 22. Compare the values of P_{AM} and P_T for the three cases (columns 7 and 9 of Table 2-1).

_____

_____

_____

_____

☐ 23. Compare the sideband powers (P_{SB}) obtained with the True RMS Voltmeter Results with the corresponding values obtained using the Spectrum Analyzer Results. Use only the dBm values for the comparison.

_____

_____

_____

☐ 24. Turn all OUTPUT LEVEL and GAIN controls to the MIN position. Place all power switches in the off (O) position and disconnect all cables.

Carrier and Sideband Power

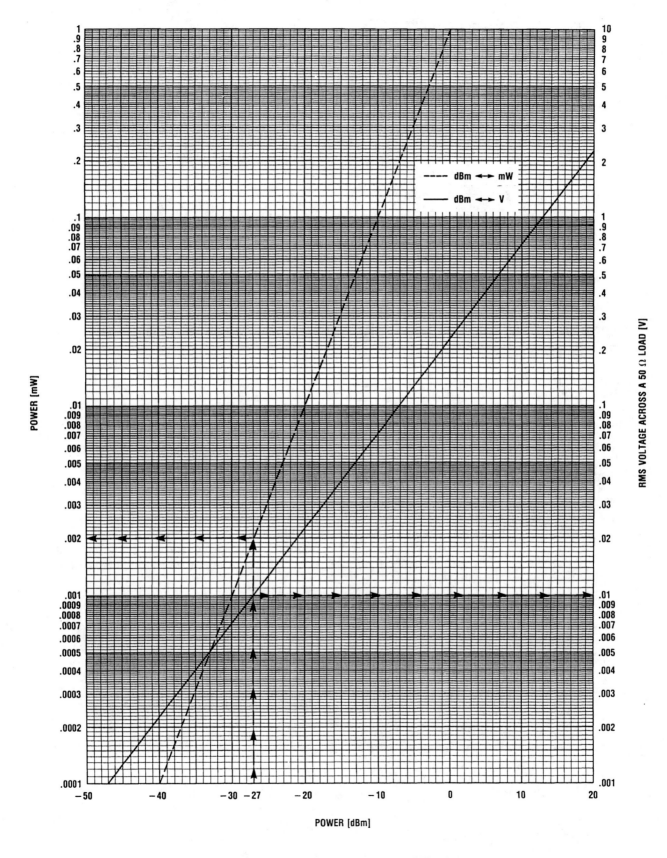

Figure 2-20. Converting dBm to mW and RMS voltage.

CONCLUSION

Because power and efficiency are directly related to the modulation index, both quantities can be determined with simple calculations, once the modulation index is known. Signal power measurements made with the True RMS Voltmeter / Power Meter and the Spectrum Analyzer have allowed you to verify the relationships and compare experimental values with theoretical calculations. The exercise has also demonstrated that a spectrum analyzer allows one to determine directly the power levels of all the components of an AM signal.

REVIEW QUESTIONS

1. Write in equation form the expression for 1) the total power of an AM signal, 2) the relationship between μ and m.

   $P_T =$ _____ $\mu =$ _____

2. The maximum transmission efficiency that can be obtained in AM is $33\frac{1}{3}\%$. Explain.

   _____

   _____

3. Spectrum analyzer measurements of an AM signal show that $P_C = 0$ dBm and $P_{LSB} = P_{USB} = -6$ dBm. Determine the modulation index.

   $m =$ _____

4. An AM signal is attenuated by 1000 before measurements are made with a spectrum analyzer. The spectrum analyzer measurements show that $P_C = 0$ dBm, and $P_{LSB} = P_{USB} = -6$ dBm. Determine P_T , the actual power of the AM signal.

   _____

   _____

   _____

   _____

Carrier and Sideband Power

5. An AM station transmits an average carrier power of 10 kW. Spectrum Analyzer measurements show that the difference between carrier and sideband power is 8 dB (Δ = 8 dB). Determine m, μ, P_T, P_{LSB} and P_{USB}. (Hint: see Figure 2-11).

_____

_____

_____

_____

_____

_____

_____

Unit Test

1. If the amplitude of a sine-wave message signal is increased with respect to the carrier amplitude in an AM signal, the modulation index

   a. will decrease.
   b. will remain the same.
   c. will increase.
   d. will increase and decrease alternatively.

2. The names intelligence, information, audio, and modulating signal all refer to

   a. the message signal.
   b. the carrier wave.
   c. the RF waveform.
   d. both b and c.

3. The modulation index (or percentage modulation) of an AM signal can be determined accurately

   a. only if the message and carrier signal amplitudes are known.
   b. with measurements of the AM waveform.
   c. using the trapezoidal method.
   d. both b and c.

4. If the difference Δ between carrier and sideband power in an AM signal is known, and P_C equals 10 kW,

   a. the modulation index can be determined.
   b. the total RF power can be determined.
   c. the transmission efficiency can be determined.
   d. all of the above.

5. Spurious sideband frequencies (sideband splatter) occur in commercial AM when

   a. the extra lobes caused by overmodulation are clipped.
   b. the message signal amplitude is too small.
   c. the modulation index is less than 1.
   d. both a and c.

6. Measurements of an AM waveform show that A equals 1.5 V and B equals 1 V. The percentage modulation is

   a. equal to 150%.
   b. equal to 67%.
   c. equal to 20%.
   d. not related to these measurements.

7. Power measurements of an AM signal indicate that sideband power is 6 dB less than carrier power. This indicates

    a. that upper and lower sideband powers are equal..
    b. that the modulation index equals 1.
    c. that the transmission efficiency equals ½.
    d. none of the above.

8. Spectrum analyzer measurements of an AM signal

    a. allow the power levels of all spectral components to be determined.
    b. do not allow the total RF power to be determined.
    c. are useful only if the modulation index is less than 1.
    d. both a and c.

9. The difference between upper and lower sideband power in an AM signal

    a. is 6 dB.
    b. is 3 dB.
    c. depends on carrier power.
    d. equals zero, since they are equal.

10. The maximum sideband power in commercial AM signals is limited to

    a. ½ of the total power.
    b. ⅓ of the total power.
    c. ¼ of the total power.
    d. different values for each station.

Reception of AM Signals

UNIT OBJECTIVE

Upon completing this unit, you will be able to explain and demonstrate the functional operations required of a superheterodyne receiver to receive, process and demodulate an AM signal.

DISCUSSION OF FUNDAMENTALS

In the previous units you became familiar with the generation and appearance of AM signals. You learned how AM radio waves are used to communicate information, and you observed AM signals in the time and frequency domains. In this unit you will learn how the transmitted information is recovered from the RF carrier wave.

The process of amplitude modulation is accompanied by frequency translation of the message signal to a position in the frequency spectrum that is centered at the carrier frequency. This means that several stations with different carrier frequencies can broadcast messages at the same time in the commercial AM band. Figure 3-1 illustrates this and shows the frequency spectra of four different AM stations.

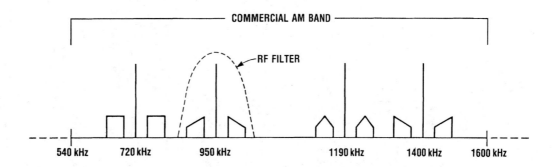

Figure 3-1. The frequency spectra of four different AM stations.

Reception of AM Signals

An AM receiver has to be able to single out or select the desired station, and then recover the information that is being broadcast. This idea is illustrated in Figure 3-2. The station broadcasting at 950 kHz is the desired station, and the basic operations required are: 1) filtering so that only the frequency contents centered at 950 kHz are selected for **demodulation** and 2) returning the frequency contents of the message signal to their original place in the frequency spectrum. When you tune in a particular AM station, this is essentially all that happens, since the theoretical process involved is mainly frequency translation.

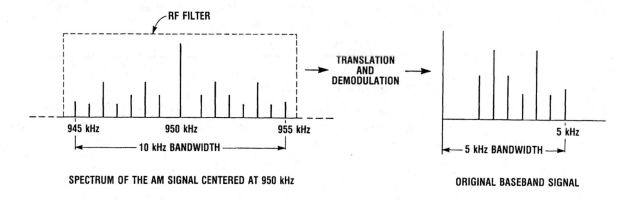

Figure 3-2. Recovering the information being broadcast.

The kind of receiver that you will use in the Analog Communications Training System is called a superheterodyne receiver. A simplified block diagram of this receiver is shown in Figure 3-3.

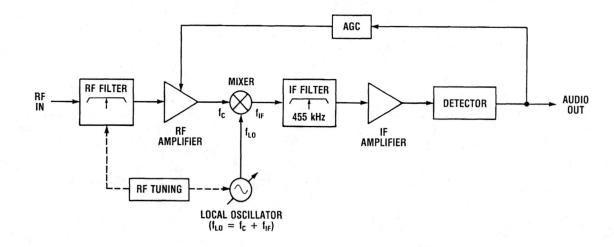

Figure 3-3. Simplified block diagram of a superheterodyne receiver.

Reception of AM Signals

The basic operation of the superheterodyne receiver is as follows. The incoming RF signals are filtered to select the desired station by adjusting the LO frequency with the RF Tuning control. This changes the center frequency of the RF Filter and can be compared to displacing a "window" (the RF Filter) in the frequency spectrum. When the "window" is positioned at the desired carrier frequency, station selection is complete and the selected RF signal is then amplified before mixing with the LO signal. The local oscillator is designed so that the LO frequency is 455 kHz (the intermediate frequency) above the station frequency, and the RF Tuning control adjusts the LO frequency at the same time as the center frequency of the RF Filter. This results in a fixed IF for all stations ($f_{LO} = f_C + f_{IF}$). Tuning the LO above the carrier frequency, instead of below, results in more linear tuning for the local oscillator. This is because it's easier to make oscillators which are linear over a 1 to 2 MHz range (a frequency ratio of 2), than it is to make them linear over a 0.1 to 1.1 MHz range (a frequency ratio of 11).

Mixing the selected RF signal with the LO signal produces sum and difference frequencies (of both input signals) at the output of the mixer. The IF filter allows only the difference frequency (f_{IF}) to pass through, and the filtered signal is then processed by the **detector** to remove the original information. The **Automatic Gain Control (AGC)** circuit helps maintain a fairly constant output level by controlling the gain of the RF amplifier. The AGC circuit in some receivers also controls the gain of the IF amplifier.

NEW TERMS AND WORDS

Automatic Gain Control (AGC) — the circuit or process used to maintain the output volume of a receiver constant, regardless of variations in the RF signal strength applied to the receiver.

demodulation — the process of removing the information contained in a modulated RF signal; also called detection.

detector — the circuit or device used to perform the process of demodulation.

IF stage — that section of a receiver contained between the mixer and the detector stage. This stage operates at the fixed intermediate frequency and it is here that most of the amplification and filtering takes place.

intraband image frequencies — image frequencies that lie inside the allocated frequency band for the type of communications involved. In AM, intraband image frequencies occur at both ends of the commercial band from 540 to 690 kHz and from 1450 to 1600 kHz.

image frequency (f_{IMAGE}) — in heterodyne receivers, an undesired input frequency equal to the station frequency plus twice the intermediate frequency ($f_{IMAGE} = f_C + 2f_{IF}$). The image frequency results in two stations being received at the same time, thus producing interference. (For receivers in which the LO is tuned below the station, $f_{IMAGE} = f_C - 2f_{IF}$).

image frequency rejection ratio — of a superheterodyne receiver, the ratio of the response at the desired frequency to the response at the image frequency.

RF stage — the first input stage of a receiver, in which primary selection, filtering and amplification of the input RF signal is performed.

selectivity — a measure of how well a receiver rejects adjacent channel signals when tuned to a particular station.

The RF Stage Frequency Response

EXERCISE OBJECTIVE

When you have completed this exercise you will be familiar with the frequency response characteristics of the RF stage in the AM / DSB Receiver.

DISCUSSION

The reception of an AM signal using a superheterodyne receiver, such as the AM / DSB Receiver, involves four principal operations. First, the desired station must be selected or "tuned in" from among all the others. Once this is done the radio signal must be frequency-translated to the intermediate frequency. The third operation is filtering and amplifying the IF signal which is almost an exact copy of the RF signal except for its frequency and amplitude.

The fourth and final operation involved in the process of AM reception is demodulation (or detection) of the information contained in the IF signal.

In this exercise, you will study the operation of the **RF stage** of the receiver – more particularly the RF filter. The RF filter is responsible for making sure that only the frequency contents centered around the selected carrier frequency pass through to be mixed with the local oscillator frequency. The RF filter is also the principal element in **image frequency (f_{IMAGE}) rejection**. This will be studied in a later exercise. An important consideration for the RF filter is its bandwidth. If the message signal contains frequencies up to 5 kHz, then the bandwidth of the RF filter must be at least 10 kHz. This is because the AM signal contains two sidebands, the USB and the LSB, both of which contain the information being transmitted. Consequently, the process of amplitude modulation doubles the bandwidth necessary for transmission of the message signal. An ordinary AM receiver needs both sidebands to demodulate the message properly. Refer to Figure 3-2 and you will see that the bandwidth of the AM signal is $955 - 945 = 10$ kHz for the baseband signal containing frequencies up to 5 kHz.

EQUIPMENT REQUIRED

DESCRIPTION	MODEL
Accessories	8948
Power Supply / Dual Audio Amplifier	9401
Frequency Counter	9403
True RMS Voltmeter / Power Meter	9404
Spectrum Analyzer	9405
AM / DSB / SSB Generator	9410
AM / DSB Receiver	9411
Oscilloscope	—

The RF Stage Frequency Response

PROCEDURE

☐ 1. Set up the modules as shown in Figure 3-4. Make sure that all OUTPUT LEVEL and GAIN controls are turned fully counterclockwise to the MIN position, and power up the equipment.

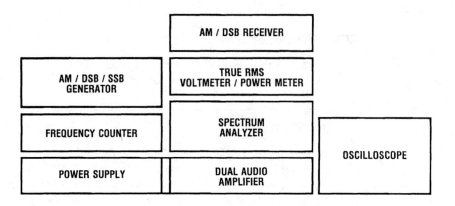

Figure 3-4. Suggested Module Arrangement.

☐ 2. Set up and calibrate the Spectrum Analyzer module around 1.0 MHz. Place the INPUT impedance switch in the 1 MΩ position. Use a BNC / BNC cable to connect the RF OUTPUT (terminal 3) of the AM / DSB Receiver to the INPUT of the Spectrum Analyzer.

☐ 3. Use the Frequency Counter to set a Local Oscillator frequency of 1405 kHz at OSC OUTPUT on the AM / DSB Receiver.

Since $f_{LO} = f_C + f_{IF}$, what carrier frequency is the receiver tuned to select?

_____ kHz

☐ 4. Place the AGC switch in the I (active) position and select the SYNC DETECTOR. Have your instructor activate Fault number 2 (FLT 2) on the AM / DSB Receiver module. This is done by opening the top panel of the module, and placing the FLT 2 switch under the small hinged cover in the I (active) position.

Note: *Once the fault has been activated, the RF TUNING knob **must not** be readjusted because the Local Oscillator has been disabled. If it is necessary to verify or readjust f_{LO} , FLT 2 must be returned to the O (inactive) position.*

☐ 5. Open the top panel of the AM / DSB / SSB Generator module and connect a × 10 oscilloscope probe at TP13. This will allow you to continuously monitor the carrier frequency with the Frequency Counter. Connect the other end to the Frequency Counter in place of the AM / DSB Receiver.

The RF Stage Frequency Response

☐ 6. Set the CARRIER LEVEL on the AM / DSB / SSB Generator at MAX, and make sure that it is pushed-in to the LINEAR OVERMODULATION position. Set the RF GAIN (amplifier A_2) at ¼ turn cw, and then connect the AM / DSB RF OUTPUT to the 50 Ω RF INPUT on the AM / DSB Receiver.

☐ 7. While adjusting the RF TUNING knob on the AM / DSB / SSB Generator to obtain a carrier frequency of 950 kHz, observe the Spectrum Analyzer display. What happens as the carrier frequency approaches 950 kHz?

_____

_____

_____

☐ 8. Use the TUNING controls on the Spectrum Analyzer to center the 950-kHz carrier in the center of the screen. Change the FREQUENCY SPAN successively to 50 kHz / V and retune the Spectrum Analyzer as necessary to keep the carrier frequency in the center of the screen.

☐ 9. Readjust the RF GAIN (amplifier A_2) on the AM / DSB / SSB Generator, if necessary, to set the height of the carrier frequency line on the Spectrum Analyzer at the − 10 dBm reference level (6th graticule line from the bottom with 0 dBm MAXIMUM INPUT).

☐ 10. Vary the RF TUNING control on the AM / DSB / SSB Generator both sides of 950 kHz. As the top of the carrier frequency line moves, it will trace out the approximate frequency response of the RF filter at 950 kHz. Use Figure 3-5 to sketch the curve traced out by the top of the line.

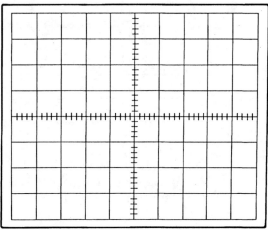

Figure 3-5. RF Filter approximate frequency response at 950 kHz.

☐ 11. What are the approximate 3-, 10-, and 20-dB bandwidths (BW)?

3-dB BW = _____ kHz − _____ kHz = _____ kHz

10-dB BW = _____ kHz − _____ kHz = _____ kHz

20-dB BW = _____ kHz − _____ kHz = _____ kHz

☐ 12. Connect the True RMS Voltmeter / Power Meter to the RF OUTPUT (terminal 3) of the AM / DSB Receiver, in place of the Spectrum Analyzer. Adjust the zero on the voltmeter module, and then place the MODE switch in the dBm position.

☐ 13. If necessary, readjust the RF GAIN (amplifier A_2) and the RF TUNING on the AM / DSB / SSB Generator to obtain a reading of − 10 dBm at 950 kHz.

☐ 14. Vary the RF TUNING to obtain the frequencies shown in Figure 3-6 and record the dBm reading for each frequency in the corresponding column.

☐ 15. Calculate the relative dB values using the relation in Figure 3-6, and sketch the frequency response curve corresponding to these values.

☐ 16. What are the 3-, 10-, and 20-dB bandwidths according to Figure 3-6?

3-dB BW = _____ kHz

10-dB BW = _____ kHz

20-dB BW = _____ kHz

☐ 17. How do these values compare with the approximate results determined in step 11?

_____

_____

_____

☐ 18. The 3-dB bandwidth must be at least twice as large as the highest frequency in the message (5 kHz in this exercise). How do your results compare with this criteria?

_____

_____

_____

The RF Stage Frequency Response

FREQUENCY	850	870	890	910	930	950	970	990	1010	1030	1050
dBm READING											
RELATIVE dB*											

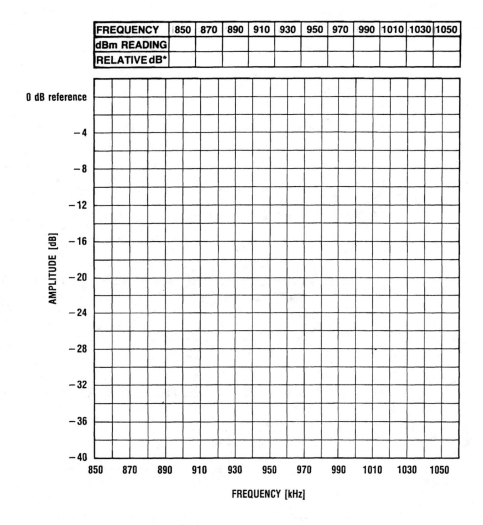

0 dB Reference = MAXIMUM dBm Reading
* Relative dB = (dBm Reading) − (0 dB Reference)

Figure 3-6. RF Filter frequency response at 950 kHz.

☐ 19. Have your instructor return FLT 2 to the O (inactive) position and check that the module operates properly before proceeding with step 20.

☐ 20. Turn all OUTPUT LEVEL and GAIN controls to the MIN position. Place all power switches in the off (O) position and disconnect all cables.

CONCLUSION

This exercise has allowed you to measure and observe the frequency response characteristics of the RF stage in a superheterodyne receiver. You have learned that the minimum bandwidth required for the RF stage depends on the frequency contents of the message signal. In general terms however, the bandwidth must be large enough to accept both sidebands of the AM signal.

The RF Stage Frequency Response

REVIEW QUESTIONS

1. What kind of receiver is the AM / DSB Receiver?

   _____

2. What are the four principal operations involved in AM reception?

   _____

   _____

   _____

   _____

3. If a message signal contains frequencies up to 3 kHz, what is the minimum bandwidth required for the RF stage if the message is to be demodulated correctly?

   _____

4. What is the result of mixing the incoming RF signal with the local oscillator signal?

   _____

   _____

   _____

   _____

5. The difference frequency of 455 kHz in the AM / DSB Receiver is called ____

   _____

The Mixer and Image Frequency Rejection

EXERCISE OBJECTIVE

When you have completed this exercise, you will be able to demonstrate the role of the mixer in a superheterodyne receiver, and explain how image frequency is related to this functional element.

DISCUSSION

The role of the mixer is to join the RF stage to the **IF stage** and to perform the necessary operations to convert (or translate) the RF signal to the fixed intermediate frequency.

As you have learned in earlier exercises the output signal of a theoretical mixer contains both the sum and the difference frequencies of the two original input signals. The output of actual mixers, however, often contains frequency components corresponding to the input signals. Figure 3-7 shows an example of this for a 950-kHz carrier modulated with a 5-kHz sine wave. Since the RF input signal to the mixer contains three frequency components, the mixer output signal will contain sum and difference frequencies for the three RF components. This results in 4 groups of frequency components in all.

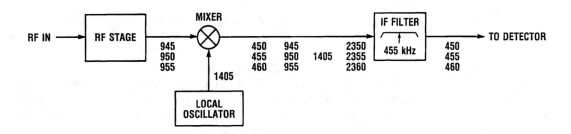

Figure 3-7. Frequency components in the output of a mixer.

Generally, the presence of these extra frequencies does not adversely affect the operation of the receiver. This is because the mixer output signal goes through a series of filters and amplifiers in the IF stage that are all tuned to the fixed IF − 455 kHz in most receivers. Also, the power levels of these frequencies are much lower than those of the main difference components situated at 455 kHz.

The Mixer and Image Frequency Rejection

One of the major disadvantages of the superheterodyne receiver is the problem of image frequency (f_{IMAGE}). Figure 3-8 illustrates how the image frequency arises and the manner in which the mixer is involved.

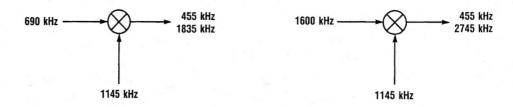

Figure 3-8. The image frequency for 950 kHz.

In this example, the carrier frequency is 690 kHz. The local oscillator frequency (f_{LO}) must be 1145 kHz in order to receive the station, since 1145 kHz − 690 kHz results in the 455 kHz IF at which the receiver operates. Now, suppose that another station operating at 1600 kHz is located in the same region, and the LO frequency remains at 1145 kHz. The difference between 1600 kHz and 1145 kHz is 455 kHz, and this new station will pass through the IF stage and interfere with the 690-kHz station. Note that for commercial AM broadcasting, image frequency problems from other AM stations occur only at both ends of the band − between 540 - 690 kHz and 1450 - 1600 kHz. However, the problem could be caused by other types of communications facilities outside the commercial band. **Intraband image frequencies** can only be eliminated when the IF frequency is such that $f_C \pm 2f_{IF}$ falls outside the band of operation. This is because the image frequency is equal to the station frequency plus (or minus) twice the intermediate frequency.

Because of the problem caused by image frequencies, one of the more important criteria for a superheterodyne receiver is the **image frequency rejection ratio**, a parameter that you will experiment in this exercise. The RF stage is responsible for most of the image frequency rejection in a superheterodyne receiver. For this reason the bandwidth of the RF stage should be no larger than is necessary for the message signal and adjacent station rejection. In this way the image frequency is greatly attenuated before the RF signal is mixed with the local oscillator signal.

EQUIPMENT REQUIRED

DESCRIPTION	MODEL
Accessories	8948
Power Supply / Dual Audio Amplifier	9401
Dual Function Generator	9402
Frequency Counter	9403
True RMS Voltmeter / Power Meter	9404
Spectrum Analyzer	9405
AM / DSB / SSB Generator	9410
AM / DSB Receiver	9411
Oscilloscope	—

The Mixer and Image Frequency Rejection

PROCEDURE

☐ 1. Set up the modules as shown in Figure 3-9. Make sure that all OUTPUT LEVEL and GAIN controls are turned fully counterclockwise to the MIN position, and power up the equipment.

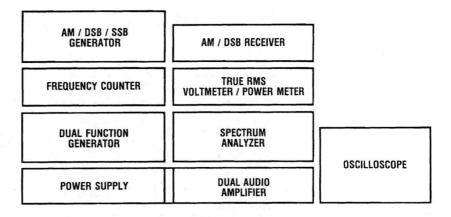

Figure 3-9. Suggested Module Arrangement.

☐ 2. Connect the AM / DSB RF OUTPUT of the AM / DSB / SSB Generator to the 50 Ω RF INPUT of the AM / DSB Receiver. Adjust the controls of both modules as follows:

AM / DSB / SSB Generator*

CARRIER LEVEL	: MAX and pushed-in
RF TUNING*	: Adjust for f_C = 690 kHz

* Use the Frequency Counter to monitor the carrier frequency with a × 10 probe connected at TP13.

AM / DSB Receiver

AGC	: O
DETECTOR	: SYNC
RF TUNING	: Adjust for f_{LO} = 1145 kHz

☐ 3. Set up and calibrate the Spectrum Analyzer module around 1.0 MHz. Place the INPUT impedance switch in the 1 MΩ position, select 0 dBm MAXIMUM INPUT and a FREQUENCY SPAN of 200 kHz / V.

☐ 4. On the Dual Function Generator adjust the channel A controls to obtain a 5-kHz sine wave. Set the OUTPUT LEVEL knob at ¼ turn cw and select the 20 dB ATTENUATOR. Connect this message signal to the AUDIO INPUT of the AM / DSB / SSB Generator.

☐ 5.   Verify that f_c is 690 kHz and that f_{LO} is 1145 kHz. Readjust the RF TUNING controls as necessary to set the frequencies within ± 0.5 kHz of the desired values.

☐ 6.   Connect the MIXER OUTPUT (terminal 5) of the AM / DSB Receiver to the INPUT of the Spectrum Analyzer and adjust the RF GAIN (amplifier A_2) on the AM / DSB / SSB Generator to obtain a spectrum as shown in Figure 3-10.

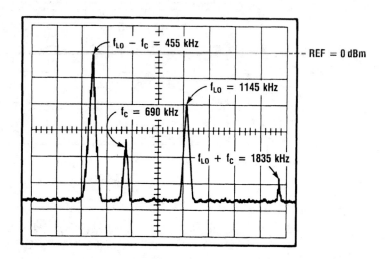

Figure 3-10. Spectrum of IF signal at MIXER OUTPUT. FREQUENCY SPAN = 200 kHz / V.

☐ 7.   Vary slightly the RF TUNING of the AM / DSB / SSB Generator and observe the signal at about 455 kHz. When the signal has reached its maximum, measure and record the approximate dBm values of the frequency components.

$f_{LO} =$ _____ dBm $f_c =$ _____ dBm

$f_{LO} + f_c =$ _____ dBm $f_{LO} - f_c =$ _____ dBm

Note: *It may be difficult to measure f_c and $f_{LO} + f_c$, as they are typically 35 – 50 dB below the difference component depending on the level of the RF input signal.*

☐ 8.   How many dB difference do you obtain between f_{LO} and the IF component at 455 kHz?

_____ dB

Do you think this is acceptable? (Remember, the mixer output signal goes through several IF filters before demodulation).

_____

_____

The Mixer and Image Frequency Rejection

☐ 9. Select the 20 dBm MAXIMUM INPUT on the Spectrum Analyzer.

☐ 10. Connect the IF OUTPUT (terminal 7) of the AM / DSB Receiver to the INPUT of the Spectrum Analyzer in place of the MIXER OUTPUT. What do you observe on the Spectrum Analyzer display?

_____

_____

What has changed with respect to the spectrum observed in step 6?

_____

_____

☐ 11. Adjust the RF GAIN (amplifier A_2) on the AM / DSB / SSB Generator to obtain a height of 10 dBm for the IF component. Depress the 40 dB ATTENUATOR for channel A on the Dual Function Generator. This will result in a lower modulation index and a more stable frequency display.

Note: *You should vary slightly the RF TUNING on the AM / DSB / SSB Generator to both sides in order to maximize the height of the spectral line.*

☐ 12. When the IF component has been properly adjusted at the 10 dBm reference level, disconnect the AM / DSB RF OUTPUT of the AM / DSB / SSB Generator from the RF INPUT of the AM / DSB Receiver.

Install a 50 Ω load at the INPUT of the True RMS Voltmeter / Power Meter and measure the dBm value of the AM signal.

P_{AM} (690 kHz) = _____ dBm

☐ 13. Reconnect the AM / DSB output to the 50 Ω RF INPUT of the AM receiver, and then adjust the RF TUNING of the AM / DSB / SSB Generator to obtain a carrier frequency of 1600 kHz.

What is this frequency called with respect to 690 kHz?

_____

☐ 14. Readjust the RF GAIN as in step 11 to obtain 10 dBm on the Spectrum Analyzer display and repeat step 12. You will notice that the RF GAIN must be set relatively high in order to obtain 10 dBm.

P_{AM} (1600 kHz) = _____ dBm

☐ 15. What is the value of P_{AM} (1600 kHz) − P_{AM} (690 kHz)?

P_{AM} (1600 kHz) − P_{AM} (690 kHz) = _____ dB

The difference in dB that you have calculated between the RF power at the image frequency and the RF power at the station frequency represents the image frequency rejection ratio.

☐ 16. Turn all OUTPUT LEVEL and GAIN control to the MIN position. Place all power switches in the off (O) position and disconnect all cables.

CONCLUSION

The mixer stage in a superheterodyne receiver allows the RF signal to be frequency-translated to a fixed IF, and it is the link between the RF and IF stages. You have seen however that the mixer does not distinguish between the station frequency and the image frequency. The image frequency rejection ratio is an indication of how well the receiver and its associated elements work together in reducing the problems caused by the image frequency.

REVIEW QUESTIONS

1. An AM receiver tuned to a station at 600 kHz uses a 455 kHz IF and the local oscillator operates above the station frequency. What is the image frequency for this station?

_____ kHz

2. The image frequency of an AM station is 2500 kHz. What is the frequency of the station if the receiver uses 455 kHz as the IF and $f_{LO} = f_C + f_{IF}$?

_____ kHz

3. What is the role of the mixer linking the RF and IF stages of a superheterodyne receiver?

_____

_____

4. Which stage of the receiver is responsible for most of the image frequency rejection?

_____

5. How can intraband image frequencies be eliminated?

_____

The IF Stage Frequency Response

EXERCISE OBJECTIVE

When you have completed this exercise you will be familiar with the frequency-response characteristics of the IF stage in the AM / DSB Receiver.

DISCUSSION

You may have wondered why the RF signal is first converted to a fixed IF in the superheterodyne receiver before demodulating the message. The principal reason is so that amplification and filtering can be performed at a fixed frequency that is independent of the RF signal frequency. This means that sensitivity is about the same for all stations, and **selectivity** criteria for the RF stage can be relaxed since more control is given to the IF stage.

The IF stage of a superheterodyne receiver is therefore responsible for most of the receiver's selectivity. The bandwidth of this stage should be only as large as required for the message signal – typically 10 kHz in commercial AM broadcasting. It is also necessary to assure proper IF shielding, because any transmission occurring at the 455-kHz intermediate frequency will interfere with proper operation, even if only a very small amount of undesirable signal gets through the RF stage. This is due mainly to the fact that the gain of the IF stage is generally very large and this section of the receiver accepts readily any signal at 455 kHz.

Because of its importance in fixing selectivity, the IF stage should have sharp roll-off characteristics in its frequency-response curve. This will enable greater rejection of stations close to the one that the receiver is tuned to. Since channel spacing for AM stations is 10 kHz, the steeper the slope of the frequency-response curve at 450 and 460 kHz, the better the selectivity will be. A station at 960 kHz, for example, will already be attenuated by the RF stage tuned to 950 kHz, and the message signal contents of this adjacent station will be further attenuated by the IF stage. Another factor coming into play is the input / output isolation of the mixer stage, which typically offers 10 to 20 dB attenuation of the input signals (since it is usually optimized to produce the difference frequency).

The IF Stage Frequency Response

EQUIPMENT REQUIRED

DESCRIPTION	MODEL
Accessories	8948
Power Supply / Dual Audio Amplifier	9401
Dual Function Generator	9402
Frequency Counter	9403
True RMS Voltmeter / Power Meter	9404
Spectrum Analyzer	9405
AM / DSB / SSB Generator	9410
AM / DSB Receiver	9411
Oscilloscope	—

PROCEDURE

☐ 1. Set up the modules as shown in Figure 3-11. Make sure that all OUTPUT LEVEL and GAIN controls are turned fully counterclockwise to the MIN position, and power up the equipment.

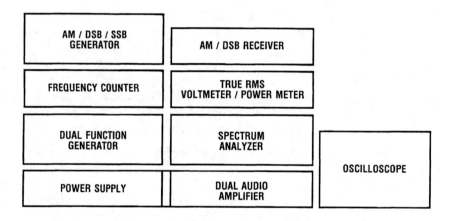

Figure 3-11. Suggested Module Arrangement.

☐ 2. Set up and calibrate the Spectrum Analyzer module around 0.5 MHz. Place the INPUT impedance switch in the 1 MΩ position. Use a BNC / BNC cable to connect the IF OUTPUT of the AM / DSB Receiver to the INPUT of the Spectrum Analyzer.

☐ 3. On the AM / DSB Receiver place the AGC switch in the O (inactive) position and select the SYNC DETECTOR. Have your instructor activate Fault 2 (FLT 2) as in Exercise 3-1, step 4.

☐ 4. Open the top panel of the AM / DSB / SSB Generator and connect a × 10 oscilloscope probe at TP13 to monitor the output frequency of the generator with the Frequency Counter.

The IF Stage Frequency Response

☐ 5. Set the CARRIER LEVEL control on the AM generator at the MAX position, and make sure that it is pushed-in to the LINEAR OVERMODULATION position. Adjust the RF GAIN (amplifier A_2) at ½ turn cw, and then connect the AM / DSB RF OUTPUT to the AUX IF INPUT (terminal 6) of the AM / DSB Receiver.

At what frequency should the carrier be adjusted if we are going to measure the frequency response of the fixed-frequency IF stage?

_____ kHz

☐ 6. Adjust the RF TUNING control on the AM / DSB / SSB Generator to obtain 455 kHz, and observe the results on the Spectrum Analyzer display.

What happens as the carrier approaches 455 kHz?

_____

_____

_____

☐ 7. Place the 455-kHz IF signal in the center of the Spectrum Analyzer display and select successively the 200, 50, 10, and 2 kHz / V FREQUENCY SPANs.

☐ 8. Adjust the RF GAIN (amplifier A_2) on the AM / DSB / SSB Generator to obtain a height of − 10 dB for the IF line on the Spectrum Analyzer. Vary the RF TUNING slightly to both sides to maximize the height of the spectral line.

At what frequency is the maximum height obtained?

_____ kHz

☐ 9. Vary the RF TUNING control on the AM / DSB / SSB Generator both sides of 455 kHz. The tip of the spectral line will trace out the approximate frequency response at 455 kHz. Use Figure 3-12 to sketch the curve traced out by the tip of the spectral line.

☐ 10. What are the approximate 3-, 10-, and 20-dB bandwidths?

3-dB BW = _____ kHz − _____ kHz = _____ kHz

10-dB BW = _____ kHz − _____ kHz = _____ kHz

20-dB BW = _____ kHz − _____ kHz = _____ kHz

The IF Stage Frequency Response

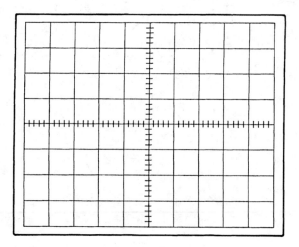

Figure 3-12. IF Stage approximate frequency response at 455 kHz.

☐ 11. Connect the True RMS Voltmeter / Power Meter to the IF OUTPUT of the AM / DSB Receiver in place of the Spectrum Analyzer. Adjust the zero on the voltmeter module, and then place the MODE switch in the dBm position.

☐ 12. If necessary, readjust the RF GAIN (amplifier A_2) and the RF TUNING on the AM / DSB / SSB Generator to obtain a reading of −10 dBm at 455 kHz. Make sure that you maximize the level of the signal using the RF TUNING control before final adjustment of the RF GAIN control.

☐ 13. Vary the RF TUNING to obtain the frequencies shown in Figure 3-13 and record the dBm reading for each frequency in the corresponding column.

☐ 14. Calculate the relative dB values using the relation in Figure 3-13, and sketch the frequency response curve corresponding to these values.

☐ 15. What are the 3-, 10-, and 20-dB bandwidths according to Figure 3-13?

    3-dB BW = _____ kHz

    10-dB BW = _____ kHz

    20-dB BW = _____ kHz

☐ 16. How do these values compare with those of step 10?

_____

_____

The IF Stage Frequency Response

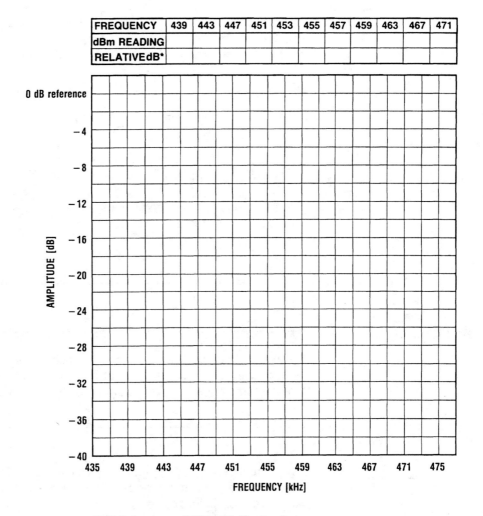

FREQUENCY	439	443	447	451	453	455	457	459	463	467	471
dBm READING											
RELATIVE dB*											

0 dB Reference = MAXIMUM dBm Reading.
* Relative dB = (dBm Reading) − (0 dB Reference)

Figure 3-13. IF Stage frequency response at 455 kHz.

☐ 17. In order to appreciate more fully how the bandwidth of the IF stage affects the message signal, you will inject a modulated signal at the AUX IF INPUT. Reconnect the IF OUTPUT of the receiver to the INPUT of the Spectrum Analyzer in place of the True RMS Voltmeter / Power Meter.

☐ 18. Make sure that the RF TUNING on the AM / DSB / SSB Generator is adjusted so that the height of the spectral line is maximum.

☐ 19. On the Dual Function Generator adjust the channel A controls to produce a 5-kHz sine wave with the OUTPUT LEVEL set at ¼ turn cw and select the 20 dB ATTENUATOR. Connect the channel A signal to the AUDIO INPUT on the AM / DSB / SSB Generator.

The IF Stage Frequency Response

☐ 20. Select the 10 kHz / V FREQUENCY SPAN on the Spectrum Analyzer and readjust the TUNING controls as necessary to keep the modulated carrier centered in the display. What do you observe on the display?

_____

_____

☐ 21. Vary the frequency of the message signal between 2 and 10 kHz using the channel A FREQUENCY control on the Dual Function Generator.

What happens to the spectral lines representing the message signal as the frequency increases?

_____

_____

_____

_____

Because of frequency-response characteristics of the IF stage, the attenuation of both spectral lines may not be identical at every point and therefore the spectrum will not be symmetrical. Does this happen in your case?

_____

☐ 22. Adjust the message signal frequency until the LSB and the USB are 3 dB less than their maximum values. Record the sideband frequencies at which the 3-dB point occurs.

f_{LSB} = _____ kHz f_{USB} = _____ kHz

☐ 23. Compare these answers with the 3-dB point on the frequency-response curve of Figure 3-13.

_____

_____

_____

☐ 24. Compare the 3-dB bandwidth of the IF stage (step 15) with the 3-dB bandwidth of the RF stage (Exercise 3-1, step 16).

_____

_____

_____

The IF Stage Frequency Response

☐ 25. Have your instructor return FLT 2 to the O (inactive) position and check that the module operates properly before proceeding with step 26.

☐ 26. Turn all OUTPUT LEVEL and GAIN controls to the MIN position. Place all power switches in the off (O) position and disconnect all cables.

CONCLUSION

This exercise has allowed you to measure and observe the frequency-response characteristics of the IF stage in a superheterodyne receiver. You have also observed the manner in which the AM sidebands are attenuated as the message signal frequency is increased beyond the design capabilities of the IF stage.

REVIEW QUESTIONS

1. The typical bandwidth required to transmit a message signal in commercial AM is 10 kHz. Explain the influence, if any, that this has on the bandwidth requirements of the IF stage.

   _____

   _____

   _____

2. The IF stage bandwidth of an AM receiver is measured and found to be 6 kHz. What effect will this have on performance during reception of commercial AM stations?

   _____

   _____

   _____

3. Which stage of a superheterodyne receiver is responsible for most of the receiver's selectivity?

   _____

   _____

   _____

4. Why can the very large gain of the IF stage cause problems in a superheterodyne receiver?

   _____

   _____

   _____

5. During frequency-response measurements of the IF stage it is found that the LSB and USB are not attenuated equally. Can this be considered normal? Explain.

_____

_____

_____

The Envelope Detector

EXERCISE OBJECTIVE

When you have completed this exercise, you will be able to demonstrate how an AM signal is demodulated using the ENVelope detector found in the AM / DSB Receiver.

DISCUSSION

Any circuit whose output follows the envelope of an AM signal can serve as a detector, and be used to demodulate the RF wave. One of the most widely used and simplest detectors is the non-linear charging circuit formed by a diode in series with the parallel RC network shown in Figure 3-14. This kind of envelope detector is also known as a diode detector.

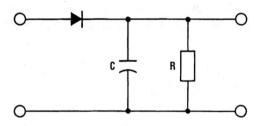

Figure 3-14. The Envelope Detector.

The circuit is designed to have a fast charge time and a slow discharge time, with the resistor controlling the discharge time constant. If the AM signal shown in Figure 3-15 is applied to the input of this circuit, it will undergo half-wave rectification as illustrated.

The Envelope Detector

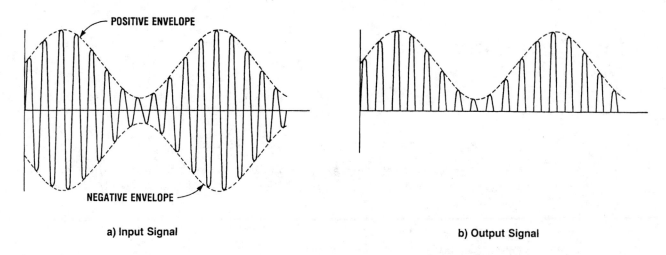

a) Input Signal

b) Output Signal

Figure 3-15. Theoretical input and output signals of the envelope detector.

The operation of the envelope detector is as follows. On the positive half cycles of the input signal, the capacitor charges to the peak value of the input. Therefore, the voltage across RC will be equal to that of the input signal since the diode is forward-biased. When the input signal drops below this value, the diode turns off and the capacitor starts to slowly discharge through the resistor at a rate determined by the RC time constant. On the next positive half-cycle of the input signal, the diode is turned on and the capacitor again charges to the new value determined by the input signal. Figure 3-16 resumes this charge-discharge process.

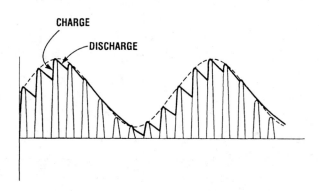

Figure 3-16. The charge-discharge process of the capacitor.

There is an optimum value for the discharge time constant RC. If the time constant is too large, or too small, the output of the detector will not follow faithfully the envelope of the input signal. Figure 3-17 shows the effects of having RC too large, or too small.

The Envelope Detector

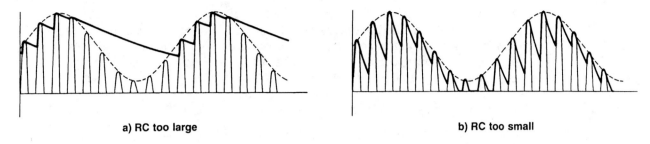

a) RC too large   b) RC too small

Figure 3-17. The effects of the discharge time constant.

The optimum value of RC is obtained when the time constant is equal to the maximum negative slope of the envelope. Because the envelope represents the message signal waveform, RC is a function of the modulating signal frequency and the modulation index. The following equation has been derived for the optimum value of the discharge time constant.

$$RC_{optimum} = \frac{1}{m \, 2\pi \, f_m}$$

After detection, the output of the envelope detector is usually filtered with a low pass filter, in order to remove ripple and the unwanted harmonic content. Often, a coupling capacitor is used to remove the dc level introduced by the carrier.

One of the major drawbacks of the envelope detector is the fact that approximately 0.6 V potential difference must exist across the diode before it conducts. This means that a 0.6 V difference between the input signal voltage and the capacitor voltage is necessary before the output begins following the input. This is more pronounced for weak input signals, and also when the modulation index is close to 100%. Figure 3-18 shows the two cases. The heavy line shows the demodulated signal waveform (before filtering) while the dashed line illustrates the envelope. The resulting audio will often be distorted and subject to fading because of this voltage loss, and weak stations may not be demodulated at all.

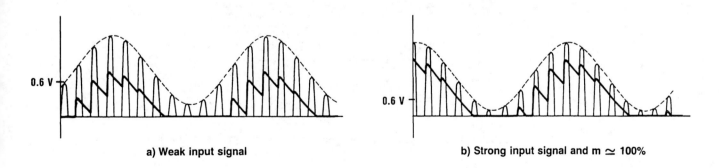

a) Weak input signal   b) Strong input signal and m $\simeq$ 100%

Figure 3-18. The effect of the diode's forward voltage drop.

The Envelope Detector

More often than not, it is the negative envelope of the AM signal that is detected with the diode detector, and the diode in Figure 3-14 is simply reversed. The reason for this is that detection of the negative envelope provides the negative AGC voltage necessary to control the gain of the RF stage. If the RF signal increases in strength, more negative feedback from the AGC circuit is sent to the RF stage to reduce its gain. In this way, the audio output level remains fairly constant in spite of variations in the strength of the RF signal.

Among the other types of detectors available is the PLL (phase-locked loop) SYN-Chronous detector. The functional block diagram of the SYNC detector used in the AM / DSB Receiver is shown in Figure 3-19 below. This type of detector provides better detection of AM signals, and allows the RF TUNING to vary over a larger frequency range before the station is lost. Coupled with the AGC circuit, it also allows greater variations in RF signal levels, and permits modulation levels approaching 100%.

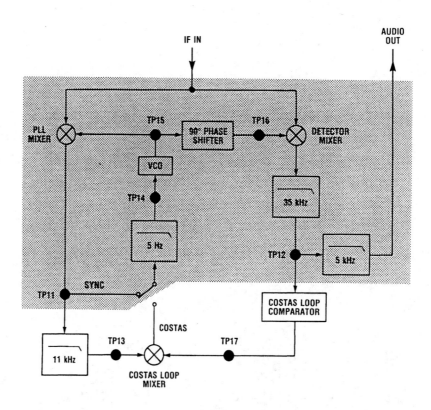

Figure 3-19. Functional block diagram of the SYNC DETECTOR (shaded).

The Envelope Detector

EQUIPMENT REQUIRED

DESCRIPTION	MODEL
Accessories	8948
Power Supply / Dual Audio Amplifier	9401
Dual Function Generator	9402
Frequency Counter	9403
AM / DSB / SSB Generator	9410
AM / DSB Receiver	9411
Oscilloscope	—

PROCEDURE

☐ 1. Set up the modules as shown in Figure 3-20. Make sure that all OUTPUT LEVEL and GAIN controls are turned fully counterclockwise to the MIN position, and power up the equipment.

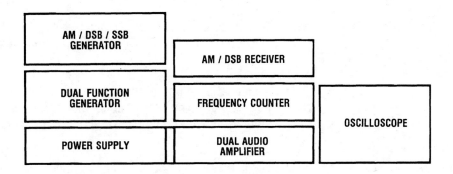

Figure 3-20. Suggested Module Arrangement.

☐ 2. Adjust the channel A controls on the Dual Function Generator to obtain a 1.0 kHz sine wave. Set the OUTPUT LEVEL control at ¼ turn cw and select the 20 dB attenuator. Connect this message signal to the AUDIO INPUT on the AM / DSB / SSB Generator.

If the modulation index (m) is equal to 1.0, what is the optimum value of the RC time constant for the 1.0 kHz message signal?

$$RC_{optimum} = \rule{2cm}{0.4pt} \mu s$$

☐ 3. Set up the AM communications system using a 950-kHz carrier frequency for the AM / DSB / SSB Generator. Monitor the carrier frequency at TP13. Set the RF GAIN (amplifier A_2) at ¼ turn cw, and make sure that the CARRIER LEVEL knob is pushed-in and at the MAX position.

The Envelope Detector

☐ 4. To what value must the LO frequency on the AM / DSB Receiver be set in order to receive the 950-kHz frequency?

LO frequency = _____ kHz

☐ 5. Adjust the RF TUNING control on the AM / DSB Receiver to 1405 kHz and connect the AM / DSB RF OUTPUT to the AM receiver's 50 Ω RF INPUT. Select the ENV DETECTOR and place the AGC switch in the I (active) position.

☐ 6. Connect the IF OUTPUT of the AM / DSB Receiver to channel 1 of the oscilloscope and the AUDIO OUTPUT to channel 2.

Set the time base control at .5 ms / DIV and set the oscilloscope to trigger on the audio signal.

☐ 7. Select dc coupling for both channels of the oscilloscope and set the sensitivity controls at 1 VOLT / DIV for channel 1 and .5 VOLT / DIV for channel 2.

As a final adjustment, position the dc reference line for channel 2 on the 2 nd graticule line (from the bottom) of the oscilloscope, and position the dc reference for channel 1 on the 5 th graticule line.

☐ 8. Verify that the carrier frequency is still at 950 kHz, and then describe the signals displayed on the oscilloscope.

_____

_____

☐ 9. Use one of the methods described in Unit 2 to determine the approximate modulation index.

m = _____

☐ 10. Vary the CARRIER LEVEL control on the AM / DSB / SSB Generator between MAX and MIN. What happens to the audio signal displayed on the oscilloscope?

_____

_____

Note: *Varying the CARRIER LEVEL produces the same kind of change in the modulation index as when the message signal level is varied. It can therefore be used to vary the modulation index.*

The Envelope Detector

☐ 11. At what position of the CARRIER LEVEL control does the demodulated audio signal begin to be affected (⅛, ¼, ½, etc.)?

_____

Determine the approximate modulation index for this position of the CARRIER LEVEL control.

m = _____

☐ 12. Overmodulate the AM signal by reducing the CARRIER LEVEL to MIN and pull the knob out to the NONLINEAR OVERMODULATION position. What effect does this have on the demodulated audio signal?

_____

_____

_____

☐ 13. Return the CARRIER LEVEL control to MAX and push it in to the LINEAR OVERMODULATION position.

☐ 14. Place the AGC switch on the receiver in the O (inactive) position, and set the RF GAIN of the AM generator ½ turn cw.

☐ 15. Vary the RF GAIN (amplifier A_2) slowly between ½ turn cw and MIN. What happens to the demodulated audio?

_____

_____

_____

☐ 16. Activate the AGC (I position) and then vary the RF GAIN (amplifier A_2) between MIN and MAX. What differences are there with respect to step 15?

_____

_____

_____

_____

☐ 17. Return the RF GAIN (amplifier A_2) to the ¼ turn cw position and set the channel 2 sensitivity control of the oscilloscope at 1 VOLT / DIV.

☐ 18. Select the SYNC DETECTOR on the AM / DSB Receiver and increase the channel A OUTPUT LEVEL of the Dual Function Generator to obtain approximately 100% modulation.

Switch between the ENV and SYNC DETECTORs and describe the differences in the demodulated audio.

_____

_____

_____

_____

☐ 19. Based on your observations which detector permits a modulation index approaching 100% before distortion of the demodulated audio signal occurs?

_____

_____

☐ 20. Turn all OUTPUT LEVEL and GAIN controls to the MIN Position. Place all power switches in the off (O) position and disconnect all cables.

CONCLUSION

As you have seen in this exercise, an envelope detector functions very well within a limited range of signal level variations, and adds little or no distortion at proper signal levels. The AGC circuit also plays an important role in detection, as it controls the input level to the detector circuit. You have also observed the operation of the SYNChronous detector, which is built around a PLL. This detector permits a wider variation in the level of the RF signal and also keeps the station tuned-in over a larger tuning range.

REVIEW QUESTIONS

1. Sketch the circuit for a simple diode detector.

The Envelope Detector

2. Explain briefly how a diode detector operates.

_____

_____

_____

3. What effect does the 0.6 V drop across the detector diode have on demodulation of the IF signal?

_____

_____

_____

4. Does an AGC circuit have any effect on the detection process? Explain.

_____

_____

_____

_____

5. Based on the results of this exercise, which detector coupled with an AGC circuit provides a demodulated audio signal having less distortion and a higher level?

_____

Unit Test

1. In a superheterodyne receiver the incoming RF signal is first converted to a fixed frequency called

   a. the LO frequency.
   b. the intermediate frequency (IF).
   c. the image frequency.
   d. none of the above.

2. The local oscillator frequency of an AM receiver is adjusted at 1045 kHz and the receiver uses 455 kHz as the IF. What station is the receiver tuned to select?

   a. 1500 kHz, if the LO is tuned below the station frequency.
   b. 690 kHz, if the LO is tuned below the station frequency.
   c. 590 kHz, if the LO is tuned above the station frequency.
   d. Either a or c.

3. The process of recovering the information contained in an AM signal is called

   a. modulation.
   b. demodulation.
   c. frequency translation.
   d. analog communications.

4. Image frequency rejection is controlled mostly by

   a. the IF stage.
   b. the detector circuit.
   c. the RF stage.
   d. maintaining the modulation index at proper levels.

5. The image frequency for an AM station at 590 kHz is 1500 kHz if

   a. the IF is 455 kHz and the LO is tuned above the carrier frequency.
   b. the IF is 455 kHz and the LO is tuned below the carrier frequency.
   c. the IF is equal to the carrier frequency.
   d. the IF is equal to the LO frequency.

6. Commercial AM stations broadcast information containing frequencies up to 5 kHz. The IF stage of an AM receiver should therefore have a 3-dB bandwidth of

   a. 20 kHz
   b. 15 kHz
   c. 10 kHz
   d. 5 kHz

7. The IF stage is responsible for most of the selectivity of a superheterodyne receiver.

   a. True.
   b. False.

8. An envelope detector for AM signals is less efficient in demodulating weak AM signals than a PLL synchronous detector. This is because of

   a. the RC time constant in the detector diode.
   b. the 0.6 V drop across the detector diode.
   c. the AGC circuit in the receiver.
   d. both b and c.

9. The AGC circuit controls

   a. the input level to the detector circuit.
   b. the output level of the receiver.
   c. the gain of the RF and / or IF stages.
   d. all of the above.

10. The optimum value for the discharge time constant of a diode detector circuit is directly related to

   a. the minimum RF power available at the input.
   b. the carrier frequency.
   c. the modulation index and the message signal frequency.
   d. both a and c.

Double Sideband Modulation – DSB

UNIT OBJECTIVE

When you have completed this unit, you will be able to explain and demonstrate DSB modulation using the AM / DSB / SSB Generator and the AM / DSB Receiver.

DISCUSSION OF FUNDAMENTALS

As a result of your work in the previous units, you should now be familiar with amplitude modulation and what it represents. Recall that for AM, the message signal is translated in frequency to a position centered around the carrier frequency as shown in Figure 4-1 (a). Figure 4-1 (b) shows the same message signal at the same position in the frequency spectrum, but now the line representing the carrier has been removed. Basically, this is all that **DSB** (double sideband) modulation really is – removing the carrier from the RF wave.

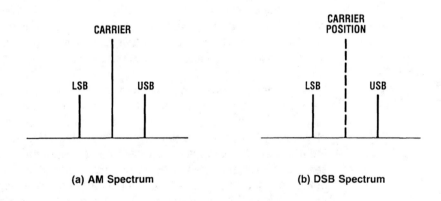

(a) AM Spectrum   (b) DSB Spectrum

Figure 4-1. Spectral representation of AM and DSB.

Double Sideband Modulation – DSB

As for the time domain representation of a DSB signal, Figure 4-2 illustrates the differences with an AM signal.

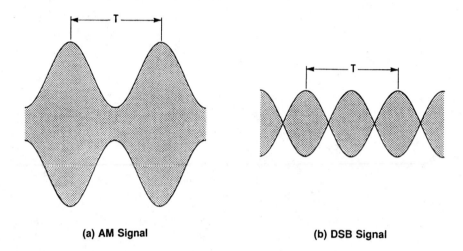

(a) AM Signal   (b) DSB Signal

Figure 4-2. The time domain representation of AM and DSB signals.

You may recall from previous exercises, that this type of waveform (DSB signal) occurred as the CARRIER LEVEL control was placed in the MIN position on the AM / DSB / SSB Generator. Reducing the carrier level produced an overmodulated AM signal, and then a DSB signal when there was negligible power left in the carrier. This brings us to the major advantage of DSB modulation – better power utilization with respect to AM. This is because there is no power "wasted" in the carrier, since all available power is placed in the message signal.

However, there is one principal disadvantage with DSB modulation. Since the carrier is absent from the spectrum, how does one go about locating and demodulating the message? Locating the message is not in itself a great problem, as scanning across the frequency spectrum with a filter will produce an output signal from the receiver at those positions where message signals are present. The difficulty lies in synchronizing the locally generated carrier (in the receiver) to the frequency of the absent carrier. Recall that a local carrier is necessary for reception because the incoming RF signal is first converted to an intermediate frequency before recovering the message. Any differences in frequency and/or phase relationship between the locally generated carrier and the RF carrier will result in distortion of the demodulated audio. Therefore, the detection circuitry in the receiver has to be more complex, so that the proper phase and frequency relationship will be maintained.

In the Analog Communications Training System, a **COSTAS loop detector** is used to demodulate a DSB signal. This kind of detector consists of a PLL combined with a COSTAS section. Figure 4-3 shows the functional block diagram of the Costas loop detector with the PLL section non-shaded. The additional section (shaded) allows the complete detector system to remain synchronized with the carrier frequency, and to detect the zero crossover (polarity change) of the message signal. Zero-crossover detection is important to prevent the PLL from interpreting this as a phase error, in which case the error signal to the VCO will cause the locally generated carrier frequency (the VCO frequency) to change, and synchronization will be lost.

Double Sideband Modulation – DSB

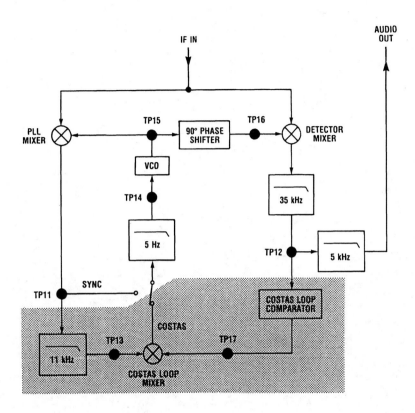

Figure 4-3. A COSTAS loop detector for DSB signals.

NEW TERMS AND WORDS

DSB — a type of modulation in which the carrier is suppressed in the RF signal.

COSTAS loop detector — a complex detector used for reception and demodulation of DSB-modulated signals.

carrier suppression — the act of reducing (suppressing) carrier power in a radio wave. The amount of carrier suppression is usually expressed in dB, and represents the difference between maximum carrier power and its minimum suppressed value.

DSB Signals

EXERCISE OBJECTIVE

When you have completed this exercise, you will be able to demonstrate DSB modulation using the AM / DSB / SSB Generator.

DISCUSSION

As stated previously, the main difference between AM and DSB is the absence of the carrier in DSB modulation. In the AM / DSB / SSB Generator, carrier power is produced by adding a dc level to the message signal. If the dc level is reduced to minimum, no carrier power (or extremely little) will be present in the RF output. The difference in dB between maximum carrier power and its minimum suppressed value is called the amount of **carrier suppression**. While having the advantage of better power utilization, DSB offers no advantage over AM as far as frequency spectrum use and bandwidth requirements are concerned. The same bandwidth is necessary for DSB as for AM.

As you will learn in this exercise, the message signal corresponds to the line traced through alternate lobes of the DSB waveform as shown in Figure 4-4. This is one of the major differences between the waveforms of a DSB signal and an AM signal.

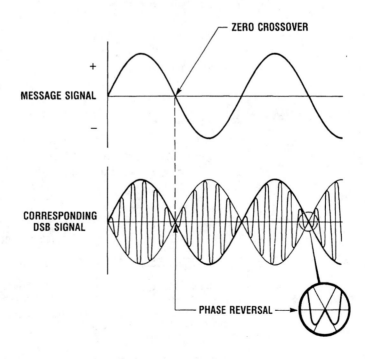

Figure 4-4. The carrier phase reverses when message signal polarity changes.

In AM it is the envelope which corresponds to the message signal. Also, in DSB, there is a phase reversal in the carrier signal each time the message signal changes polarity since a sign change from positive to negative (and vice versa) corresponds to a 180° phase change. Although the phase reversal may be difficult to observe in the time domain (because of the frequencies involved), it is the means used by the receiver to maintain frequency and phase synchronization, and thus detect the zero crossover of the message signal.

Another distinguishing feature of DSB modulation is the effect of message signal amplitude on RF power. For AM signals, maximum RF power occurs at 100% modulation. At this point, sideband power is maximum but is represents only one-third of the total RF power. The other two-thirds of the total power are "wasted" in the carrier (see Exercise 2-3). If the modulating signal amplitude is now reduced, the sideband power will decrease in accordance with the reduction, but the total RF power will be less affected. This is because the carrier power has remained constant. The total RF power for a DSB signal, however, consists entirely of sideband power because there is no carrier power (or very little) in the RF signal. Consequently, any increase or decrease in sideband power by changing the message signal amplitude will lead to an immediate change in RF power in the same proportion.

EQUIPMENT REQUIRED

DESCRIPTION	MODEL
Accessories	8948
Power Supply / Dual Audio Amplifier	9401
Dual Function Generator	9402
Frequency Counter	9403
Spectrum Analyzer	9405
AM / DSB / SSB Generator	9410
Oscilloscope	—

PROCEDURE

☐ 1. Set up the modules as shown in Figure 4-5. Make sure that all OUTPUT LEVEL and GAIN controls are turned fully counterclockwise to the MIN position, and power up the equipment.

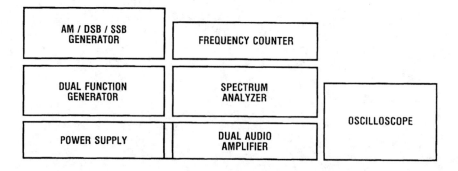

Figure 4-5. Suggested Module Arrangement.

DSB Signals

☐ 2. Adjust the channel A controls on the Dual Function Generator to produce a 10-kHz sine wave with the OUTPUT LEVEL control set at ¼ turn cw. Select the 20 dB ATTENUATOR.

☐ 3. Connect this 10-kHz sine wave to both the AUDIO INPUT of the AM / DSB / SSB Generator and to channel 1 of the oscilloscope. Place the VOLTS / DIV control for channel 1 at .2 V, and set the TIME / DIV control at 20 μs.

What do you observe on the oscilloscope?

_____

☐ 4. Use the Frequency Counter to monitor the carrier frequency of the AM / DSB / SSB Generator at TP13, and adjust the RF TUNING control to obtain f_C = 1000 kHz. Place the RF GAIN (amplifier A_2) at ½ turn cw and *set the CARRIER LEVEL control at MIN.* Make sure that it is pushed-in to the LINEAR OVERMODULATION position.

☐ 5. Connect the AM / DSB RF OUTPUT to channel 2 of the oscilloscope and place the VOLTS / DIV control at .2 V. Set the oscilloscope to trigger on the audio signal, and select dc coupling for both channels, as well as the ALT position for the display.

What do you observe on the oscilloscope?

_____

_____

☐ 6. Adjust the oscilloscope so that the dc reference lines for both channels coincide with the center graticule line of the oscilloscope.

☐ 7. Adjust the RF GAIN (amplifier A_2) on the AM / DSB / SSB Generator so that the RF waveform has the same amplitude as the 10-kHz sine wave. Use Figure 4-6 to sketch the waveforms displayed on the screen.

☐ 8. For an AM waveform, the envelope of the RF waveform corresponds to the message signal. What do you notice about the correspondence between the DSB waveform and the message signal?

_____

_____

_____

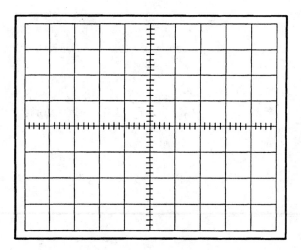

Figure 4-6. The DSB waveform and its modulating signal.

☐ 9. Vary the CARRIER LEVEL on the AM / DSB / SSB Generator between MIN and MAX and return it to the MIN position.

What effect does this have on the RF waveform displayed on the oscilloscope screen?

_____

_____

_____

☐ 10. Vary the channel A OUTPUT LEVEL between MIN and MAX and return it to the ¼ turn cw position.

What effect does this have on the RF waveform displayed on the oscilloscope screen?

_____

_____

_____

☐ 11. Vary the frequency of the message signal between 1 and 10 kHz and readjust it at 10 kHz.

What effect does this have on the RF waveform displayed on the oscilloscope screen?

_____

_____

DSB Signals

☐ 12. Observe the DSB waveform produced with a triangle wave message signal. Vary the amplitude and frequency of the message signal as in steps 10 and 11. Do the same for a ramp signal and describe your observations for both message signals.

_____

_____

_____

_____

☐ 13. Are the effects produced by changes in the amplitude and frequency of these different message signals similar to those caused by a sine wave? Explain.

_____

_____

_____

☐ 14. Readjust the Dual Function Generator controls to obtain a 10-kHz sine wave with the OUTPUT LEVEL set at ¼ turn cw.

☐ 15. Disconnect the oscilloscope and set up and calibrate the Spectrum Analyzer around 1.0 MHz. Make sure that the INPUT impedance switch is in the 50 Ω position.

☐ 16. Connect the AM / DSB RF OUTPUT to the INPUT of the Spectrum Analyzer and adjust the TUNING controls to place the spectrum of the DSB signal in the center of the screen.

☐ 17. Choose successively the 200, 50 and 10 kHz / V FREQUENCY SPANs, and readjust the TUNING controls as necessary to keep the DSB signal centered.

What do you observe on the screen?

_____

_____

☐ 18. Vary the CARRIER LEVEL between MIN and MAX and record the difference in dB between both levels. This difference corresponds to the carrier suppression in dB.

Carrier suppression = _____ dB

DSB Signals

☐ 19. Return the CARRIER LEVEL control to MIN and measure the power levels of the upper and lower sidebands.

LSB power level = _____ dBm

USB power level = _____ dBm

☐ 20. Increase the OUTPUT LEVEL for channel A of the Dual Function Generator to ½ turn cw. What effect does this have on the power levels of the sidebands?

_____

_____

_____

☐ 21. Measure and record the USB and LSB power levels when the RF GAIN is set at ½ turn cw.

LSB power level = _____ dBm

USB power level = _____ dBm

☐ 22. By how much has the carrier power changed between steps 19 and 21?

_____

☐ 23. By what amount has RF power changed between steps 19 and 21?

_____

☐ 24. Vary the frequency of the message signal between 1 and 10 kHz and describe the effects produced in the frequency spectrum.

_____

_____

_____

☐ 25. According to your observations in step 24, what do you conclude concerning the bandwidth requirements of DSB signals versus the bandwidth required for AM signals?

_____

_____

_____

DSB Signals

□ 26. Turn all OUTPUT LEVEL and GAIN controls to the MIN position. Place all power switches in the off (O) position and disconnect all cables.

CONCLUSION

As you have seen in this exercise, DSB modulation produces an RF waveform which is easily distinguished from that of an AM waveform. The frequency spectrum is also quite different. Increasing message-signal power leads to a much greater increase in RF power for DSB modulation than it does in AM, thus showing that DSB modulation allows much better power utilization. Bandwidth requirements for a DSB signal, however, are identical to those of ordinary AM.

REVIEW QUESTIONS

1. Draw a frequency spectrum sketch showing the main difference between an AM signal and a DSB signal. Both signals are modulated by the same single-tone sine wave.

2. What is the major advantage of DSB modulation over AM?

   _____

   _____

3. To transmit a message signal frequency of 5 kHz, is it better to use DSB modulation, or AM, to reduce bandwidth requirements? Explain.

   _____

   _____

   _____

4. Explain why RF power increases in a greater proportion for a DSB signal than an AM signal when the message signal amplitude is doubled.

   _____

   _____

   _____

5. The frequency spectrum of a signal shows that carrier power is 40 dB less than sideband power. If this is the spectrum of a DSB signal, the 40 dB difference corresponds to the _____ .

Reception and Demodulation of DSB Signals

EXERCISE OBJECTIVE

When you have completed this exercise, you will be able to explain and demonstrate reception and demodulation of DSB signals with a COSTAS loop detector.

DISCUSSION

In Exercise 4-1, you saw that the message signal corresponds to the line drawn through alternate lobes of the DSB signal waveform. This leads to a problem in demodulation since a way must be found to indicate the polarity change of the message signal. If this is not done, the demodulated audio signal will consist of the external envelope of the DSB signal and will be severly distorted. Figure 4-7 shows the audio waveforms for both correct and incorrect demodulation.

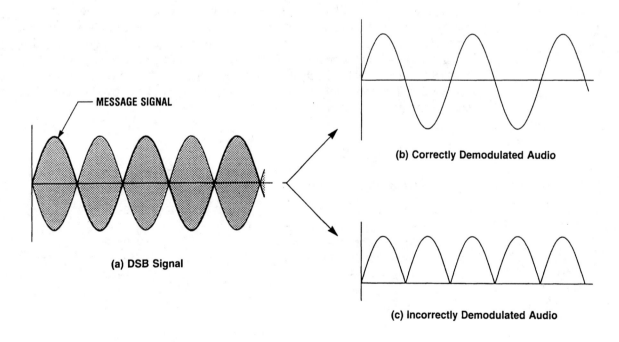

Figure 4-7. Audio waveforms for correct and incorrect demodulation.

Reception and Demodulation of DSB Signals

As shown in the figure, the waveform of the incorrectly demodulated audio signal corresponds to a rectified version of the original sine wave, and the frequency is twice that of the original message signal. This is because the detector being used is not synchronized to detect the polarity changes (zero crossover) of the message signal, and is therefore not able to demodulate the DSB signal.

An ordinary envelope detector will not allow proper demodulation of a DSB signal because it consists essentially of a rectifier diode which "strips off" the envelope of the RF waveform. The demodulated audio will be similar to the rectified waveform shown in Figure 4-7 (c). A PLL synchronous detector will not work properly either, since the phase reversal of the carrier signal will be taken as a phase error. This will result in an error signal being fed back to the VCO forcing the VCO output frequency to change in response to the phase change. The end result will be an incorrectly demodulated audio signal as in Figure 4-7 (c).

The COSTAS loop detector will allow proper recovery of the audio signal. As shown in Figure 4-8, the PLL synchronous detector has been modified to include a COSTAS LOOP MIXER and a COSTAS LOOP COMPARATOR. The PLL MIXER output, instead of going directly through the 5-Hz filter to the VCO, now passes through the 11-kHz filter, to be combined in the COSTAS loop mixer with the output of the COSTAS loop comparator. The output of the COSTAS loop mixer now becomes the new error signal for the VCO. The COSTAS loop comparator maintains a constant amplitude signal at one of the COSTAS loop mixer's inputs. This input signal changes polarity in synchronization with the message signal. The other input to the COSTAS loop mixer is the former error signal, and it changes polarity when phase reversal of the carrier occurs. Since both signals at the inputs of the COSTAS loop mixer have now changed sign (polarity), the sign of the mixer output signal remains constant. (Remember, operation of a mixer in the time domain is mathematically equivalent to multiplication). In this way the error signal is prevented from indicating a phase error, and the VCO remains synchronized with the carrier frequency.

EQUIPMENT REQUIRED

DESCRIPTION	MODEL
Accessories	8948
Power Supply / Dual Audio Amplifier	9401
Dual Function Generator	9402
Frequency Counter	9403
AM / DSB / SSB Generator	9410
AM / DSB Receiver	9411
Oscilloscope	—

Reception and Demodulation of DSB Signals

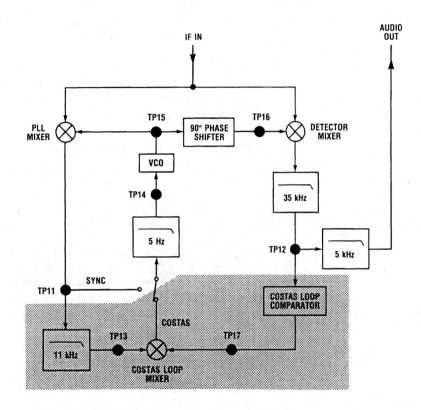

Figure 4-8. A COSTAS loop detector.

PROCEDURE

☐ 1. Set up the modules as shown in Figure 4-9. Make sure that all OUTPUT LEVEL and GAIN controls are turned fully counterclockwise to the MIN position, and power up the equipment.

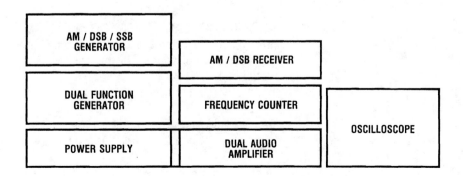

Figure 4-9. Suggested Module Arrangement.

☐ 2. Adjust the channel A controls on the Dual Function Generator to produce a 1.5 kHz sine wave with the OUTPUT LEVEL control set at ¼ turn cw. Select the 20 dB ATTENUATOR.

☐ 3. Connect the 1.5-kHz signal to both the AUDIO INPUT of the AM / DSB / SSB Generator and to channel 1 of the oscilloscope. Place the VOLTS / DIV control for channel 1 at .2 V, and set the TIME / DIV control at .1 ms.

What do you observe on the oscilloscope?

_____

_____

☐ 4. Use the Frequency Counter to monitor the carrier frequency of the AM / DSB / SSB Generator at TP13, and adjust the RF TUNING control to obtain $f_c = 1000$ kHz. Place the RF GAIN (amplifier A_2) at ¼ turn clockwise and *set the CARRIER LEVEL control at MIN.* Make sure that it is pushed-in to the LINEAR OVERMODULATION position.

☐ 5. Connect the AM / DSB RF OUTPUT to the 50 Ω RF INPUT of the AM / DSB Receiver.

☐ 6. The AM receiver must now be tuned to the carrier frequency. At what frequency must the local oscillator be set to accomplish this?

$f_{LO} =$ _____ kHz

☐ 7. Adjust the RF TUNING on the AM / DSB Receiver to measure 1455 kHz at OSC OUTPUT so as to tune the receiver to the carrier frequency. Reconnect the Frequency Counter to TP13 on the AM / DSB / SSB Generator when f_{LO} has been set to 1455 kHz.

☐ 8. Select the COSTAS DETECTOR on the AM / DSB Receiver, and place the AGC switch in the I (active) position. Connect the AUDIO OUTPUT of the receiver to channel 2 of the oscilloscope, and set the VOLTS / DIV control at 1 V.

☐ 9. Set the oscilloscope to trigger on the original audio signal (CH 1). Select dc coupling for both channels, as well as the ALT position for the display.

What do you observe on the oscilloscope?

_____

_____

Reception and Demodulation of DSB Signals

Note: *It may be very difficult at first to obtain a stable display, because the COSTAS detector requires that the carrier frequency be within 700 Hz (approx) of the frequency to which the receiver is tuned. The fact that the local oscillator frequency of the receiver is more stable, and drifts much less with time, will allow you to concentrate only on readjusting the carrier frequency. As the RF carrier frequency comes within the 1.4 kHz capture range of the COSTAS loop detector, the "hopping" on the oscilloscope display will become more rapid, until finally it stops and the signal is locked-in.*

☐ 10. Adjust the position controls so that the original message signal is centered on the sixth graticule line, and the demodulated signal is centered on the second.

Readjust carefully the RF TUNING on the AM / DSB / SSB Generator until the oscilloscope display for channel 2 becomes stable and stops "hopping" up and down.

☐ 11. When the carrier frequency has been adjusted to provide a stable display for the demodulated audio signal, sketch the waveforms of both signals in Figure 4-10.

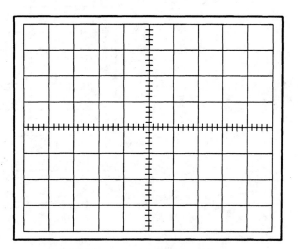

Figure 4-10. Original and recovered signals with DSB modulation.

☐ 12. Compare the original and demodulated message signals.

_____

_____

_____

☐ 13. Readjust the RF TUNING on the AM / DSB / SSB Generator as necessary to maintain synchronization between the generator and the receiver. Because of the very selective nature of the COSTAS loop detector this will probably be required often.

With the generator and receiver properly synchronized, disactivate and activate the AGC switch several times before returning it to the I (active) position. What happens?

_____

_____

_____

☐ 14. With the generator and receiver properly synchronized, select the SYNC detector on the AM / DSB Receiver. Sketch the waveform of the demodulated audio signal in Figure 4-11.

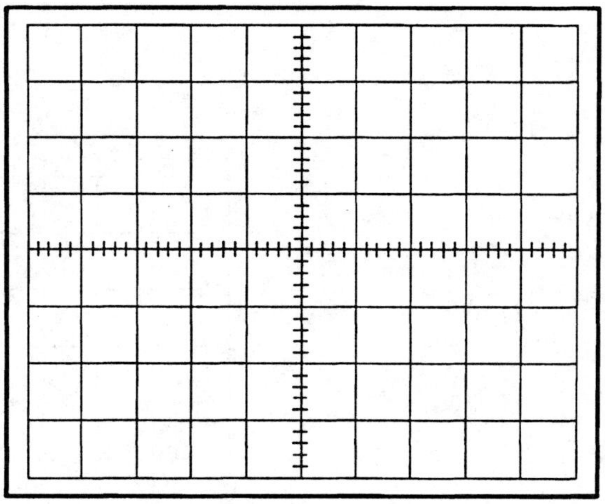

Figure 4-11. Demodulated DSB signal obtained with the SYNC detector.

☐ 15. With the generator and receiver properly synchronized, select the ENV detector on the AM / DSB Receiver. Sketch the waveform of the demodulated audio signal in Figure 4-12.

☐ 16. What are your observations concerning the results obtained with the ENV, SYNC, and COSTAS detectors?

_____

_____

_____

_____

Reception and Demodulation of DSB Signals

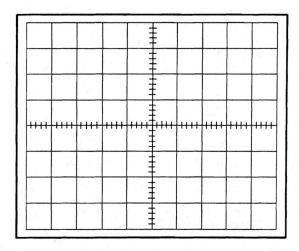

Figure 4-12. Demodulated DSB signal obtained with the ENV detector.

☐ 17. Select the COSTAS DETECTOR. Use a BNC T-connector and a BNC cable to connect the AUDIO OUTPUT of the AM / DSB Receiver to the Dual Audio Amplifier to monitor the demodulated audio signal with the head-phones.

☐ 18. With the generator and receiver properly synchronized, what do you hear?

_____

_____

☐ 19. What happens to the sound when you try to demodulate the DSB signal using the ENV and SYNC DETECTORs?

_____

_____

_____

☐ 20. Disconnect the AM / DSB RF OUTPUT and connect a telescopic antenna to the 50 kΩ RF INPUT and try to tune-in a local AM station. Use the SYNC DETECTOR and once a station has been tuned in (if possible), select the COSTAS DETECTOR. What happens to the sound of the demodulated audio?

_____

_____

☐ 21. Turn all OUTPUT LEVEL and GAIN controls to the MIN position. Place all power switches in the off (O) position and disconnect all cables.

CONCLUSION

DSB modulation requires the use of a more complex receiver for demodulation and a COSTAS loop detector is the central element of such a receiver. The COSTAS loop detector ensures that proper phase and frequency synchronization is maintained between the RF carrier and the locally generated carrier. The use of a COSTAS loop detector requires that the RF carrier frequency be highly stable, since the frequency range over which the detector can maintain proper synchronization is usually small. When a DSB-modulated signal is demodulated using an envelope detector, or a synchronous detector, the recovered message signal is highly distorted.

REVIEW QUESTIONS

1. What type of detector is required to demodulate DSB signals?

   _____

2. The envelope of an AM signal corresponds to the waveform of the message signal. What does the waveform of the message signal correspond to in a DSB signal?

   _____

   _____

3. Sketch the audio waveform that will be obtained if an envelope detector is used to demodulate a DSB signal.

4. Carrier phase reversal and message signal polarity changes occur in synchronization in a DSB signal. Control signals indicating these changes are combined through the COSTAS LOOP MIXER. What effect does the mixer output signal have on the VCO generating the local carrier? Explain.

   _____

   _____

   _____

Reception and Demodulation of DSB Signals

5. Why does a PLL synchronous detector cause the VCO to change the locally generated carrier frequency when this type of detector is used to demodulate a DSB signal?

_____

_____

_____

Unit Test

1. In the frequency spectrum of a DSB signal

   a. no carrier is present.
   b. only one sideband is present.
   c. the carrier is at least 3 dB higher than the sidebands.
   d. the USB has been suppressed.

2. The external envelope of a DSB waveform corresponds

   a. to the message signal waveform.
   b. to the carrier signal waveform.
   c. partially to the message signal waveform.
   d. to harmonics of the carrier signal.

3. The great difficulty in demodulating DSB signals is

   a. locating the broadcast frequency of the station.
   b. following the message signal variations rapidly.
   c. obtaining sufficient RF signal power.
   d. synchronizing the receiver's locally generated carrier to the RF carrier.

4. The detector used to demodulate DSB signals is called

   a. an envelope detector.
   b. a PLL detector.
   c. a COSTAS loop detector.
   d. a synchronous AM detector.

5. The major advantage of DSB modulation is

   a. better power utilization.
   b. more efficient use of the frequency spectrum.
   c. easier to build and less complex receivers.
   d. both a and c.

6. The difference in dB between maximum carrier power and its minimum suppressed value (for DSB signals) is called

   a. carrier power ratio.
   b. the increase in transmission efficiency.
   c. the amount of carrier suppression.
   d. the reduction ratio.

7. A line drawn through alternate lobes of a DSB waveform obtained with a sine-wave message signal corresponds to

a. the message signal waveform.
b. the frequency of the sine-wave.
c. the modulated carrier.
d. both a and b.

8. Receivers capable of demodulating DSB signals are

a. less complex than ordinary AM receivers.
b. more complex than ordinary AM receivers.
c. not very efficient.
d. none of the above.

9. Control signals indicating carrier phase reversal and message signal polarity changes are combined through the COSTAS loop mixer in the COSTAS loop detector. The mixer output signal

a. controls the VCO frequency.
b. controls the phase of the VCO signal.
c. prevents the VCO from losing synchronization with the RF carrier.
d. all of the above.

10. The use of a COSTAS loop detector usually requires that the carrier frequency

a. be lower than 1 MHz.
b. be greater than 500 kHz.
c. be highly stable.
d. not drift rapidly over a 50-kHz range.

Single Sideband Modulation – SSB

UNIT OBJECTIVE

When you have completed this unit, you will be capable of explaining and demonstrating SSB modulation using the AM / DSB / SSB Generator and the SSB Receiver.

DISCUSSION OF FUNDAMENTALS

The concept of **SSB** modulation can be represented as shown in Figure 5-1. The spectrum of an SSB signal can be theoretically obtained in the manner suggested by first removing the carrier from the AM signal to produce the DSB spectrum shown in Figure 5-1 (b). Then, by removing one of the two sidebands from the DSB signal, one of the SSB spectra of Figure 5-1 (c) will be obtained. The advantages of SSB modulation are 1) there is no carrier present in the spectrum of an SSB signal, and 2) only half the frequency bandwidth is required for communication since only one sideband is transmitted. Therefore, SSB offers efficient power utilization and economic bandwidth use. These advantages are offset, however, by the fact that transmission and reception equipment is much more complex.

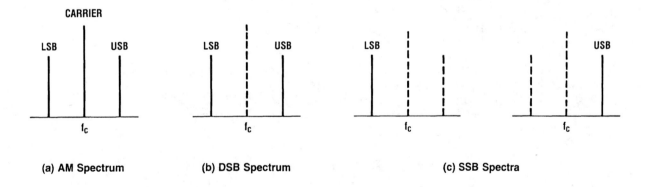

(a) AM Spectrum   (b) DSB Spectrum   (c) SSB Spectra

Figure 5-1. The concept of SSB modulation.

Single Sideband Modulation – SSB

In practice it is simpler and easier to start with DSB, since this type of modulation is obtained directly when a message signal is combined with an RF carrier through a balanced mixer. To produce an SSB signal, all that remains to do is filter out one of the sidebands before the RF signal is transmitted. Figure 5-2 illustrates this theoretical process, which is known as the filter method of generating SSB signals.

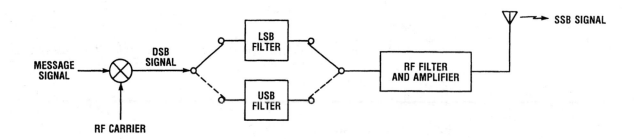

Figure 5-2. SSB generation by the filter method.

The way in which this process is accomplished in the Analog Communications Training System is shown in the functional block diagram of Figure 5-3. The diagram is a modified version of the functional representation shown on the front panel of the AM / DSB / SSB Generator.

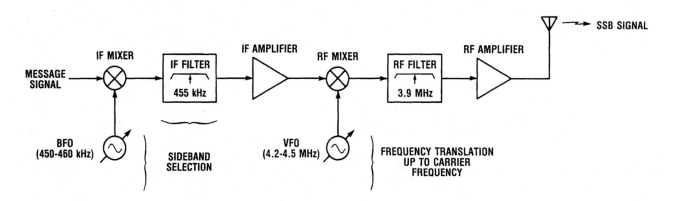

Figure 5-3. Functional block diagram for generating an SSB signal.

The message signal is combined with the **Beat Frequency Oscillator (BFO)** signal, thus producing a DSB output centered at the BFO frequency. Sideband selection begins by adjusting the BFO frequency within its 450-460 kHz range. This causes the frequency contents of the message signal to be shifted relative to the passband of the fixed IF filter. Since the 455-kHz IF filter has a narrow 6-kHz bandwidth and sharp roll-off characteristics, the effect of frequency displacement (caused by varying the BFO frequency) is to "push" one of the sidebands outside the passband of the IF filter. Once the desired sideband has been selected, the SSB signal is frequency-translated up to the carrier frequency determined by the **Variable Frequency Oscillator (VFO)**. For the AM / DSB / SSB Generator, the SSB carrier frequency lies in the 80-meter amateur band (3.7-4.0 MHz).

Single Sideband Modulation — SSB

The final operations that are performed before transmission are RF filtering and amplification. The RF stage of the SSB section is designed to allow only the transmission of the difference frequency from the RF MIXER. This is necessary since the desired sideband selected at the IF stage has been reproduced by the second mixing operation. Recall that the combining of two signals through a balanced mixer always produces the sum and the difference frequencies at the output. Figure 5-4 illustrates this situation.

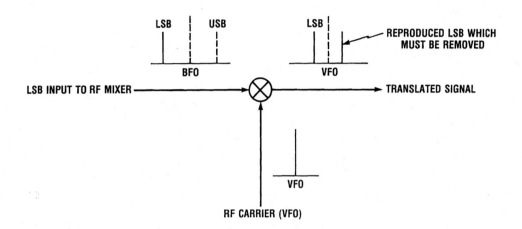

Figure 5-4. RF mixing reproduces the selected sideband.

NEW TERMS AND WORDS

Beat Frequency Oscillator (BFO) — the narrow-range oscillator used to displace the spectrum of the message signal so as to position one of the sidebands outside the passband of the selective IF filter.

sideband reversal — a phenomenon occurring in SSB modulation when the SSB receiver is adjusted to demodulate the opposite sideband relative to the transmitted sideband. For example, the SSB transmission is USB and the receiver is adjusted to demodulate the LSB (and vice versa).

SSB — a type of modulation in which the carrier is suppressed and only one of the two sidebands is transmitted, either the LSB or the USB.

Variable Frequency Oscillator (VFO) — the oscillator that determines the SSB carrier frequency.

Generating SSB Signals by the Filter Method

EXERCISE OBJECTIVE

When you have completed this exercise, you will be able to explain and demonstrate the filter method of generating SSB signals using the AM / DSB / SSB Generator.

DISCUSSION

As stated earlier, SSB signals can be generated by filtering out one of the sidebands of a DSB signal. The following examples, illustrated in Figure 5-5, explain how this is done. The message signal is a 2.5-kHz sine wave and it will be combined with the BFO signal through the IF MIXER (see Figure 5-3). The BFO signal is a sine wave whose frequency can be adjusted anywhere between 450 and 460 kHz. The mixer output signal contains the sum and the difference frequencies of the two input signals, and the mixer's DSB output is filtered through the narrow-bandwidth IF filter before frequency translation up to the carrier frequency. Three cases of BFO frequency adjustment (452.5, 455.0, and 457.5 kHz) are shown in Figure 5-5.

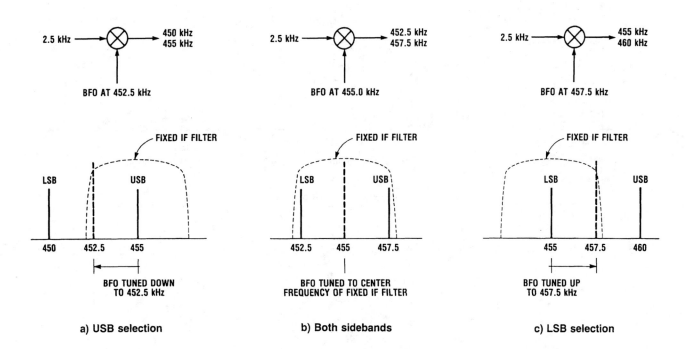

Figure 5-5. Sideband selection by mixing with a BFO signal.

Generating SSB Signals by the Filter Method

Analysis of Figure 5-5 shows that the whole operation of sideband selection consists essentially in moving the frequency contents of the message signal so that only one of the sidebands is placed inside the passband of the fixed IF filter. When the BFO is tuned down to 452.5 kHz, Figure 5-5 (a), the LSB has been displaced to 450 kHz and outside the passband of the IF filter. At the same time the USB has been positioned in the center of the filter's passband. The LSB has therefore been rejected (or greatly attenuated), and only the USB of the message signal remains for frequency translation up to the carrier frequency.

In Figure 5-5 (b), the BFO has been tuned to 455.0 kHz, and because the maximum frequency of the message signal is 2.5 kHz, both sidebands lie within the 6-kHz passband of the IF filter. If this signal is frequency-translated up to the carrier frequency, the resulting RF output will be a DSB signal.

LSB selection is illustrated in Figure 5-5 (c). The BFO frequency has been tuned up to 457.5 kHz. This shifts the USB to 460 kHz, and outside the passband of the IF filter. The LSB has been positioned in the center of the passband, thus completing the selection process. The selected LSB is then frequency-translated up to the carrier frequency and processed for transmission.

Figure 5-6 illustrates the selection process for SSB transmission of voice signals. The selection process is the same, and the only real difficulty arises when the sidebands of the message signal are improperly positioned within the IF filter's passband. If the desired sideband is not positioned correctly, a part of the other sideband will be transmitted. This will result in a distorted and perhaps unintelligible output at the receiver when the RF signal is demodulated.

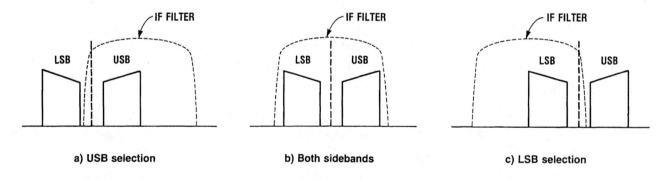

a) USB selection   b) Both sidebands   c) LSB selection

Figure 5-6. Sideband selection of voice signals.

EQUIPMENT REQUIRED

DESCRIPTION	MODEL
Accessories	8948
Power Supply / Dual Audio Amplifier	9401
Dual Function Generator	9402
Frequency Counter	9403
Spectrum Analyzer	9405
AM / DSB / SSB Generator	9410
Oscilloscope	—

Generating SSB Signals by the Filter Method

PROCEDURE

☐ 1. Set up the modules as shown in Figure 5-7. Make sure that all OUTPUT LEVEL and GAIN controls are turned fully counterclockwise to the MIN position, and power up the equipment.

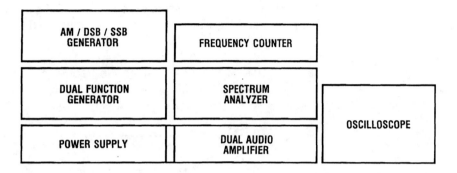

Figure 5-7. Suggested Module Arrangement.

☐ 2. Adjust the channel A controls on the Dual Function Generator to produce a 2.5-kHz sine wave with the OUTPUT LEVEL control set at ¼ turn cw. Select the 20 dB ATTENUATOR, and then connect the message signal to the AUDIO INPUT of the AM / DSB / SSB Generator.

☐ 3. Turn the CARRIER LEVEL control on the AM / DSB / SSB Generator to the MIN position, making sure that it is pushed in to the LINEAR OVERMODULATION position. Set the SSB RF GAIN (amplifier A_3) at ½ turn cw.

☐ 4. Adjust the BFO TUNING control to measure a frequency of 452.5 kHz at the BFO OUTPUT (terminal 2). Record the reading of the Frequency Counter.

$f_{BFO} =$ _____ kHz

☐ 5. Adjust the VFO TUNING control to measure a frequency of 4355 kHz at the VFO OUTPUT (terminal 5). Record the reading of the Frequency Counter. For this exercise, any value between 4350 and 4360 kHz is acceptable.

$f_{VFO} =$ _____ kHz

☐ 6. Set up and calibrate the Spectrum Analyzer around 0.5 MHz. Set the INPUT impedance switch in the 1 MΩ position and select the 10 dBm MAXIMUM INPUT.

☐ 7. Connect the MIXER OUTPUT (terminal 3) of the SSB section to the INPUT of the Spectrum Analyzer. Use the TUNING controls to place the frequency spectrum at 455 kHz in the center of the screen.

☐ 8. Depress successively the 200, 50, 10 and 2 kHz / V FREQUENCY SPAN switches successively, and retune the Spectrum Analyzer as necessary to keep the frequency spectrum centered in the screen.

☐ 9. Use Figure 5-8 to sketch the frequency spectrum observed at the FRE-QUENCY SPAN setting of 2 kHz / V.

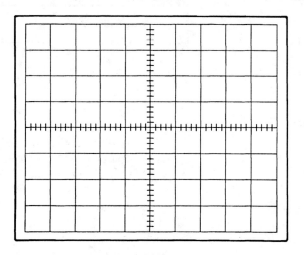

Figure 5-8. The frequency spectrum at the MIXER OUTPUT.

Describe the frequency spectrum, and determine the frequencies of the LSB and the USB.

_____

_____

f_{LSB} = _____ kHz f_{USB} = _____ kHz

☐ 10. Observe the frequency spectrum of the signal at the IF OUTPUT (terminal 4). Describe it, and explain what has happened.

_____

_____

_____

_____

Generating SSB Signals by the Filter Method

☐ 11. Adjust f_{BFO} to 455 kHz using the BFO TUNING control. Explain what happens to the frequency spectrum as f_{BFO} approaches 455 kHz.

_____

_____

_____

☐ 12. With f_{BFO} set at 455 kHz, increase the message signal frequency up to 3.5 kHz. Explain the changes in the frequency spectrum.

_____

_____

_____

☐ 13. Readjust the message signal frequency to 2.5 kHz, and then tune the BFO to obtain f_{BFO} = 457.5 kHz. Explain what happens as f_{BFO} is increased from 455 to 457.5 kHz.

_____

_____

_____

☐ 14. Use the BFO TUNING control to vary f_{BFO} between 453 and 457 kHz. What changes take place in the frequency spectrum as f_{BFO} varies between 453 and 457 kHz?

_____

_____

_____

☐ 15. Place the INPUT impedance switch on the Spectrum Analyzer in the 50 Ω position and select the 1 MHz / V FREQUENCY SPAN. Select the −10 dBm MAXIMUM INPUT. Observe the frequency spectrum of the signal at the SSB RF OUTPUT (terminal 7) with the Spectrum Analyzer. (Readjust f_{BFO} at 455 kHz).

☐ 16. Center the spectrum of the RF signal in the screen, and select the 200, 50, 10 and 2 kHz / V FREQUENCY SPANs successively. Retune the Spectrum Analyzer as necessary to keep the image centered.

Generating SSB Signals by the Filter Method

☐ 17. Describe the frequency spectrum observed at the FREQUENCY SPAN setting of 2 kHz / V.

_____

_____

_____

☐ 18. Vary f_{BFO} between 453 and 457 kHz as in step 14. Compare the effect this produces with the results obtained in step 14.

_____

_____

_____

☐ 19. What can you conclude about the effect caused by adjusting f_{BFO} at 452.5 or 457.5 kHz with a message signal frequency of 2.5 kHz?

_____

_____

_____

☐ 20. Based on your results and observations in the frequency domain, what is the time domain waveform for an SSB signal modulated by a single-tone sine wave? (Recall that the frequency spectrum of a sine wave is a single line in the frequency spectrum).

_____

_____

_____

☐ 21. Disconnect the Spectrum Analyzer and use the oscilloscope to observe the waveform of the SSB signal at the SSB RF OUTPUT of the AM / DSB / SSB Generator when f_{BFO} = 452.5 kHz.

How does the waveform compare with your predictions of step 20?

_____

_____

_____

☐ 22. Turn all OUTPUT LEVEL and GAIN controls to the MIN position. Place all power switches in the off (O) position and disconnect all cables.

Generating SSB Signals by the Filter Method

CONCLUSION

This exercise has allowed you to demonstrate the generation of SSB signals by the filter method. You have seen that sideband selection is obtained by displacing the sidebands of a message signal relative to the passband of a fixed IF filter. Frequency displacement is accomplished by mixing the message signal with a BFO signal, whose frequency adjustment determines the position of the message signal spectrum. This shifts the LSB or USB outside the filter's passband, thus producing an SSB signal containing the remaining sideband. Another mixing operation with the VFO signal then frequency-translates the SSB signal up to the carrier frequency.

REVIEW QUESTIONS

1. Sketch the frequency spectrum of an SSB signal (LSB or USB), and list the differences between an SSB spectrum and those of an AM spectrum and a DSB spectrum.

   _____

   _____

2. What are the two principal advantages of SSB modulation over AM and DSB?

   _____

   _____

3. Describe briefly the filter method of generating SSB signals used in the Analog Communications Training System.

   _____

   _____

   _____

   _____

   _____

4. Observation of the spectrum at the output of an SSB generator shows that the spectrum is identical to that of a DSB signal. Explain the problem with the generator.

_____

_____

_____

_____

5. The IF section of an SSB generator used for voice communications is tuned for operation at 455 kHz. The bandwidth of the IF stage is 2 kHz. What effect, if any, will the very narrow passband have on communications?

_____

_____

_____

_____

Exercise 5-2

Reception and Demodulation of SSB Signals

EXERCISE OBJECTIVE

When you have completed this exercise, you will be able to set up an SSB communications system, using the AM / DSB / SSB Generator and the SSB Receiver, to demonstrate reception and demodulation of SSB signals.

DISCUSSION

In the previous exercise, you learned that producing an SSB signal using the filter method was mainly a matter of selecting the LSB or the USB, and then frequency-translating the selected sideband up to the carrier frequency. Based on the knowledge gained in previous units of this manual, you should now realize that the receiver must reverse the operations performed by the transmitter in order to recover the original information. Figure 5-9 shows the functional block representation of the manner in which the SSB Receiver reverses the modulation process to recover the transmitted information.

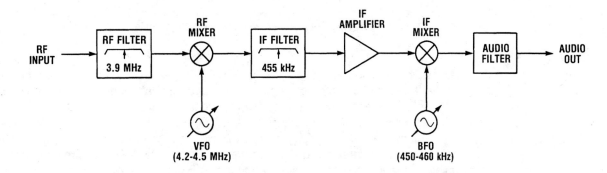

Figure 5-9. Functional block diagram for demodulating an SSB signal.

Reception and Demodulation of SSB Signals

Frequency-translation of the incoming RF signal is fairly straight-forward, being just a matter of tuning the VFO to *exactly* the same frequency as that used by the transmitter. The IF signal present at the output of the IF filter represents the transmitted sideband, either the LSB or the USB. Up to this point, the process of reception is about the same as for AM or DSB signals. The next step in demodulation is translating the message signal spectrum back to its proper position in the frequency spectrum. Figure 5-10 helps illustrate the process of recovering the message information from the IF signal. The message signal is a 2.5-kHz sine wave, and the transmitter BFO (BFO-TX) has been adjusted for USB transmission.

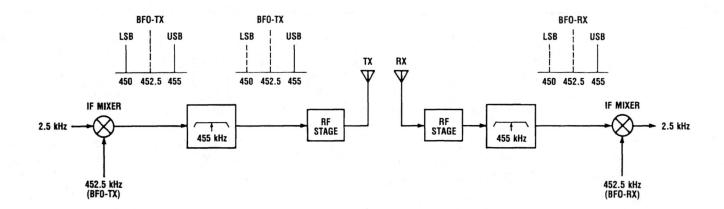

Figure 5-10. Message signal recovery from an SSB signal.

As shown in the figure, the receiver BFO (BFO-RX) is tuned to the same frequency as the transmitter BFO. This conserves the spectral relationship between the BFO and the USB that has been established at the transmitter. Since BFO-TX is tuned 2.5 kHz below the USB at the transmitter, BFO-RX must be tuned 2.5 kHz below the USB at the receiver. *For proper SSB communications the spectral relationship must be maintained at the receiver.* If it is not, frequency errors resulting in unintelligible audio will be present when the SSB signal is demodulated. Complete **sideband reversal** is even possible!

To understand the effects of frequency errors and sideband reversal, a quick review of normal spectral behaviour will be useful. Figure 5-11 shows the spectrum of a DSB signal obtained when a 2.5-kHz sine wave is mixed with a 455-kHz BFO signal. As shown in Figure 5-11 (a), decreasing the message signal frequency (f_m) causes the sidebands to approach each other. Increasing the message signal frequency causes the sidebands to spread apart, as in Figure 5-11 (b). This is normal spectral behaviour as dictated by physical laws, and it conforms with the results you obtained in previous exercises. The USB frequency increases or decreases as the message signal frequency is increased or decreased, while the LSB frequency does the opposite.

Reception and Demodulation of SSB Signals

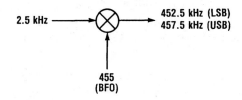

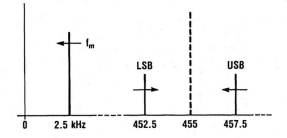

a) Decreasing f_m decreases distance between sidebands.

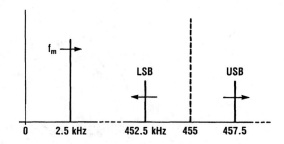

b) Increasing f_m increases distance between sidebands.

Figure 5-11. Normal LSB and USB movement when f_m is varied.

If sideband reversal occurs the normal spectral behaviour shown in Figure 5-11 will be reversed. When the message signal frequency is decreased the sidebands will spread apart instead of approaching each other. It's as if the DSB spectra in Figure 5-11 (a) and (b) have been interchanged with each other, resulting in a reversal of normal spectral behaviour. This is what happens when the receiver BFO is tuned to reverse the spectral relationship set up at the transmitter. Figure 5-12 illustrates the situation where BFO-RX is tuned for LSB reception instead of USB reception.

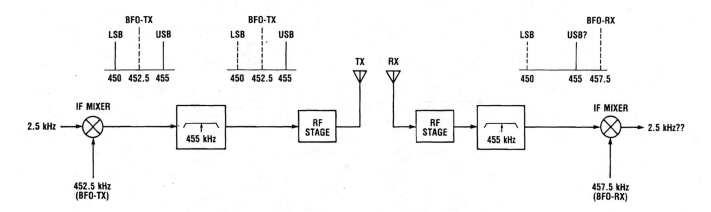

Figure 5-12. Receiver BFO tuned for LSB reception of a USB transmission.

Reception and Demodulation of SSB Signals

As shown in the figure, BFO-RX is tuned at 457.5 kHz, which is 2.5 kHz above the spectral position of the transmitted USB. This reverses the established spectral relationship since the USB has been shifted to the opposite position with respect to the transmitter BFO.

The result of this is to reverse the frequency characteristics of the demodulated signal. *When the frequency of the message signal is increased at the transmitter, the frequency of the demodulated signal decreases, and vice versa.* By mislocating the USB below the BFO in the frequency spectrum, the USB now occupies the position that would normally be held by the LSB had it been transmitted. High and low frequency content has been interchanged, and spectral behaviour is reversed. This characteristic of spectral reversal causes speech to be unintelligible and the principle is used in scrambling speech to ensure privacy of communications.

EQUIPMENT REQUIRED

DESCRIPTION	MODEL
Accessories	8948
Power Supply / Dual Audio Amplifier	9401
Dual Function Generator	9402
Frequency Counter	9403
Spectrum Analyzer	9405
AM / DSB / SSB Generator	9410
AM / DSB Receiver	9411
SSB Receiver	9412
Oscilloscope	—

PROCEDURE

☐ 1. Set up the modules as shown in Figure 5-13. Make sure that all OUTPUT LEVEL and GAIN controls are turned fully counterclockwise to the MIN position, and power up the equipment.

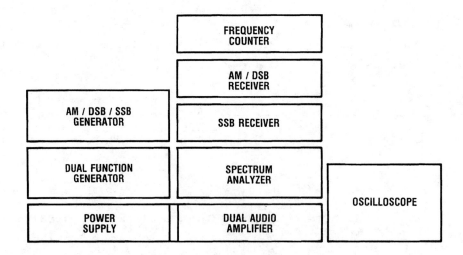

Figure 5-13. Suggested Module Arrangement.

Reception and Demodulation of SSB Signals

☐ 2. Adjust the channel A controls on the Dual Function Generator to produce a 2.5-kHz sine wave with the OUTPUT LEVEL control set at ¼ turn cw. Select the 20 dB ATTENUATOR, and then connect the message signal to the AUDIO INPUT of the AM / DSB / SSB Generator.

☐ 3. Turn the CARRIER LEVEL control on the AM / DSB / SSB Generator to the MIN position, making sure that it is pushed in to the LINEAR OVERMODULATION position. Set the SSB RF GAIN (amplifier A_3) at ½ turn cw.

☐ 4. Adjust the BFO TUNING control on the AM / DSB / SSB Generator to measure a frequency of 452.5 kHz at BFO OUTPUT. Record the reading.

$$f_{BFO} = \underline{\hspace{1cm}} \text{ kHz}$$

☐ 5. Adjust the VFO TUNING on the AM / DSB / SSB Generator to obtain 4355.0 kHz at VFO OUTPUT and record the reading.

Note: *Any value between 4350.0 and 4360.0 is acceptable for the exercise, as long as the VFO frequency on the SSB Receiver is tuned to within ±0.5 kHz of the value set on the AM / DSB / SSB Generator.*

$$f_{VFO} = \underline{\hspace{1cm}} \text{ kHz}$$

☐ 6. Connect the SSB RF OUTPUT of the AM / DSB / SSB Generator to the 50 Ω RF INPUT on the SSB Receiver. Place the AGC on the receiver module in the I (active) position.

☐ 7. Adjust the VFO TUNING on the SSB Receiver to *obtain the same VFO frequency ±0.5 kHz as set on the AM / DSB / SSB Generator*. Measure the frequency at VFO OUTPUT (terminal 3) and record the reading.

$$f_{VFO} = \underline{\hspace{1cm}} \text{ kHz}$$

☐ 8. Adjust the BFO TUNING on the SSB Receiver to obtain a frequency of 452.5 kHz at BFO OUTPUT (terminal 7) and record the reading.

Note: *The BFO frequency of the SSB Receiver must be adjusted to within ±0.1 kHz of the BFO frequency on the AM / DSB / SSB Generator.*

$$f_{BFO} = \underline{\hspace{1cm}} \text{ kHz}$$

☐ 9. Connect the AUDIO OUTPUT of the SSB Receiver to the Frequency Counter. Measure the frequency of the demodulated audio signal.

$f_{demod.}$ = _____ kHz

How does the frequency compare with that of the message signal?

_____

_____

☐ 10. Readjust the BFO TUNING on the SSB Receiver slightly, if necessary, to obtain identical readings on the Frequency Counter and the FREQUENCY display of the Dual Function Generator. Vary the message signal frequency (f_m) between 2 and 3 kHz.

What happens to the frequency of the demodulated audio signal as f_m is varied between 2 and 3 kHz?

_____

_____

_____

☐ 11. Readjust the message signal frequency to 2.5 kHz. Install a BNC T-connector at OUTPUT A of the Dual Function Generator and use a BNC / BNC cable to connect the original message signal to channel 1 of the Dual Audio Amplifier. Next, install a BNC T-connector at the AUDIO OUTPUT of the SSB Receiver and use a BNC / BNC cable to connect the demodulated audio signal to channel 2 of the Dual Audio Amplifier.

☐ 12. Make sure that the speaker disconnect switch in the off (O) position, and use the headphones to monitor both signals. Adjust the A_1 and A_2 GAIN controls for a comfortable listening level.

What do you hear in the headphones?

_____

_____

☐ 13. Readjust slightly the BFO TUNING on the SSB Receiver, if necessary, to obtain identical sounds in both earpieces.

Vary the message signal frequency between 2 and 3 kHz. What happens to the sound in both earpieces?

_____

_____

_____

Reception and Demodulation of SSB Signals

☐ 14. Readjust the message signal frequency to 2.5 kHz and then connect the Frequency Counter to BFO OUTPUT (terminal 7) on the SSB Receiver.

Adjust the BFO TUNING to obtain a BFO frequency of 457.5 kHz, and take note of the changes in the sound of the demodulated audio signal as the BFO frequency changes between 452.5 and 457.5 kHz.

What happens to the sound of the demodulated audio signal?

_____

_____

_____

☐ 15. Adjust the BFO frequency around 457 kHz to obtain identical frequency readings for both audio signals. Reconnect the Frequency Counter to read the frequency of the demodulated audio signal at the AUDIO OUTPUT of the SSB Receiver. Now, vary the frequency of the message signal upwards between 2.5 and 3 kHz, and then downwards between 2.5 and 2 kHz. What happens to the sound and frequency of the demodulated audio signal when

f_m is increased? _____

_____

_____

_____

f_m is decreased? _____

_____

_____

_____

☐ 16. Set up and calibrate the Spectrum Analyzer around 0 Hz. Set the INPUT impedance switch in the 1 MΩ position and select the 10 dBm MAXIMUM INPUT.

☐ 17. Disconnect the AUDIO OUTPUT of the SSB Receiver from the Dual Audio Amplifier and connect it instead to the INPUT of the Spectrum Analyzer.

☐ 18. Center the spectrum of the demodulated audio signal in the screen, and select the 200, 50, 10 and 2 kHz / V FREQUENCY SPANs successively. Retune the Spectrum Analyzer as necessary to keep the image centered.

Reception and Demodulation of SSB Signals

Describe the frequency spectrum observed at the FREQUENCY SPAN setting of 2 kHz / V.

_____

_____

_____

☐ 19. Vary the message signal frequency upwards from 2 to 3 kHz, and then downwards from 3 to 2 kHz. What changes take place in the frequency spectrum when

f_m is increased? _____

_____

_____

f_m is decreased? _____

_____

_____

_____

☐ 20. Explain the behaviour observed in step 19.

_____

_____

_____

☐ 21. Readjust the BFO frequency on the SSB Receiver at 452.5 kHz and observe the frequency spectrum as BFO-RX changes from 457 kHz to 452 kHz. What happens?

_____

_____

_____

☐ 22. With BFO-RX adjusted at 452.5 kHz, vary the message signal frequency in the same manner as in step 19. What is different about the changes in the frequency spectrum as compared to step 19? Explain.

_____

_____

_____

Reception and Demodulation of SSB Signals

☐ 23. Place a telescopic antenna at the high-impedance input of the AM / DSB Receiver and connect the AUDIO OUTPUT of the receiver to channel 1 of the Dual Audio Amplifier. Tune in a local AM station, if possible, and then use a BNC T-connector to connect the AUDIO OUTPUT of the AM / DSB Receiver to the AUDIO INPUT of the AM / DSB / SSB Generator, in place of the sine wave message signal.

Note: *If you are unable to tune in a local AM station the following "complex" message signal can be produced with the Dual Function Generator. Set the channel B controls to produce a 10-Hz square wave signal with OUTPUT LEVEL B at ½ turn cw, and select the 0 dB ATTENUATOR. Connect OUTPUT B to the FREQUENCY MODULATION INPUT and set the DEVIATION control at MAX. Now, set the channel A controls for a 200-Hz sine wave with OUTPUT LEVEL A at ½ turn cw. Select the 0 dB ATTENUATOR. The complex message signal now available at OUTPUT A can be used as the AUDIO INPUT for the AM / DSB / SSB Generator and the Dual Audio Amplifier (channel 1).*

☐ 24. Connect the demodulated AUDIO OUTPUT of the SSB Receiver to channel 2 of the Dual Audio Amplifier, and use the headphones to monitor both channels. Readjust the BFO tuning of the SSB Receiver around 452.5 kHz, if necessary, until the sounds in both earpieces appear to be the same.

Compare the sound of the demodulated SSB signal to that of the original message.

_____

_____

_____

☐ 25. Adjust the BFO tuning on the SSB Receiver to obtain a BFO frequency of 457.5 kHz. What differences do you notice in the sound of the demodulated audio as the BFO frequency is increased towards 457.5 kHz?

_____

_____

_____

☐ 26. When the BFO on the SSB Receiver is tuned at 457.5 kHz, high and low frequencies have been interchanged since it is the USB that is being transmitted. What changes does this produce in the sound of the demodulated audio signal?

_____

_____

_____

☐ 27. Turn all OUTPUT LEVEL and GAIN controls to the MIN position. Place all power switches in the off (O) position, and disconnect all cables.

CONCLUSION

This exercise has allowed you to demonstrate reception and demodulation of SSB signals. You have seen that the receiver BFO must be adjusted to the same frequency as the transmitter BFO for proper demodulation to occur. Adjusting the receiver BFO frequency above or below the BFO frequency at the transmitter causes frequency errors in the demodulated audio signal. If the receiver BFO frequency is adjusted to reverse the spectral relationship between the BFO and the transmitted sideband (established at the transmitter), high and low frequency content is interchanged. This reverses the sidebands and results in an unintelligible output at the receiver. Sideband reversal was demonstrated by adjusting the receiver BFO for LSB reception of a USB transmission. This lead to a reversal in behaviour of the demodulated signal, since its frequency decreased when the message signal frequency increased, and vice versa.

REVIEW QUESTIONS

1. A 2.5-kHz message signal is transmitted SSB using the Analog Communications Training System equipment. The transmitter BFO is adjusted at 457.5 kHz. Which sideband is being transmitted? (The transmitter VFO is adjusted at 4355.0 kHz).

   _____

2. To which frequency must the BFO on the SSB Receiver be adjusted to demodulate correctly the LSB transmission of a 2.5 kHz message signal by the AM / DSB / SSB Generator. The VFO frequencies of both modules are adjusted at 4355.0 kHz.

   _____

3. A 2.5 kHz message signal is transmitted SSB and BFO-TX is adjusted at 457.5 kHz. What is the effect of adjusting BFO-RX at 452.5 kHz? (VFO-TX and VFO-RX are adjusted at 4355.0 kHz).

   _____

   _____

   _____

Reception and Demodulation of SSB Signals

4. The transmitter BFO is adjusted for USB transmission and the VFO frequency is set at 4355.0 kHz. A 2.5 kHz message signal is transmitted and the receiver BFO is adjusted at 452.5 kHz. (VFO-RX is adjusted at 4355.0 kHz). When the message signal frequency at the transmitter is increased, what effect will this have on the frequency of the demodulated audio at the receiver?

_____

_____

_____

5. The audio output from an SSB transmitter is completely unintelligible. The audio appears to be music with the drum beats having a high pitched sound, and the violin producing very low notes. What is the probable cause for this problem? Explain.

_____

_____

_____

_____

Unit Test

1. The frequency spectrum of an RF signal contains only a single spectral line. This means that the signal is

   a. an SSB signal.
   b. a DSB signal having 50% modulation.
   c. an AM signal, which is not modulated.
   d. either an SSB signal or an unmodulated carrier signal.

2. The filter method is one way of generating

   a. AM signals.
   b. SSB signals.
   c. DSB signals.
   d. unmodulated AM signals.

3. A message signal is combined in a mixer with a BFO signal. If the BFO frequency is varied, the message signal spectrum at the mixer output will be

   a. displaced in the frequency spectrum.
   b. filtered according to the amount of change in the BFO frequency.
   c. attenuated according to the amount of change in the BFO frequency.
   d. split up into different frequency bands.

4. A 2.5-kHz sine wave is combined in a balanced mixer with a BFO signal at 457.5 kHz. The mixer output signal is filtered with a narrow-bandwidth (5 kHz) IF filter centered at 455 kHz. The frequency spectrum of the signal at the output of the filter will show

   a. a single spectral line at 460 kHz.
   b. a single spectral line at 455 kHz.
   c. that this is an SSB signal.
   d. both b and c.

5. The AM / DSB / SSB Generator is adjusted for USB transmission of a 2.5 kHz sine-wave message signal. The BFO frequency is therefore

   a. 457.5 kHz
   b. 455.0 kHz
   c. 452.5 kHz
   d. 450.0 kHz

6. An SSB communications system using the Analog Communications Training System modules is set up for LSB transmission of a 2.5 kHz sine wave. The BFO frequency at the receiver is adjusted at 452.5 kHz. This means that

   a. sideband reversal will occur.
   b. normal reception will take place.
   c. the equipment is being operated outside its specifications.
   d. none of the above.

7. The sound of the demodulated SSB signal from an SSB receiver is completely unintelligible. It is known that the transmitter is set up for USB transmission. The probable cause for the problem with the audio is that

    a. the receiver is tuned for LSB reception.
    b. sideband reversal has taken place.
    c. the BFO and VFO frequencies at the receiver are too close to each other.
    d. both a and b.

8. Adjusting the receiver BFO frequency at 457.5 kHz to receive the LSB transmission of a 2.5 kHz message signal from the AM / DSB / SSB Generator will result in

    a. proper demodulation of the message signal.
    b. sideband reversal.
    c. unintelligible audio from the receiver.
    d. both b and c.

9. Compared to ordinary AM and DSB, SSB modulation

    a. offers no advantages.
    b. offers better power utilization and reduces bandwidth.
    c. is too complicated to be widely used for communications.
    d. none of the above.

10. The transmitter VFO frequency is adjusted at 4355.0 kHz. For correct reception the receiver VFO frequency must be adjusted at

    a. 4810.0 kHz
    b. 4375.5 kHz
    c. 4355.0 kHz
    d. 4352.5 kHz

Troubleshooting AM Communications Systems

UNIT OBJECTIVE

When you have completed this unit, you will be able to locate instructor-inserted faults in the AM communications modules and identify the defective functional block using standard test equipment.

DISCUSSION

The AM communications trainers have provisions for manually inserting a number of faults. Each fault is controlled by a switch located under the small hinged cover inside the module. In order to assist in the troubleshooting procedure, test points have been provided to allow easy access to major circuit paths and functions within the trainers.

Troubleshooting communications equipment is basically the same as troubleshooting any other electrical, electronic, or mechanical device. Good troubleshooting techniques depend on a sound knowledge of the system or device and the way it normally operates, as well as a procedure that limits the number of signals tested. For example, you may be familiar with the joke about the person who called the TV repairman to come and fix the new TV. When the technician arrived, he plugged the TV into the wall outlet and then presented the customer with his bill. The moral of the story is, "Don't overlook the obvious" when troubleshooting. If the digital display on an instrument doesn't light up, maybe its power supply is defective.

Individual initiative and imagination, coupled with effective and efficient troubleshooting techniques, are important elements in successful troubleshooting. Troubleshooting can be structured according to four levels of activity designed to identify, locate, and correct a problem. Each level brings us closer to the problem source. The levels of activity, listed in order are:

1. System Function
2. Signal Flow Tracing
3. Voltage / Resistance Measurements
4. Substitution / Replacement

In this unit, you will concentrate on the first three levels of activity, with special emphasis being placed on signal flow tracing and voltage / resistance measurements.

Troubleshooting AM Communications Systems

To successfully perform any troubleshooting activity, it is necessary to understand the equipment and its operation. The best way to start any troubleshooting job is to read through the instruction manual, which will tell you how the equipment should operate. Often, the manual will have lists of typical faults and probable causes. This kind of information, along with electrical schematics and functional block diagrams, can be useful and time saving.

In all cases, troubleshooting should be approached using two fundamental rules as a guide. First, observe the symptoms of the problem, and second, relate the problem to specific functional blocks. This will usually lead you to the particular area of the system or device that is at fault.

NEW TERMS AND WORDS

troubleshooting — locating and diagnosing malfunctions or breakdowns in equipment by means of systematic checking or analysis.

Troubleshooting Techniques

EXERCISE OBJECTIVE

When you have completed this exercise, you will be able to apply a systematic technique of signal flow tracing to isolate a fault in the AM / DSB / SSB Generator module.

DISCUSSION

Signal flow tracing and voltage / resistance measurements are the principal techniques applied in troubleshooting, once a problem has been determined and enough information concerning the problem and its symptoms has been gathered. To assist you in the troubleshooting procedures, the list of test points, their location, and the schematic diagrams for the AM communications modules, are included in Appendix D of the Manual. Diagrams showing the location of test points have been repeated in the exercises. Reviewing previous exercises can provide valuable information concerning equipment operation, and lead to more efficient troubleshooting.

The technique of signal flow tracing consists in analyzing signals at different points along their path. In many cases, an oscilloscope, a frequency counter, and a spectrum analyzer, along with an audio generator and a VOM, are the only test equipment needed to troubleshoot communications equipment. The choice of which signal to analyze, and where to analyze it, should never be done on a random basis. A straight-forward, logical approach leads to quicker identification and correction of a problem. Knowing the operating principles of the equipment also reduces the time and effort required to isolate a fault.

Signal flow tracing can be approached in two ways. They are basically the same except for the direction followed in analysis.

1. Signal flow tracing from *input to output*.

2. Signal flow tracing from *output to input*.

Depending on the ability and training of the troubleshooter, and the functional complexity of the equipment, one or the other of the two approaches will be preferred. Extensive knowledge of equipment operating principles is necessary to trace signals from output to input, while troubleshooting equipment with only one output and multiple inputs can often be better performed in this way.

Troubleshooting Techniques

A more rapid technique used by experienced personnel is the divide-in-half method. Basically, this method requires that the input and output of the equipment be checked to verify defective operation. Next, the complete circuit path is divided-in-half and signals near the center are checked to determine if the problem is in the first or the second half. Following this, the defective section is again divided-in-half to further locate the problem. This successive divide-in-half approach is applied until the last remaining functional block is checked and the fault located. Figure 6-1 illustrates the procedure for a problem located at functional block B. The dotted lines show where signals are checked and the circled numbers indicate the steps in sequential order.

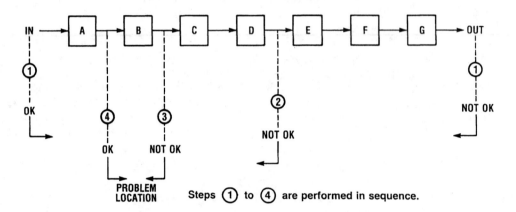

Figure 6-1. The divide-in-half method of troubleshooting.

The sequence of steps that should be followed for effective troubleshooting of the AM communications modules are:

1. Identify the defective module (generator or receiver), and perform a visual inspection for loose or damaged wires, connectors and components.

2. Check the module's input power at the 9-pin connector.

3. Check the module's internal regulated power at the identified test points.

4. Inject typical test signals at appropriate inputs.

5. Trace and analyze the signals along their flow path from input to output (or the reverse) using proper test equipment.

6. Verify that the signal has been transformed to correctly reflect the operation of the previous functional block. If not, diagnose the fault to determine the possible causes.

7. If another input branch meets at the point where faulty operation was discovered, verify that this branch is fault-free before concluding that the fault discovered in step 6 is the real problem.

EQUIPMENT REQUIRED

DESCRIPTION	MODEL
Accessories	8948
Power Supply / Dual Audio Amplifier	9401
Dual Function Generator	9402
Frequency Counter	9403
Spectrum Analyzer	9405
AM / DSB / SSB Generator	9410
Oscilloscope	—

PROCEDURE

☐ 1. Set up the modules as shown in Figure 6-2. Make sure that all OUTPUT LEVEL and GAIN controls are turned fully counterclockwise to the MIN position, and power up the equipment.

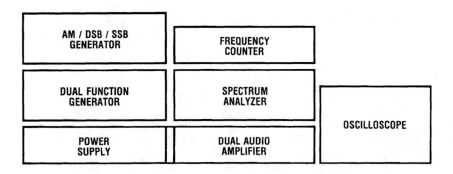

Figure 6-2. Suggested Module Arrangement.

☐ 2. Examine Figure 6-3. It shows the location of all test points in the AM / DSB / SSB Generator on a more-detailed functional block diagram.

Note: *Test points shown to coincide with front panel terminals may provide different signal levels than those found at the front panel terminal. This is because of protection and buffering devices which have been added.*

☐ 3. What is the advantage of measuring the carrier frequency at TP13 instead of TP11?

_____

_____

_____

Troubleshooting Techniques

TEST POINT	DESCRIPTION
TP1	BFO Output
TP2	BFO Tuning Control (dc voltage)
TP3	SSB IF Filter Output
TP4	SSB IF Output
TP5	SSB IF Mixer Output
TP6	SSB RF Amplifier Output (before output filter)
TP7	SSB RF Filter output
TP8	SSB RF Output
TP9	SSB RF Mixer Output
TP10	Carrier Level Control (dc voltage)
TP11	AM / DSB RF Output
TP12	Audio Input
TP13	VCO Square Wave (carrier frequency)
TP14	Audio Amplifier Output
TP15	RF Tuning Control (dc voltage)
TP16	AM / DSB RF Mixer Output
TP17	VFO Output

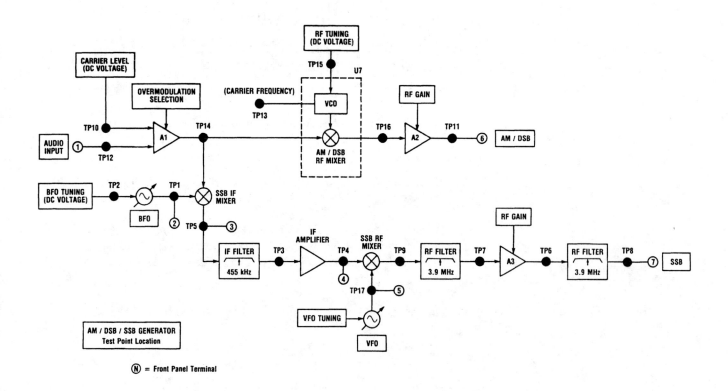

Figure 6-3. Test point locations – AM / DSB / SSB Generator.

Troubleshooting Techniques

☐ 4. What difference should exist between the signals at TP16 and TP11, according to the functional representation shown in Figure 6-3?

_____

_____

☐ 5. Adjust the Dual Function Generator to provide a 2.5-kHz sine wave with an amplitude of 400 mV p-p at OUTPUT A.

☐ 6. Adjust the RF TUNING control to measure a carrier frequency of 1000 kHz at TP13 with the Frequency Counter. Set the CARRIER LEVEL and RF GAIN (amplifier A_2) controls at MAX, and make sure the CARRIER LEVEL knob is pushed-in to the LINEAR OVERMODULATION position.

☐ 7. Inject the 2.5-kHz test signal at the AUDIO INPUT of the AM / DSB / SSB Generator. Observe the AM / DSB RF OUTPUT with the oscilloscope to confirm that the module operates normally.

☐ 8. The green LED lights automatically to indicate that unregulated input power is applied to the module. Is it on?

   ☐ Yes   ☐ No

What should you check if the green LED is off?

_____

_____

_____

☐ 9. Check the internal regulated voltages. Oscilloscope accuracy is sufficient in this case.

   + 15 V   ☐ OK   ☐ Not OK
   − 15 V   ☐ OK   ☐ Not OK

☐ 10. Open the top cover of the AM / DSB / SSB Generator, and ask your instructor to activate Fault 11 (FLT 11). Use a × 10 probe for signal observation at the various test points.

Note: _Do not use uncompensated (× 1) oscilloscope probes. They place a capacitive load on the test point. This capacitive load corresponds to the input capacitance of the measurement instrument. A × 10 probe provides 10 times less loading on the circuit being examined. While the test points provided in the AM communications modules are highly insensitive to capacitive loads, it is good lab practice to use a × 10 probe with unknown RF equipment._

Troubleshooting Techniques

☐ 11. Examine the test points and their location through the top cover. The U-shaped metal rings corresponding to the test points are accessed through the holes in the transparent cover fastened to the PC Board. Relate the test points to Figure 6-3.

☐ 12. Observe the AM / DSB RF OUTPUT with the oscilloscope to confirm that a fault has been inserted.

What are the symptoms of the problem as indicated by oscilloscope observation of the output waveform at terminal 6?

_____

_____

_____

☐ 13. You will now isolate the fault by performing signal flow tracing from the input to the output. Note that the simultaneous use of the oscilloscope and the spectrum analyzer is possible if two oscilloscopes are available.

☐ 14. Use the oscilloscope to observe the test signal at TP12. Compare it to the original test signal.

_____

_____

☐ 15. At TP14, the effect of adjusting the carrier level can be observed. Verify that the CARRIER LEVEL control operates normally by observing the effect at TP14. Return the control to the position set in step 6 when operation has been verified.

☐ 16. Have you observed faulty operation to this point?

☐ Yes   ☐ No

☐ 17. At TP16, you should observe that the audio signal is now combined with the high frequency carrier. Observe the waveform and/or frequency spectrum of the signal at TP16 to verify that they are correct. Use the information in Units 1, 2 and 3 as the reference for correct operation.

☐ 18. Do the results obtained in step 17 confirm proper operation?

☐ Yes   ☐ No

Troubleshooting Techniques

Explain _____

_____

_____

_____

☐ 19. All test results so far should confirm that the AM / DSB / SSB Generator is operating normally – up to and including TP16. Vary the RF GAIN (amplifier A_2) and compare the signals present at TP16 and TP11.

_____

_____

_____

_____

☐ 20. Based on your observations, what do you conclude?

_____

_____

_____

☐ 21. Compare your observations and conclusions with the description concerning Fault 11 given at the end of the Review Questions.

☐ 22. Have your instructor return FLT 11 to the inactive position and check that the module operates properly before proceeding with step 23.

☐ 23. Turn all OUTPUT LEVEL and GAIN controls to the MIN Position. Place all power switches in the off (O) position, and disconnect all cables.

CONCLUSION

You have applied a systematic, step-by-step approach to troubleshooting a fault in the AM / DSB / SSB Generator. The exercise has allowed you to acquire useful knowledge concerning troubleshooting, and you have been able to verify that a sound approach leads to quicker identification of the problem source. While you should not neglect any personal talents for troubleshooting that you may have discovered, it is important to combine these talents with the fundamental principles given in the exercise. This will reduce the chances of making errors when troubleshooting.

Troubleshooting Techniques

REVIEW QUESTIONS

1. Define troubleshooting.

   _____

   _____

   _____

2. Six of the seven steps for effective troubleshooting of the AM communications modules are listed below. Write in the missing step, and indicate the sequence in which each should be performed.

   _____ Check the module's input power at the 9-pin connector.

   _____ If another input branch meets at the point where faulty operation was discovered, verify that this branch is fault-free before concluding that the fault discovered in step 6 is the real problem.

   _____ Inject typical test signals at appropriate inputs.

   _____ Identify the defective module (generator or receiver), and perform a visual inspection for loose or damaged wires, connectors and components.

   _____ Check the module's internal regulated power at the identified test points.

   _____ Verify that the signal has been transformed to correctly reflect the operation of the previous functional block. If not, diagnose the fault to determine the possible causes.

   _____ _____

            _____

            _____

3. Why is signal flow tracing from output to input instead of from input to output a more difficult method to apply in troubleshooting?

   _____

   _____

   _____

4. What is the principal advantage of using a × 10 probe in troubleshooting unknown RF equipment?

   _____

   _____

   _____

Troubleshooting Techniques

5. What are two fundamental rules that should be used as a guide in any troubleshooting job?

_____

_____

_____

DESCRIPTION FOR FAULT 11

The effect of Fault 11 is to short the input of the RF amplifier stage to ground, causing a very weak RF signal. This simulates a transmitter with no output (except for feedthrough) from the final stage.

Troubleshooting the AM / DSB Section of the AM / DSB / SSB Generator

EXERCISE OBJECTIVE

When you have completed this exercise you will be able to locate instructor-inserted faults in the AM / DSB section of the AM / DSB / SSB Generator using the methods developed in Exercise 6-1.

DISCUSSION

There are five (5) instructor-insertable faults in the AM / DSB / SSB Generator that apply to the AM / DSB section. Fault 11 was used in the previous exercise. The knowledge gained in Exercise 6-1, and the familiarity with AM communications acquired through Units 1 to 5, should now be sufficient to allow you to trace these faults to the appropriate functional blocks. Therefore, the exercise procedures in this exercise, and those that follow, are centered around the use of troubleshooting worksheets. Specific procedure steps are given only where necessary.

EQUIPMENT REQUIRED

DESCRIPTION	MODEL
Accessories	8948
Power Supply / Dual Audio Amplifier	9401
Dual Function Generator	9402
Frequency Counter	9403
Spectrum Analyzer	9405
AM / DSB / SSB Generator	9410
Oscilloscope	—

Troubleshooting the AM / DSB Section
of the AM / DSB / SSB Generator

PROCEDURE

☐ 1. Set up the modules as shown in Figure 6-4. Make sure that all OUTPUT LEVEL and GAIN controls are turned fully counterclockwise to the MIN position, and power up the equipment.

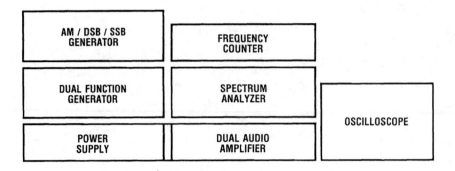

Figure 6-4. Suggested Module Arrangement.

☐ 2. Adjust the appropriate controls on the modules to provide an RF carrier frequency of 1000 kHz, and use a 2.5-kHz sine wave at 400 mV p-p as the modulating signal.

Note: *Since the communications mode may be AM or DSB, ensure that the CARRIER LEVEL control is in the appropriate position – MIN for DSB or MAX for AM. The control must also be pushed-in to the LINEAR OVERMODULATION position and the RF GAIN should be set at MAX.*

☐ 3. Verify that the module is operating normally.

☐ 4. Open the top cover of the AM / DSB / SSB Generator and ask your instructor to activate a fault.

☐ 5. Use Figure 6-5 and the Troubleshooting Worksheet to isolate the fault. Use a × 10 probe for signal observation at the various test points.

☐ 6. If troubleshooting for other faults is required, use additional worksheets and repeat the troubleshooting process.

☐ 7. Make sure that all fault switches are returned to the inactive position and check that the module operates properly before proceeding with step 8.

☐ 8. Turn all OUTPUT LEVEL and GAIN controls to the MIN position. Place all power switches in the off (O) position, and disconnect all cables.

Troubleshooting the AM / DSB Section
of the AM / DSB / SSB Generator

TEST POINT	DESCRIPTION
TP1	BFO Output
TP2	BFO Tuning Control (dc voltage)
TP3	SSB IF Filter Output
TP4	SSB IF Output
TP5	SSB IF Mixer Output
TP6	SSB RF Amplifier Output (before output filter)
TP7	SSB RF Filter output
TP8	SSB RF Output
TP9	SSB RF Mixer Output
TP10	Carrier Level Control (dc voltage)
TP11	AM / DSB RF Output
TP12	Audio Input
TP13	VCO Square Wave (carrier frequency)
TP14	Audio Amplifier Output
TP15	RF Tuning Control (dc voltage)
TP16	AM / DSB RF Mixer Output
TP17	VFO Output

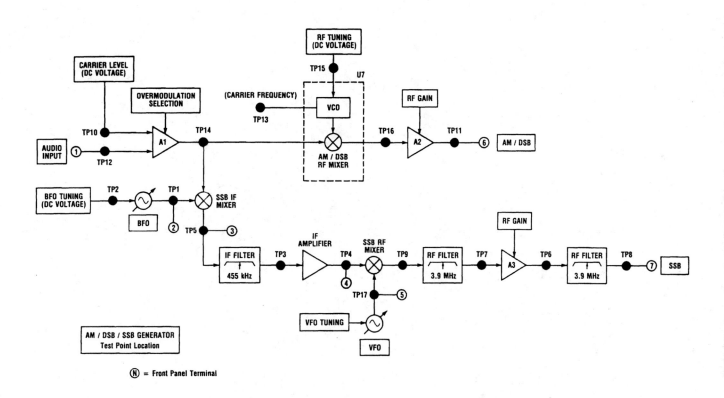

Figure 6-5. Test point locations – AM / DSB / SSB Generator.

Troubleshooting the AM / DSB Section
of the AM / DSB / SSB Generator

☐ 9. Notes and comments _____

_____

_____

_____

_____

_____

TROUBLESHOOTING WORKSHEET – AM / DSB / SSB

Type of Communications : ☐ AM ☐ DSB ☐ SSB

Problem With : ☐ Transmitter ☐ Receiver

Name of Module : _____

Fault Number* (or description) : _____

Fault Activated By : _____

Student's Name : _____

Steps Completed in Troubleshooting Sequence (See Exercise 6-1):

☐ 1 ☐ 2 ☐ 3 ☐ 4 ☐ 5 ☐ 6 ☐ 7

Problem Description and Symptoms †: _____

_____

_____

_____

_____

_____

_____

_____

_____

Defective Functional Block: _____

Instructor's Comments: _____

_____

_____

_____

_____

Notes: _____

_____

_____

_____

*At instructor's discretion.
†Sketch waveforms and spectra on reverse side.

TROUBLESHOOTING WORKSHEET – AM / DSB / SSB WAVEFORMS AND SPECTRA

Notes: _____

_____

_____

Notes: _____

_____

_____

Notes: _____

_____

_____

Notes: _____

_____

_____

Notes: _____

_____

_____

Notes: _____

_____

_____

Troubleshooting the SSB Section of the AM / DSB / SSB Generator

EXERCISE OBJECTIVE

When you have completed this exercise, you will be able to locate instructor-inserted faults in the SSB section of the AM / DSB / SSB Generator.

DISCUSSION

There are seven (7) instructor-insertable faults in the AM / DSB / SSB Generator that apply to the SSB section. These faults affect all major sections of the SSB generator – the BFO, the VFO, the IF section and the RF section. When troubleshooting SSB equipment, it is important to remember that negligeable carrier power is supposed to be present in the RF signal, and that the RF signal consists only of the upper sideband (USB) or the lower sideband (LSB).

EQUIPMENT REQUIRED

DESCRIPTION	MODEL
Accessories	8948
Power Supply / Dual Audio Amplifier	9401
Dual Function Generator	9402
Frequency Counter	9403
Spectrum Analyzer	9405
AM / DSB / SSB Generator	9410
Oscilloscope	—

Troubleshooting the SSB Section
of the AM / DSB / SSB Generator

PROCEDURE

☐ 1. Set up the modules as shown in Figure 6-6. Make sure that all OUTPUT LEVEL and GAIN controls are turned fully counterclockwise to the MIN position, and power up the equipment.

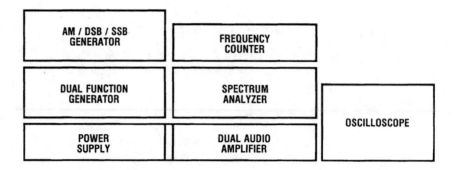

Figure 6-6. Suggested Module Arrangement.

☐ 2. Adjust the controls of the SSB section of the AM / DSB / SSB Generator to obtain a BFO frequency of 452.5 kHz and a VFO frequency of 4.355 MHz. *Make sure that the CARRIER LEVEL knob is turned fully ccw to MIN, and that it is pushed-in to the LINEAR OVERMODULATION position.*

☐ 3. Set the RF GAIN (amplifier A_3) at MAX.

☐ 4. Inject a 2.5-kHz sine wave with an amplitude of 200 mV p-p at the AUDIO INPUT of the AM / DSB / SSB Generator.

☐ 5. Verify that the module is operating normally.

☐ 6. Open the top cover of the AM / DSB / SSB Generator and ask your instructor to activate a fault.

☐ 7. Use Figure 6-7 and the Troubleshooting Worksheet to isolate the fault. Use a ×10 probe for signal observation at the various test points.

☐ 8. If troubleshooting for other faults is required, use additional worksheets and repeat the troubleshooting process.

☐ 9. Make sure that all fault switches are returned to the inactive position and check that the module operates properly before proceeding with step 10.

Troubleshooting the SSB Section
of the AM / DSB / SSB Generator

TEST POINT	DESCRIPTION
TP1	BFO Output
TP2	BFO Tuning Control (dc voltage)
TP3	SSB IF Filter Output
TP4	SSB IF Output
TP5	SSB IF Mixer Output
TP6	SSB RF Amplifier Output (before output filter)
TP7	SSB RF Filter output
TP8	SSB RF Output
TP9	SSB RF Mixer Output
TP10	Carrier Level Control (dc voltage)
TP11	AM / DSB RF Output
TP12	Audio Input
TP13	VCO Square Wave (carrier frequency)
TP14	Audio Amplifier Output
TP15	RF Tuning Control (dc voltage)
TP16	AM / DSB RF Mixer Output
TP17	VFO Output

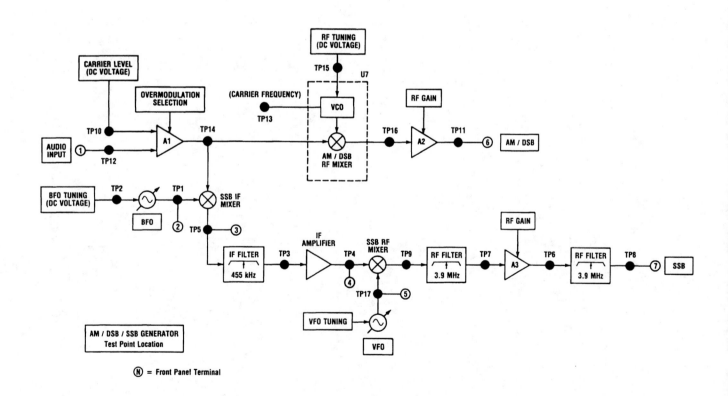

Figure 6-7. Test point locations — AM / DSB / SSB Generator.

☐ 10. Turn all OUTPUT LEVEL and GAIN controls to the MIN position. Place all power switches in the off (O) position, and disconnect all cables.

☐ 11. Notes and comments _____

_____

_____

_____

_____

_____

TROUBLESHOOTING WORKSHEET – AM / DSB / SSB

Type of Communications   : ☐ AM   ☐ DSB   ☐ SSB

Problem With   : ☐ Transmitter   ☐ Receiver

Name of Module   : _____

Fault Number* (or description)   : _____

Fault Activated By   : _____

Student's Name   : _____

Steps Completed in Troubleshooting Sequence (See Exercise 6-1):

☐ 1   ☐ 2   ☐ 3   ☐ 4   ☐ 5   ☐ 6   ☐ 7

Problem Description and Symptoms †: _____

_____

_____

_____

_____

_____

_____

_____

_____

Defective Functional Block: _____

Instructor's Comments: _____

_____

_____

_____

_____

Notes: _____

_____

_____

_____

*At instructor's discretion.
†Sketch waveforms and spectra on reverse side.

TROUBLESHOOTING WORKSHEET – AM / DSB / SSB WAVEFORMS AND SPECTRA

Notes: _____

_____

_____

Notes: _____

_____

_____

Notes: _____

_____

_____

Notes: _____

_____

_____

Notes: _____

_____

_____

Notes: _____

_____

_____

Troubleshooting the AM / DSB Receiver

EXERCISE OBJECTIVE

When you have completed this exercise, you will be able to locate instructor-inserted faults in the AM / DSB Receiver.

DISCUSSION

There are eight (8) instructor-insertable faults in the AM / DSB Receiver, and they affect all major sections of the receiver – the RF and IF stages, the Local Oscillator, the AGC, and the Detector circuits.

EQUIPMENT REQUIRED

DESCRIPTION	MODEL
Accessories	8948
Power Supply / Dual Audio Amplifier	9401
Dual Function Generator	9402
Frequency Counter	9403
Spectrum Analyzer	9405
AM / DSB / SSB Generator	9410
AM / DSB Receiver	9411
Oscilloscope	—

Troubleshooting the AM / DSB Receiver

PROCEDURE

☐ 1. Set up the modules as shown in Figure 6-8. Make sure that all OUTPUT LEVEL and GAIN controls are turned fully counterclockwise to the MIN position, and power up the equipment.

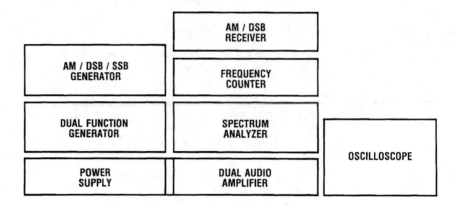

Figure 6-8. Suggested Module Arrangement.

☐ 2. Adjust the controls on the AM / DSB / SSB Generator to provide an RF carrier frequency of 1000 kHz, and use a 2.5-kHz sine wave at 400 mV p-p as the modulating signal.

   Note: *Since the communications mode may be AM or DSB, ensure that the CARRIER LEVEL control is in the appropriate position – MIN for DSB or MAX for AM. The control must also be pushed-in to the LINEAR OVERMODULATION position and the RF GAIN should be set at MAX.*

☐ 3. Verify that the module is operating normally.

☐ 4. Connect the RF OUTPUT of the AM / DSB / SSB Generator to the 50 Ω RF INPUT on the AM / DSB Receiver and ensure that the RF GAIN (amplifier A_2) is not set higher than ¼ turn cw.

☐ 5. Tune the AM / DSB Receiver to pick up the 1000-kHz carrier and verify that the module is operating normally.

☐ 6. Open the top cover of the AM / DSB Receiver and ask your instructor to activate a fault.

☐ 7. Use Figure 6-9 and the Troubleshooting Worksheet to isolate the fault. Use a ×10 probe for signal observation at the various test points.

Troubleshooting the AM / DSB Receiver

TEST POINT	DESCRIPTION
TP1	50 Ω RF Input
TP2	RF Filter Output
TP3	RF Output
TP4	IF Filter Output
TP5	IF Output
TP6	RF Mixer Output
TP7	Local Oscillator Output
TP8	Envelope Detector Output (unfiltered)
TP9	Audio Output
TP10	DC Control Voltage from AGC
TP11	PLL Mixer Output
TP12	Detector Mixer Output (filtered)
TP13	PLL Mixer Output (filtered)
TP14	VCO Input
TP15	VCO Output
TP16	VCO Output (after phase shifter)
TP17	Output of Costas Loop Comparator

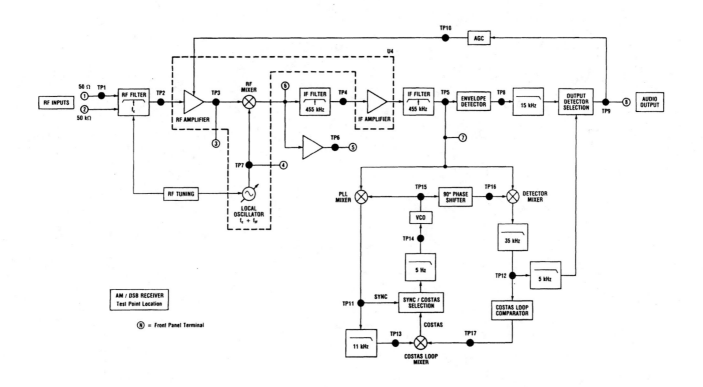

Figure 6-9. Test point locations – AM / DSB Receiver.

Troubleshooting the AM / DSB Receiver

☐ 8. If troubleshooting for other faults is required, use additional worksheets and repeat the troubleshooting process.

☐ 9. Make sure that all fault switches are returned to the inactive position and check that the module operates properly before proceeding with step 10.

☐ 10. Turn all OUTPUT LEVEL and GAIN controls to the MIN position. Place all power switches in the off (O) position, and disconnect all cables.

☐ 11. Notes and comments _____

_____

_____

_____

_____

_____

TROUBLESHOOTING WORKSHEET – AM / DSB / SSB

Type of Communications   : ☐ AM   ☐ DSB   ☐ SSB

Problem With   : ☐ Transmitter   ☐ Receiver

Name of Module   : _____

Fault Number* (or description)   : _____

Fault Activated By   : _____

Student's Name   : _____

Steps Completed in Troubleshooting Sequence (See Exercise 6-1):

☐ 1   ☐ 2   ☐ 3   ☐ 4   ☐ 5   ☐ 6   ☐ 7

Problem Description and Symptoms †: _____

_____

_____

_____

_____

_____

_____

_____

_____

_____

Defective Functional Block: _____

Instructor's Comments: _____

_____

_____

_____

_____

Notes: _____

_____

_____

_____

*At instructor's discretion.
†Sketch waveforms and spectra on reverse side.

TROUBLESHOOTING WORKSHEET – AM / DSB / SSB WAVEFORMS AND SPECTRA

Notes: _____

_____

_____

Notes: _____

_____

_____

Notes: _____

_____

_____

Notes: _____

_____

_____

Notes: _____

_____

_____

Notes: _____

_____

_____

Troubleshooting the SSB Receiver

EXERCISE OBJECTIVE

When you have completed this exercise, you will be able to locate instructor-inserted faults in the SSB Receiver.

DISCUSSION

There are eight (8) instructor-insertable faults in the SSB Receiver, and they affect all major sections – the BFO, the VFO, the IF section, and the RF section.

EQUIPMENT REQUIRED

DESCRIPTION	MODEL
Accessories	8948
Power Supply / Dual Audio Amplifier	9401
Dual Function Generator	9402
Frequency Counter	9403
Spectrum Analyzer	9405
AM / DSB / SSB Generator	9410
SSB Receiver	9412
Oscilloscope	—

PROCEDURE

☐ 1. Set up the modules as shown in Figure 6-10. Make sure that all OUTPUT LEVEL and GAIN controls are turned fully counterclockwise to the MIN position, and power up the equipment.

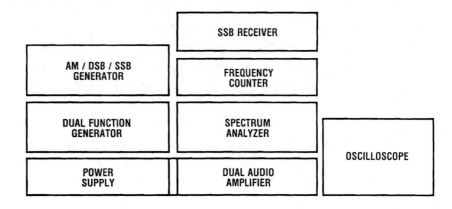

Figure 6-10. Suggested Module Arrangement.

Troubleshooting the SSB Receiver

☐ 2. Adjust the controls on the SSB section of the AM / DSB / SSB Generator to obtain a BFO frequency of 452.5 kHz and a VFO frequency of 4.355 MHz. Make sure that the CARRIER LEVEL knob is turned fully ccw to MIN, and that it is pushed-in to the LINEAR OVERMODULATION position.

☐ 3. Set the RF GAIN (amplifier A_3) at ¼ turn cw.

☐ 4. Inject a 2.5-kHz sine wave with an amplitude of 200 mV p-p at the AUDIO INPUT of the AM / DSB / SSB Generator.

☐ 5. Connect the SSB RF OUTPUT of the AM / DSB / SSB Generator to the 50 Ω RF INPUT on the SSB Receiver.

☐ 6. Tune the BFO and the VFO on the SSB Receiver to 452.5 kHz and 4.355 MHz respectively, and verify that the module is operating normally.

   Note: *The BFO and the VFO on the SSB Receiver* **must** *be tuned to the same frequency as their counterparts on the AM / DSB / SSB Generator.*

☐ 7. Open the top cover of the SSB Receiver and ask your instructor to activate a fault.

☐ 8. Use Figure 6-11 and the Troubleshooting Worksheet to isolate the fault. Use a × 10 probe for signal observation at the various test points.

☐ 9. If troubleshooting for other faults is required, use additional worksheets and repeat the troubleshooting process.

☐ 10. Make sure that all fault switches are returned to the inactive position and check that the module operates properly before proceeding with step 11.

☐ 11. Turn all OUTPUT LEVEL and GAIN controls to the MIN position. Place all power switches in the off (O) position, and disconnect all cables.

Troubleshooting the SSB Receiver

TEST POINT	DESCRIPTION
TP1	VFO Output
TP2	RF Filter Output
TP3	50 Ω RF Input
TP4	IF Filter Output
TP5	DC Control Voltage from AGC
TP6	Auxiliary IF Input
TP7	IF Signal after First IF Amplifier Stage
TP8	IF Output
TP9	RF Mixer Output
TP10	Emitter of IF Mixer Transistor
TP11	IF Mixer Output
TP12	Audio Output
TP13	BFO Tuning Control (dc voltage)
TP14	BFO Output

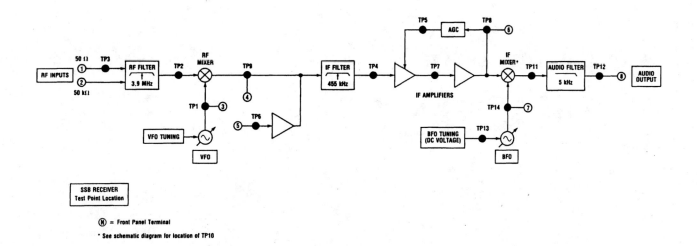

Figure 6-11. Test point locations – SSB Receiver.

Troubleshooting the SSB Receiver

☐ 12.　Notes and comments _____

_____

_____

_____

_____

_____

TROUBLESHOOTING WORKSHEET – AM / DSB / SSB

Type of Communications : ☐ AM ☐ DSB ☐ SSB

Problem With : ☐ Transmitter ☐ Receiver

Name of Module : _____

Fault Number* (or description) : _____

Fault Activated By : _____

Student's Name : _____

Steps Completed in Troubleshooting Sequence (See Exercise 6-1):

☐ 1   ☐ 2   ☐ 3   ☐ 4   ☐ 5   ☐ 6   ☐ 7

Problem Description and Symptoms †: _____

_____

_____

_____

_____

_____

_____

_____

_____

Defective Functional Block: _____

Instructor's Comments: _____

_____

_____

_____

_____

Notes: _____

_____

_____

_____

*At instructor's discretion.
†Sketch waveforms and spectra on reverse side.

TROUBLESHOOTING WORKSHEET – AM / DSB / SSB WAVEFORMS AND SPECTRA

Notes: _____

_____

_____

Notes: _____

_____

_____

Notes: _____

_____

_____

Notes: _____

_____

_____

Notes: _____

_____

_____

Notes: _____

_____

_____

Troubleshooting an AM / DSB Communications System

EXERCISE OBJECTIVE

When you have completed this exercise, you will be able to locate instructor-inserted faults in an AM / DSB communications system made up of the AM / DSB / SSB Generator and the AM / DSB Receiver.

DISCUSSION

There are a total of 13 faults which can be activated in the AM / DSB communications system using the AM / DSB / SSB Generator and the AM / DSB Receiver – 5 in the generator and 8 in the receiver. In your troubleshooting, it is important to determine with certainty which module is defective in the beginning. Once the defective module has been isolated, inject a typical test signal (2.5-kHz sine wave at 400 mV p-p) at the AUDIO INPUT of the generator and set the operating controls for a carrier frequency of 1000 kHz, AM or DSB communications, and LINEAR OVERMODULATION. Note that the RF GAIN (amplifier A_2) control *should not be set* any higher than ¼ turn cw when the AM / DSB Receiver is connected by a BNC / BNC cable to the AM / DSB / SSB Generator. The reason for this is because the higher harmonic power levels present with the RF GAIN set above ¼ allow the sensitive AM / DSB Receiver to capture and demodulate spurious signals instead of the true carrier.

It should be remembered to select the right detector for the type of communications (ENV or SYNC for AM, and COSTAS for DSB), and the AGC should normally be in the I (active) position. The local oscillator frequency should be adjusted according to the carrier frequency, and it is generally useful to monitor the AUDIO OUTPUT of the receiver with the Dual Audio Amplifier. Exercises 6-1, 6-2 and 6-4 should be reviewed as required when you troubleshoot a complete AM / DSB communications system.

EQUIPMENT REQUIRED

DESCRIPTION	MODEL
Accessories	8948
Power Supply / Dual Audio Amplifier	9401
Dual Function Generator	9402
Frequency Counter	9403
Spectrum Analyzer	9405
AM / DSB / SSB Generator	9410
AM / DSB Receiver	9411
Oscilloscope	—

Troubleshooting an AM / DSB Communications System

PROCEDURE

☐ 1. Set up the modules as shown in Figure 6-12. Make sure that all OUTPUT LEVEL and GAIN controls are turned fully counterclockwise to the MIN position, and power up the equipment.

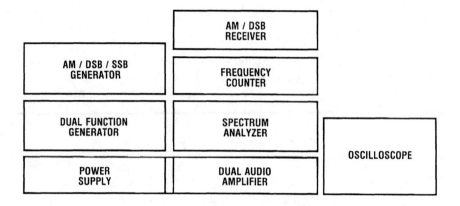

Figure 6-12. Suggested Module Arrangement.

☐ 2. Verify that both modules operate normally by setting up an AM (or DSB) communications system in accordance with your instructor's directives.

☐ 3. When you have verified that the communications system operates normally, ask your instructor to activate a fault in the system.

☐ 4. Use Figures 6-13 and 6-14 with the Troubleshooting Worksheet to isolate the fault. Use a × 10 probe for signal observation at the various test points.

☐ 5. If troubleshooting for other faults is required, use additional worksheets and repeat the troubleshooting process.

☐ 6. Make sure that all fault switches are returned to the inactive position and check that the module operates properly before proceeding with step 7.

☐ 7. Turn all OUTPUT LEVEL and GAIN controls to the MIN position. Place all power switches in the off (O) position, and disconnect all cables.

☐ 8. Notes and comments _____

_____

_____

_____

Troubleshooting an AM / DSB Communications System

TEST POINT	DESCRIPTION
TP1	BFO Output
TP2	BFO Tuning Control (dc voltage)
TP3	SSB IF Filter Output
TP4	SSB IF Output
TP5	SSB IF Mixer Output
TP6	SSB RF Amplifier Output (before output filter)
TP7	SSB RF Filter output
TP8	SSB RF Output
TP9	SSB RF Mixer Output
TP10	Carrier Level Control (dc voltage)
TP11	AM / DSB RF Output
TP12	Audio Input
TP13	VCO Square Wave (carrier frequency)
TP14	Audio Amplifier Output
TP15	RF Tuning Control (dc voltage)
TP16	AM / DSB RF Mixer Output
TP17	VFO Output

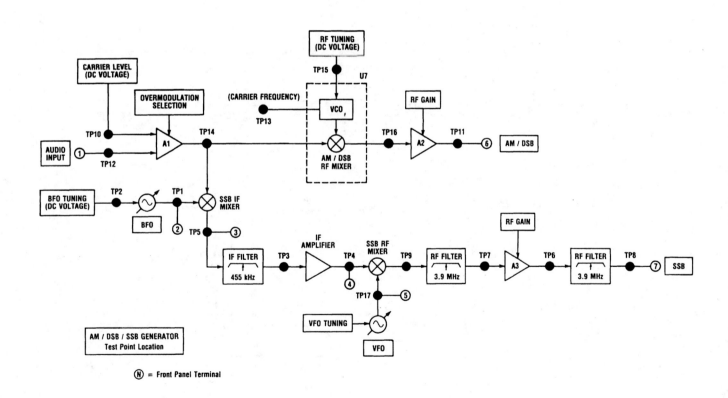

Figure 6-13. Test point locations – AM / DSB / SSB Generator.

Troubleshooting an AM / DSB Communications System

TEST POINT	DESCRIPTION
TP1	50 Ω RF Input
TP2	RF Filter Output
TP3	RF Output
TP4	IF Filter Output
TP5	IF Output
TP6	RF Mixer Output
TP7	Local Oscillator Output
TP8	Envelope Detector Output (unfiltered)
TP9	Audio Output
TP10	DC Control Voltage from AGC
TP11	PLL Mixer Output
TP12	Detector Mixer Output (filtered)
TP13	PLL Mixer Output (filtered)
TP14	VCO Input
TP15	VCO Output
TP16	VCO Output (after phase shifter)
TP17	Output of Costas Loop Comparator

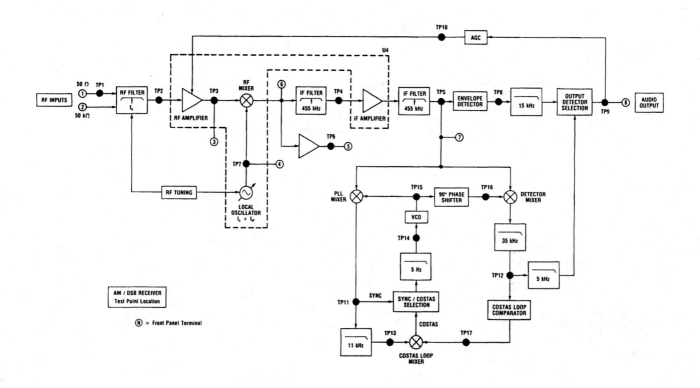

Figure 6-14. Test point locations – AM / DSB Receiver.

TROUBLESHOOTING WORKSHEET – AM / DSB / SSB

Type of Communications   : □ AM   □ DSB   □ SSB

Problem With   : □ Transmitter   □ Receiver

Name of Module   : _____

Fault Number* (or description)   : _____

Fault Activated By   : _____

Student's Name   : _____

Steps Completed in Troubleshooting Sequence (See Exercise 6-1):

□ 1   □ 2   □ 3   □ 4   □ 5   □ 6   □ 7

Problem Description and Symptoms †: _____

_____

_____

_____

_____

_____

_____

_____

_____

Defective Functional Block: _____

Instructor's Comments: _____

_____

_____

_____

_____

Notes: _____

_____

_____

*At instructor's discretion.
†Sketch waveforms and spectra on reverse side.

TROUBLESHOOTING WORKSHEET – AM / DSB / SSB WAVEFORMS AND SPECTRA

Notes: _____

_____

_____

Notes: _____

_____

_____

Notes: _____

_____

_____

Notes: _____

_____

_____

Notes: _____

_____

_____

Notes: _____

_____

_____

Troubleshooting an SSB Communications System

EXERCISE OBJECTIVE

When you have completed this exercise, you will be able to locate instructor-inserted faults in an SSB communications system made up of the AM / DSB / SSB Generator and the SSB Receiver.

DISCUSSION

There are a total of 15 faults which can be activated in the SSB communications system using the AM / DSB / SSB Generator and the SSB Receiver — 7 in the generator and 8 in the receiver. Use the same test signal (2.5 kHz sine wave at 200 mV p-p) as in Exercise 6-3, and review the material of that exercise as well as Exercise 6-5.

EQUIPMENT REQUIRED

DESCRIPTION	MODEL
Accessories	8948
Power Supply / Dual Audio Amplifier	9401
Dual Function Generator	9402
Frequency Counter	9403
Spectrum Analyzer	9405
AM / DSB / SSB Generator	9410
SSB Receiver	9412
Oscilloscope	—

Troubleshooting an SSB Communications System

PROCEDURE

☐ 1. Set up the modules as shown in Figure 6-15. Make sure that all OUTPUT LEVEL and GAIN controls are turned fully counterclockwise to the MIN position, and power up the equipment.

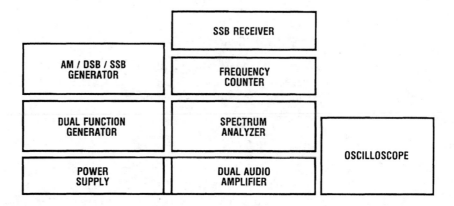

Figure 6-15. Suggested Module Arrangement.

☐ 2. Verify that both modules operate normally by setting up an SSB communications system in accordance with your instructor's directives.

☐ 3. When you have verified that the communications system operates normally, ask your instructor to activate a fault in the system.

☐ 4. Use Figure 6-16 and 6-17 with the Troubleshooting Worksheet to isolate the fault. Use a × 10 probe for signal observation at the various test points.

☐ 5. If troubleshooting for other faults is required, use additional worksheets and repeat the troubleshooting process.

☐ 6. Make sure that all fault switches are returned to the inactive position and check that the module operates properly before proceeding with step 7.

☐ 7. Turn all OUTPUT LEVEL and GAIN controls to the MIN position. Place all power switches in the off (O) position, and disconnect all cables.

☐ 8. Notes and comments _____

_____

_____

_____

_____

Troubleshooting an SSB Communications System

TEST POINT	DESCRIPTION
TP1	BFO Output
TP2	BFO Tuning Control (dc voltage)
TP3	SSB IF Filter Output
TP4	SSB IF Output
TP5	SSB IF Mixer Output
TP6	SSB RF Amplifier Output (before output filter)
TP7	SSB RF Filter output
TP8	SSB RF Output
TP9	SSB RF Mixer Output
TP10	Carrier Level Control (dc voltage)
TP11	AM / DSB RF Output
TP12	Audio Input
TP13	VCO Square Wave (carrier frequency)
TP14	Audio Amplifier Output
TP15	RF Tuning Control (dc voltage)
TP16	AM / DSB RF Mixer Output
TP17	VFO Output

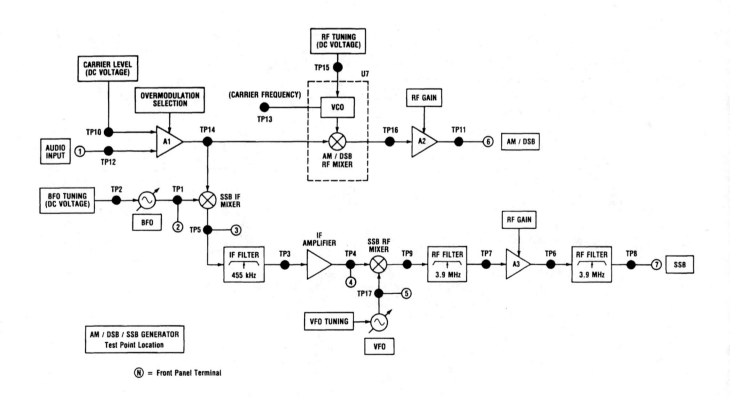

Figure 6-16. Test point locations – AM / DSB / SSB Generator.

Troubleshooting an SSB Communications System

TEST POINT	DESCRIPTION
TP1	VFO Output
TP2	RF Filter Output
TP3	50 Ω RF Input
TP4	IF Filter Output
TP5	DC Control Voltage from AGC
TP6	Auxiliary IF Input
TP7	IF Signal after First IF Amplifier Stage
TP8	IF Output
TP9	RF Mixer Output
TP10	Emitter of IF Mixer Transistor
TP11	IF Mixer Output
TP12	Audio Output
TP13	BFO Tuning Control (dc voltage)
TP14	BFO Output

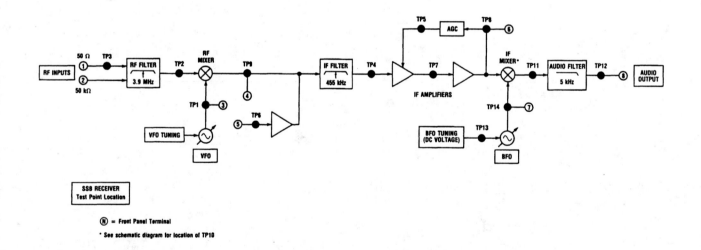

Figure 6-17. Test point locations – SSB Receiver.

TROUBLESHOOTING WORKSHEET – AM / DSB / SSB

Type of Communications : ☐ AM ☐ DSB ☐ SSB

Problem With : ☐ Transmitter ☐ Receiver

Name of Module : _____

Fault Number* (or description) : _____

Fault Activated By : _____

Student's Name : _____

Steps Completed in Troubleshooting Sequence (See Exercise 6-1):

☐ 1 ☐ 2 ☐ 3 ☐ 4 ☐ 5 ☐ 6 ☐ 7

Problem Description and Symptoms †: _____

_____

_____

_____

_____

_____

_____

_____

_____

_____

Defective Functional Block: _____

Instructor's Comments: _____

_____

_____

_____

_____

Notes: _____

_____

_____

_____

*At instructor's discretion.
†Sketch waveforms and spectra on reverse side.

TROUBLESHOOTING WORKSHEET – AM / DSB / SSB WAVEFORMS AND SPECTRA

Notes: _____

_____

_____

Notes: _____

_____

_____

Notes: _____

_____

_____

Notes: _____

_____

_____

Notes: _____

_____

_____

Notes: _____

_____

_____

Unit Test

1. Troubleshooting communications equipment is basically the same as troubleshooting any other electrical, electronic, or mechanical device.

   a. True.
   b. False.

2. Before troubleshooting any equipment the best way to start is to

   a. check that the power is on.
   b. call the manufacturer of the equipment.
   c. read through the manual to learn how the equipment operates.
   d. check that the power is off.

3. Equipment manuals usually

   a. do not help in troubleshooting.
   b. contain only general information.
   c. supply a lot of troubleshooting methods and theory.
   d. contain valuable information concerning normal operation and typical faults.

4. To successfully perform troubleshooting it is necessary to

   a. be familiar with the particular equipment.
   b. understand the equipment and its operation.
   c. talk to the equipment manufacturer.
   d. have the equipment manual.

5. Locating and diagnosing equipment malfunctions by systematic checking is known as

   a. regular maintenance.
   b. equipment checking.
   c. equipment repair.
   d. troubleshooting.

6. The divide-in-half technique of troubleshooting is

   a. well adapted for use by inexperienced personnel.
   b. a very difficult method to use.
   c. much more rapid, but requires good knowledge of the equipment.
   d. a time saving method because it takes only half as long to locate the fault.

7. One of the first things to verify when troubleshooting is

   a. the equipment's power input.
   b. the electric company's line voltage.
   c. the frequency of the ac power circuit.
   d. none of the above.

8. When troubleshooting a complete AM communications system (transmitter-receiver), it is important to first check

   a. the transmitter.
   b. the receiver.
   c. that a message signal is present.
   d. the output of both transmitter and receiver to determine which half of the system is at fault.

9. The use of a x 10 oscilloscope probe when troubleshooting unknown RF equipment is

   a. likely to cause problems.
   b. good lab practice because less circuit loading is caused.
   c. no different from using a x 1 probe.
   d. both b and c.

10. Signal flow tracing from input to output

   a. is exactly the same as signal flow tracing from-output to input.
   b. is more difficult than the divide-by-half method.
   c. doesn't require extensive knowledge of equipment operating principles.
   d. is a method used only to maintain communications equipment.

Answers to Procedure Step Questions

A-2

Answers to Procedure Step Questions

Note: *All measurements, calculations and figures given as Answers to Procedure Step Questions are approximate, and should be considered only as a guide. These results may differ considerably from one Analog Communications Training System to another. The results of calculations have been rounded off to the appropriate number of significant digits.*

Exercise 1-1

□ 2. The information signal or message.

□ 3. The carrier.

□ 4. The transmission line or channel.

□ 8. You should hear a 2-kHz audio signal.

□ 9. The sound changes in frequency and will probably seem louder around 3 kHz because of the characteristics of human hearing.

□ 10. Both displays should track closely and show the same readings at all times (up to the frequency limit of the AM / DSB Receiver).

□ 11. The waveforms of Figure 1-4 should be very similar. The recovered information signal will probably show some deformation and it will not be exactly in phase with the original information signal.

□ 12. There should be no marked difference in sound between both signals.

Exercise 1-2

□ 2. The frequency of the RF carrier changes as the RF TUNING control is varied. You will probably also notice amplitude variations in the waveform as the control is varied between its extreme positions.

□ 3. $f_{lower} < 400$ kHz, $f_{upper} > 1800$ kHz.

□ 4. Both controls affect the amplitude of the RF waveform.

Answers to Procedure Step Questions

☐ 7. The effect should be identical since the RF GAIN controls the amplitude of the RF waveform.

☐ 8. The amplitude and the form of the RF waveform changes, but that of the envelope (message signal) does not. When the relative amplitude of the message signal becomes greater than the amplitude of the non-modulated carrier, overmodulation occurs.

☐ 9. The frequency of the envelope (the number of peaks and valleys) follows the frequency of the message signal.

☐ 12. f_{LO} (f_C = 1000 kHz) = 1455 kHz ±3 kHz

☐ 13. f_{LO} (f_C = 1510 kHz) = 1965 kHz

☐ 15. f_{LO} (f_C = 1100 kHz) = 1555 kHz ± 3 kHz

☐ 16. You should obtain an answer very close to 455 kHz in both cases, and the answers confirm the fact that the local oscillator is tuned 455 kHz above the frequency of the RF signal.

☐ 21. As the FREQUENCY SPAN is decreased, more and more detail is revealed concerning the frequency content of the RF signal. Finally, at the lowest spans, it becomes clear that the input signal is an AM signal modulated by a single-tone message signal.

☐ 22. As the CARRIER LEVEL control is decreased towards MIN, the height of the carrier line on the frequency spectrum display decreases. At the MIN position the carrier is more than 35 dB below its maximum level.

☐ 23. The Spectrum Analyzer shows that all the frequency components of the RF signal are affected by the RF GAIN. When the control is tuned towards MIN, all components decrease equally, and vice versa.

☐ 24. If the Spectrum Analyzer is accurately calibrated, f_{LSB} and f_{USB} will be equal to their theoretical values, that is, 1098 kHz and 1102 kHz.

Answers to Procedure Step Questions

☐ 25. When the frequency of the message signal increases, the sidebands spread apart. The distance between each sideband and the carrier frequency changes equally in response to the increase in f_m. When f_m decreases, the sidebands come closer together, and the distance between each sideband and the carrier decreases.

☐ 26. The approximate range should be around 350 to 1900 kHz.

☐ 27. Yes, harmonic frequencies at intervals of 1 MHz do appear. These harmonics are not easily detected in the time domain, especially at low power levels, but a spectrum analyzer provides a clear picture of their presence.

Exercise 1-3

☐ 5. $f_{LSB} = 1098$ kHz, $f_{USB} = 1102$ kHz

☐ 6. If the Spectrum Analyzer is accurately calibrated, f_{LSB} and f_{USB} will be equal to their theoretical values.

☐ 7. With the Spectrum Analyzer set to the 2 kHz / V FREQUENCY SPAN, you should be able to distinguish clearly both messages that are centered around the carrier frequency. You would not be able to hear the messages individually with an ordinary AM receiver because they have been translated to the same position in the frequency spectrum, that is, centered around a single carrier.

☐ 12. An ordinary AM receiver will allow you to hear both messages individually because two different carriers are being used. Therefore, the receiver can be tuned to select one or the other of the "stations".

☐ 14. If the AM receiver is properly tuned to the carrier frequency of the AM generator, you should hear clearly the 2-kHz tone.

☐ 15. The sound should change to a 3-kHz tone as you tune in the other "station". This demonstrates that different messages can be tuned in separately when they are broadcast using two different carriers. The frequency contents of each message have been translated to different places in the frequency spectrum.

Answers to Procedure Step Questions

☐ 16. The frequency contents of the 3-kHz message can be superimposed over those of the 2-kHz message. When the spectra of the messages are too close together the sound becomes garbled and unintelligible. The original message information is therefore lost because of the interference caused by the other signal, and the resulting sound is a combination of the two original messages.

☐ 17. The minimum distance is around 8-10 kHz.

Exercise 2-1

☐ 2. The message signal, audio, intelligence.

☐ 4. The waveform is that of a high frequency (1100 kHz) sine wave carrier.

☐ 5.

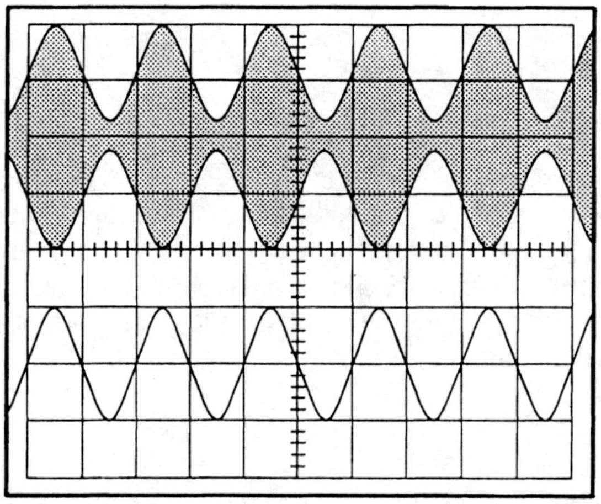

Figure 2-6. Waveforms of the modulating and modulated signals.

☐ 6. The envelope of the AM waveform corresponds to the waveform of the square wave signal.

☐ 7. In each case, the AM waveform corresponds to the waveform of the message signal.

☐ 8. The frequency of the envelope varies in accordance with the frequency of the information signal.

Answers to Procedure Step Questions

☐ 9. The amplitude of the AM waveform changes as shown in Figure 2-4. When the amplitude of the information signal is increased, the difference in height between the peaks and valleys of the envelope increases, and vice versa. This corresponds to a change in the modulation index.

☐ 10. The modulation index.

☐ 12.

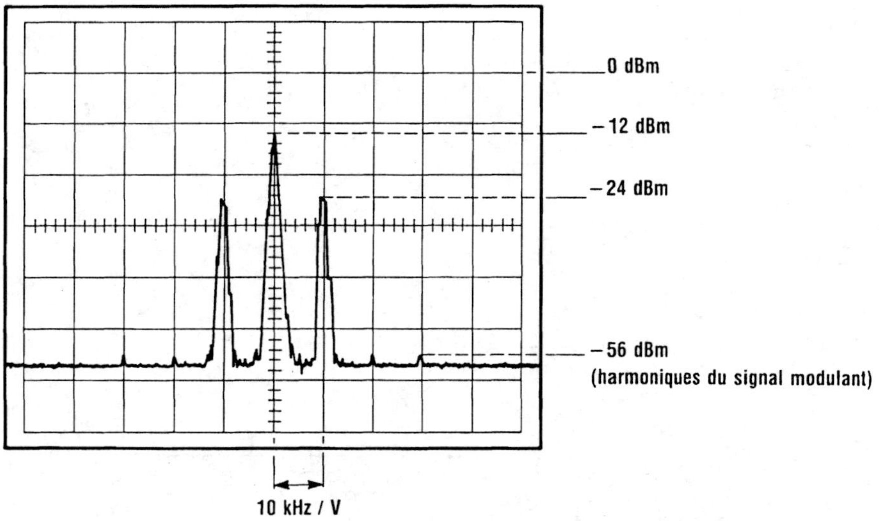

10 kHz / V

Figure 2-7. The frequency spectrum of an 1100-kHz carrier modulated by a 10-kHz sine wave.

☐ 13. The frequency spectrum should be very similar to the idealized version shown in Figure 2-3. The main differences will be the physical width of the spectral lines, and also the relative amplitudes of the carrier and the sidebands. You may also notice some low level harmonics of the message signal.

☐ 14. When the message signal frequency is increased, the sidebands spread apart in the same proportion as the frequency increase, and vice versa. This shows that increasing f_m increases the bandwidth necessary for transmission of the message signal.

☐ 15. When the amplitude of the message signal is increased, the power level of the sidebands increase in proportion. The power level of the carrier is not affected, nor the frequency of the spectral components. Beyond a certain amplitude level (approx ⅜ turn cw here), harmonics of the modulating signal begin to appear.

Answers to Procedure Step Questions

□ 16. The power level of the sidebands varies directly with the change in the modulation index. Increasing the modulation index causes their power level to increase, and vice versa. The power level of the carrier is not affected by varying the modulation index, unless the carrier amplitude is varied to adjust the modulation index.

□ 17. You should observe a "complex" spectrum, typical of a square wave, in which the fundamental and the odd-numbered harmonics of decreasing amplitude are present. (See Exercise 2-4 of Volume 1 – Instrumentation).

Exercise 2-2

□ 2. 0.4 V p-p.

□ 4. 1.16 V p-p.

□ 5.
$$\% \text{ Mod.} = \frac{0.4}{1.16} \times 100\% = 34.5\%$$

□ 6.

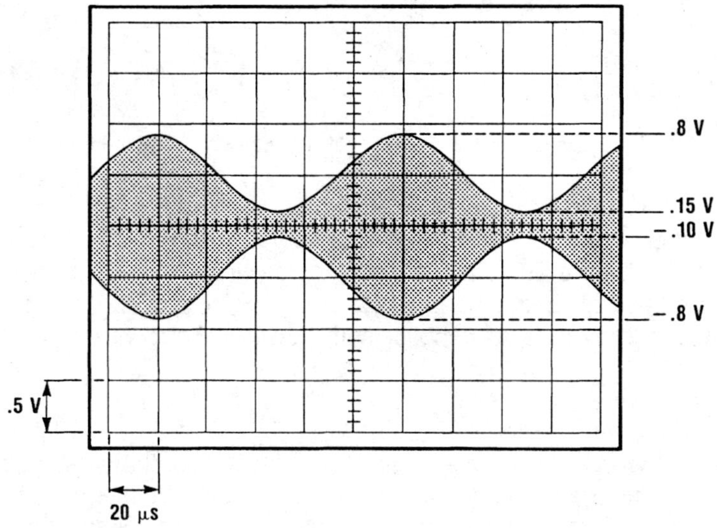

A = 1.6 V

B = .25 V

$$m = \frac{1.6 - .25}{1.6 + .25} = .730 \text{ or } 73.0\%$$

Figure 2-16. The AM signal waveform.

The modulation index in step 6 is 2.12 (.730/.345) times the value obtained in step 5, thus confirming the fact that the amplitude actually affecting the carrier is different from the value measured at the input. Note that the normal range of variation for this ratio is about 1.8 to 2.5.

Answers to Procedure Step Questions

☐ 7. A = 1.9 V and B = 0.29 V, therefore m = .735 or 73.5% which compares very well with the value obtained in step 6.

☐ 8. For m = 0.20: A = 1.34 V, B = 0.9 V, thus m = 0.196

For m = 0.33: A = 1.48 V, B = 0.72 V, thus m = 0.345

For m = 0.75: A = 1.95 V, B = 0.25 V, thus m = 0.773

☐ 12. Δ = 9 dB and according to Figure 2-11, % Mod ≃ 71%.

☐ 13. The answer is step 12 compares well with the value set in step 8.

☐ 14. Δ_1 = 11 dB and m_1 = 0.57; Δ_2 = 19 dB and m_2 = 0.225.

☐ 15. You should observe a spectrum similar to that shown in Figure 2-13, in which harmonics of the modulating signal (spurious frequencies) are visible.

☐ 16. When the percentage modulation becomes greater than 100%, harmonics of the modulating signal appear.

☐ 17. When the modulation index becomes greater than 1, the AM waveform changes to the form shown in Figure 2-13, in which clipping occurs.

☐ 18. The results are similar to Figure 2-14, in which the extra lobes of the AM waveform are not clipped when the signal is overmodulated.

☐ 19. When the modulation index becomes greater than 1, the trapezoid pattern changes to the typical form obtained with an overmodulated signal – two triangles "nose-to-nose". The appearance of the smaller triangle on the right is positive confirmation of overmodulation.

Answers to Procedure Step Questions

☐ 20.

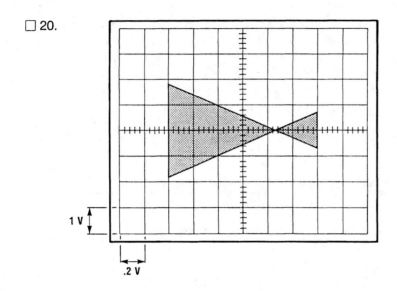

Figure 2-17. Trapezoidal pattern when m > 1.

☐ 21. When the knob is pulled out to the NONLINEAR OVERMODULATION position, the small triangle on the right disappears, and is replaced by a straight line.

Exercise 2-3

☐ 8, 9, 10, 14, 15, 16, 17, 18, 19, 20.

				TRUE RMS VOLTMETER RESULTS				SPECTRUM ANALYZER RESULTS							
m	μ	P_{SB}/P_T*	V_{AUDIO}	P_C (unmodulated)		P_{AM} (modulated)		$P_T = P_C + P_{SB}$**		P_C		P_{LSB}		P_{USB}	
—	$m^2/2 + m^2$	%	V_{rms}	dBm	mW	dBm	mW	dBm	mW	dBm	mW	dBm	mW	dBm	mW
.50	11.1%	13	.100	−10	0.1	−9.5	.115	−12.7	.055	−13	.05	−26	.0024	−26	.0024
.75	21.9%	20	.145	−10	0.1	−9.0	.125	−12.2	.058	−13	.05	−24	.004	−24	.004
1.00	33.3%	33	.190	−10	0.1	−8.3	.150	−11.7	.066	−13	.05	−21	.008	−21	.008
1	2	3	4	5	6	7	8	9	10	11	12	13	14	15	16

Table 2-1.

☐ 21. When you compare the theoretical and measured results for the transmission efficiency μ, they should be very close (within experimental error), thus confirming the fact that the modulation index is a useful tool for determining the transmission efficiency.

Answers to Procedure Step Questions

□ 22. The theoretical values of P_T and P_{AM} should be identical in each of the three cases. However, because of equipment tolerances, experimental errors, etc., this will be unlikely. You will probably observe an offset of 1 to 4 dB between the voltmeter and the spectrum analyzer results, which is normal. In any event, the results of Table 2-1 should confirm the fact that the relative increase in power level is identical in each case.

□ 23. The relative dBm values for P_{SB} in each of the three cases should correspond closely. Because of the probable offset between the frequency domain and the time domain measurements, the absolute power levels will certainly be different. Note that P_{SB} for the True RMS Voltmeter Results is the difference in dB between P_{AM} (modulated) and P_C (unmodulated), while P_{SB} for the Spectrum Analyzer Results is the dB difference between P_T and P_C.

Exercise 3-1

□ 3. 950 kHz.

□ 7. The spectral line corresponding to the carrier frequency starts to appear on the frequency spectrum display. The height of the spectral line reaches its maximum value when f_C equals 950 kHz, showing that the incoming RF signal is centered in the bandwidth of the RF filter.

□ 10.

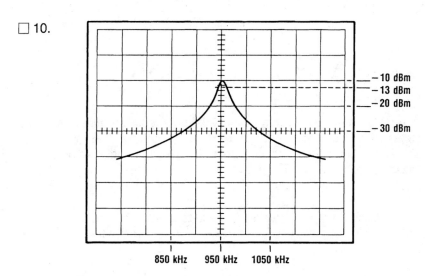

Figure 3-5. RF Filter approximate frequency response at 950 kHz.

□ 11. 3-dB BW = 962 − 943 = 19 kHz

10-dB BW = 974 − 933 = 41 kHz

20-dB BW = 1030 − 870 = 160 kHz

Answers to Procedure Step Questions

☐ 15.

FREQUENCY	850	870	890	910	930	950	970	990	1010	1030	1050
dBm READING	−31.3	−29.9	−27.2	−23.9	−19.3	−10	−16.7	−23.2	−27.0	−28.6	−30.8
RELATIVE dB*	−21.3	−19.9	−17.2	−13.9	−9.3	0	−6.7	−13.2	−17.0	−18.6	−20.8

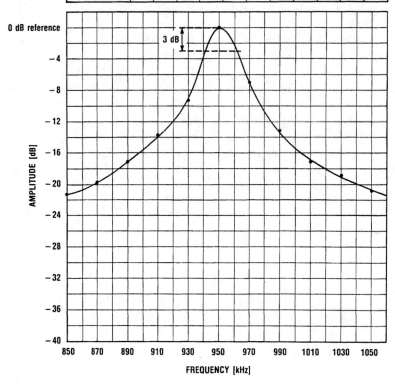

Figure 3-6.

☐ 16. 3-dB BW = 19 kHz, 10-dB BW = 50 kHz, 20-dB BW = 170 kHz.

☐ 17. The results should confirm the approximate results obtained with the Spectrum Analyzer in step 11. The main reason for any differences is due to the difficulty in interpreting the Spectrum Analyzer display to determine an absolute number.

☐ 18. The 3-dB bandwidth is approximately 20 kHz and the minimum required is 10 kHz. Any baseband signal up to 5 kHz will pass freely through the RF filter without distortion.

Exercise 3-2

☐ 7. f_{LO} = −20 dB, f_C = −34 dB, f_{LO} + f_C = −50 dB, f_{LO} − f_C = −2 dB.

Answers to Procedure Step Questions

☐ 8. 18 dB, which is acceptable since the mixer output signal will be further processed and filtered by the IF stage before reaching the detector stage.

☐ 10. You should observe a single spectral line at 455 kHz that is at a relatively high power level. This shows that the IF stage has eliminated the other frequency components in the mixer output signal and amplified the resulting IF signal.

☐ 12. −33 dBm

☐ 13. The 690 kHz image frequency.

☐ 14. −11.7 dBm

☐ 15. 21 dB

Exercise 3-3

☐ 5. 455 kHz

☐ 6. The spectral line corresponding to the IF signal starts to appear on the frequency spectrum display. The line reaches a maximum height at a frequency of 455 kHz showing that the signal is centered in the bandwidth of the IF filter.

☐ 8. 456 kHz

☐ 9.

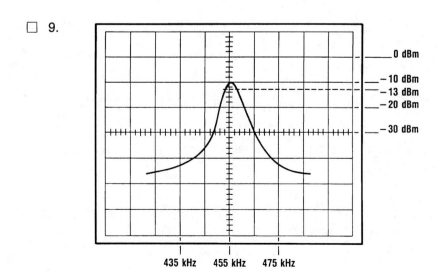

Figure 3-11. IF Stage approximate frequency response at 455 kHz.

Answers to Procedure Step Questions

☐ 10. 3-dB BW = 459 − 453 = 6 kHz
        10-dB BW = 461 − 452 = 9 kHz
        20-dB BW = 465 − 449 = 16 kHz

☐ 14.

FREQUENCY	439	443	447	451	453	455	457	459	463	467	471
dBm READING	−43.2	−38.6	−32	−24.3	−17.6	−10.4	−10	−11.9	−23.5	−31.0	−37.9
RELATIVE dB*	−33.2	−28.6	−22	−14.3	−7.6	−0.4	0	−1.9	−13.5	−21.0	−27.9

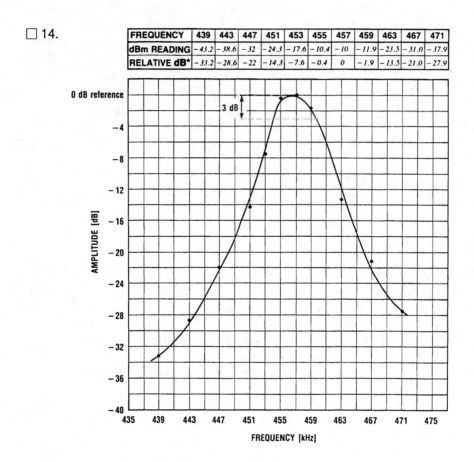

Figure 3-12.

☐ 15. 3-dB BW = 6 kHz , 10-dB BW = 10 kHz, 20-dB BW = 18 kHz.

☐ 16. The results obtained in step 15 should confirm the approximate results of step 10.

☐ 20. You should observe a typical AM spectrum centered at 455 kHz with the LSB and USB clearly visible each side of the carrier.

Answers to Procedure Step Questions

☐ 21. When the message signal frequency exceeds 5 kHz, the amplitudes of the sidebands decrease rapidly. This shows that the message signal frequency has exceeded the bandwidth of the IF stage. The lop-sided appearance of the spectrum that may be present depends on the modulating signal frequency and the frequency-response characteristics of individual IF stages.

☐ 22. LSB 3-dB point = 453 kHz, USB 3-dB point = 459 kHz.

☐ 23. The answers are very similar, thus confirming the earlier results.

☐ 24. The 3-dB bandwidth of the IF stage is about 4 times smaller than that of the RF stage. This shows that the IF stage effectively filters the frequency contents centered at the intermediate frequency and controls unwanted signals which might be adjacent to the RF carrier.

Exercise 3-4

☐ 2. 159 µs

☐ 4. 1405 kHz

☐ 8. The oscilloscope display should show the AM signal and the 1-kHz sine wave. You will notice that the negative side of the AM envelope corresponds closely to the original sine wave message signal.

☐ 9. The modulation index should be approximately 0.50.

☐ 10. The positive alternance of the demodulated audio becomes distorted when the carrier level drops below a certain value. This is because of the 0.6 V drop across the envelope detector diode.

☐ 11. The approximate position at which the demodulated audio begins to be affected is ⅝ turn cw. This corresponds to a modulation index of about 0.65.

☐ 12. With the CARRIER LEVEL control at MIN and set for NONLINEAR OVERMODULATION, the positive alternance of the demodulated audio signal is clipped showing severe distortion. There is a small range from about ¾ turn cw to MAX in which there is little or no evidence of distortion in the audio signal.

Answers to Procedure Step Questions

☐ 15. There is a variation in the amplitude of the audio signal due to the variation of RF signal power at the receiver output.

☐ 16. A much wider range of variation in the level of the RF input signal is possible because of the action of the AGC. The demodulated audio signal is much less affected by variations in the RF signal level.

☐ 18. The SYNC detector allows proper demodulation with much less distortion than the ENV detector. The audio output amplitude is also greater because there is much less power being lost in the detector circuit, as is the case for the envelope detector.

☐ 19. The SYNC detector.

Exercise 4-1

☐ 3. You should observe the 10-kHz sine wave message signal.

☐ 5. The display should show both the sine wave signal, as well as the DSB signal.

☐ 7.

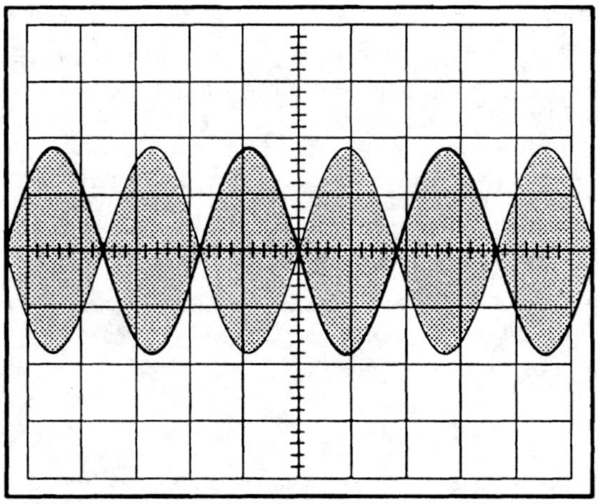

Figure 4-6. The DSB waveform and its modulating signal.

☐ 8. Proper adjustment of the controls allows you to position the original message signal to demonstrate that it corresponds to the line drawn through alternate lobes of the DSB waveform.

Answers to Procedure Step Questions

☐ 9. With the CARRIER LEVEL control at MAX, a typical AM waveform is obtained. As the control is turned towards MIN, thus reducing carrier power, the waveform changes to a linearly overmodulated AM signal. When carrier power has been reduced to minimum the waveform has become that of a DSB signal.

☐ 10. The amplitude of the RF waveform follows exactly the amplitude of the message signal, thus demonstrating that modulating signal amplitude directly controls the RF amplitude.

☐ 11. The waveform of the DSB signal follows exactly the variations in message signal frequency, as is the case for the envelope of an AM signal.

☐ 12. Your observations should confirm that the message signal waveform is composed of the line traced through alternate lobes of the DSB waveform. Message signal frequency affects the DSB waveform the same way as in step 11.

☐ 13. The effects produced by changes in the amplitude and frequency of these message signals are the same as those produced by a sine wave. When the message signal amplitude increases, the amplitude of the DSB waveform increases in the same proportion. When the message signal frequency is varied, the envelope of the DSB waveform follows the variation in frequency.

☐ 17. You should be able to observe the typical frequency spectrum of a DSB signal, in which carrier power is negligible.

☐ 18. Carrier suppression = 40 dB

☐ 19. LSB power level = USB power level = − 22 dBm

☐ 20. The power levels of the sidebands increase as the modulating signal level increases.

☐ 21. LSB power level = USB power level = − 14 dBm

☐ 22. The carrier power should not increase at all since this is a DSB spectrum. Also, carrier power is completely independent of message signal amplitude.

Answers to Procedure Step Questions

☐ 23. RF power has increased by the same amount as sideband power in direct proportion to the increase in message signal amplitude. In this particular case, RF power has increased by 8 dB between steps 19 and 21.

☐ 24. The sidebands are displaced from the carrier frequency position by an amount equal to the message signal frequency. The amount of frequency space taken up by the message signal is in direct proportion to the modulating signal frequency, which is the same as for AM.

☐ 25. Bandwidth requirements (frequency space) are the same for DSB as for AM.

Exercise 4-2

☐ 3. You should observe a 1.5 kHz, 400 mV p-p sine wave signal.

☐ 6. 1455 kHz

☐ 9. You will probably observe an oscilloscope display that is unstable with the waveform of the demodulated signal "hopping" up and down. Once the generator and receivers are properly synchronized the "hopping" will stop and a demodulated signal closely ressembling the original message signal will be obtained.

☐ 11.

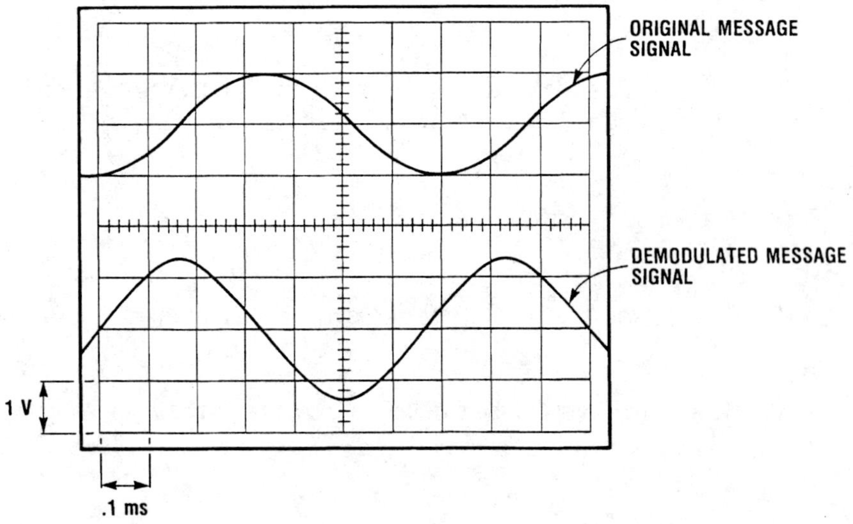

Figure 4-10. Original and recovered signals with DSB modulation.

Answers to Procedure Step Questions

☐ 12. The demodulated signal waveform should be almost identical to the original message signal waveform, and there will probably be a noticeable phase shift between the two waveforms.

☐ 13. Since it is a sensitive circuit, the COSTAS loop detector usually falls out of synchronization because of the large variation in amplitude when the AGC circuit is switched on and off. If this does not happen, you will observe the large amplitude variation and a certain amount of distortion in the demodulated signal.

☐ 14.

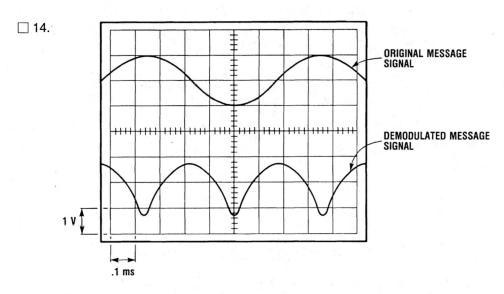

Figure 4-11. Demodulated DSB signal obtained with the SYNC detector.

☐ 15.

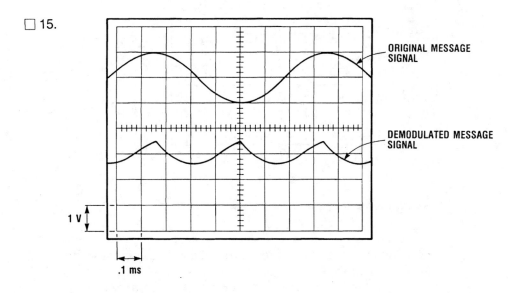

Figure 4-12. Demodulated DSB signal obtained with the ENV detector.

Answers to Procedure Step Questions

☐ 16. As shown by the various waveforms obtained with the other detectors, only the COSTAS detector is capable of properly demodulating a DSB signal. The ENV and SYNC detectors produce distorted versions of the original message signal waveform.

☐ 18. You should hear the original sine wave tone clearly, and there should be little distortion in the sound.

☐ 19. The sound of the demodulated signal doubles in frequency because both the ENV and SYNC detectors rectify a portion of the original signal. You will probably also notice a clicking noise which occurs each time the message signal changes polarity from positive to negative, and vice versa.

☐ 20. The demodulated audio should be understandable, but there will be a clicking noise present, as well as distortion in the sound.

Exercise 5-1

☐ 4. 452.5 kHz

☐ 5. 4354 kHz

☐ 9.

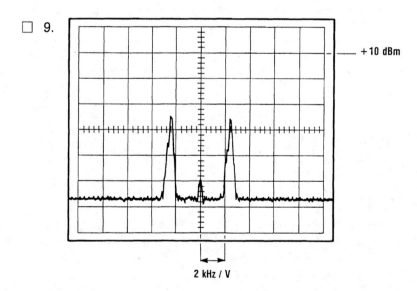

+10 dBm

2 kHz / V

Figure 5-8. The frequency spectrum at the MIXER OUTPUT.

The frequency spectrum is that of a typical DSB signal with a small amount of carrier power showing in the spectrum. Since the BFO is adjusted at 452.5 kHz and the message signal frequency is 2.5 kHz, the frequencies of the LSB and the USB are 450 and 455 kHz, respectively.

Answers to Procedure Step Questions

☐ 10. The frequency spectrum of the signal at the IF OUTPUT contains only one frequency component, which represents the USB. The IF filter has effectively removed the residual carrier power and the LSB that was positioned at 450 kHz.

☐ 11. As f_{BFO} approaches 455 kHz, the LSB reappears since it is being positioned to fall within the passband of the IF filter. When f_{BFO} is adjusted at 455 kHz, a DSB spectrum is obtained because both sidebands lie within the passband of the IF filter.

☐ 12. Both sidebands disappear because the message signal frequency becomes greater than the bandwidth capacity of the IF filter.

☐ 13. The USB is gradually placed outside the passband of the IF filter at the same time as the LSB is being positioned inside. The frequency spectrum shows the USB gradually disappearing as the LSB appears.

☐ 14. As f_{BFO} is varied between 453 and 457 kHz, sideband selection is being performed. Around 453 kHz, the USB is selected, while tuning f_{BFO} around 457 kHz selects the LSB.

☐ 17. You should observe a DSB spectrum similar to that obtained in step 11. The sidebands are positioned 2.5 kHz each side of the RF carrier frequency.

☐ 18. The effect produced is identical to that obtained in step 14, thus showing that the sideband selection performed at the IF stage (with the BFO) is conserved at the RF carrier frequency.

☐ 19. When f_{BFO} is adjusted at 452.5 kHz, the USB is selected, while adjusting f_{BFO} at 457.5 kHz selects the LSB.

☐ 20. The time domain waveform for an SSB signal is a high frequency sine wave when the modulating signal is a single-tone sine wave.

☐ 21. The waveform is that of a high-frequency sine wave.

Exercise 5-2

☐ 4. 452.5 kHz

Answers to Procedure Step Questions

☐ 5. 4355.1 kHz

☐ 7. 4355.1 kHz

☐ 8. 452.5 kHz

☐ 9. The measured frequency of the demodulated signal is 2.3 kHz which compares favorably with the message signal frequency of 2.5 kHz. However, the fact that the frequencies are not identical indicates that there is a slight misadjustment in the BFO and / or VFO frequencies between the generator and receiver.

☐ 10. When the message signal frequency is varied between 2 and 3 kHz, the frequency of the demodulated audio signal follows the variation exactly.

☐ 12. You should hear identical 2.5 kHz tones in both earpieces, if the BFO and VFO frequencies are well adjusted.

☐ 13. The sound in both earpieces changes identically, increasing or decreasing in pitch with the increase or decrease in message signal frequency.

☐ 14. The sound decreases in pitch, becoming more and more bass until it disappears. The sound then reappears and increases in pitch. When the BFO frequency has reached 457.5 kHz the sound appears to be identical to that of the original message signal.

☐ 15. When the message signal frequency increases, the sound and frequency of the demodulated audio signal decreases, and vice versa. This indicates that sideband reversal has taken place because normal spectral behavior is reversed.

☐ 18. The frequency spectrum shows the 2.5 kHz baseband signal each side of the 0-Hz reference line.

☐ 19. When the message signal frequency is increased and decreased, the spectral behavior suggested by the results obtained in step 15 is observed. Increasing f_m causes the spectral line to move towards the 0-Hz reference line indicating a decrease in frequency and vice versa. This is a reversal of normal spectral behavior.

Answers to Procedure Step Questions

☐ 20. Since BFO-RX is adjusted for LSB reception, it reverses the spectral relationship between the BFO and the USB that has been established at the transmitter. This causes sideband reversal and is demonstrated by the fact that normal spectral behavior is reversed.

☐ 21. The spectral lines each side of the 0-Hz reference line move towards each other and seem to exchange positions when they cross over the 0-Hz reference line. They then move apart from each other as the BFO frequency is adjusted towards 452.5 kHz.

☐ 22. The spectral behavior is now normal. When the message signal frequency is increased, the spectral lines move away from the 0-Hz reference line, and vice versa. This shows that the spectral relationship between the BFO and the transmitted sideband has been conserved at the receiver.

☐ 24. If you have been able to tune in a local AM station, you should be able to tune BFO-RX so that the original and the demodulated signals sound almost identical. If you have used the complex message signal suggested in step 23, it may be more difficult to judge this. Checking that the BFO and the VFO frequencies on both modules are adjusted properly at their corresponding values is a method of verification in this case.

☐ 25. The sound deteriorates rapidly and becomes completely unintelligible. When the BFO frequency is adjusted at 457.5 kHz, the sound is still mostly unintelligible but it seems more regular and it is evident that this is intelligent information being communicated. Note that this answer concerns the results obtained with the audio from an AM broadcast. For the complex message signal of step 23, results will be more difficult to interpret.

☐ 26. If the message signal is the audio from an AM broadcast, the sound of the demodulated signal will indicate clearly that high and low frequencies have been interchanged. Women's voices will sound like those of men, and drum beats will have a high-pitched sound. Violins will produce strange, low notes.

Exercise 6-1

☐ 3. Measuring the carrier frequency at TP13 instead of TP11 allows continuous monitoring of f_c without the necessity of disconnecting input signals. Measuring f_c at the output while an input signal is connected could cause inaccurate results.

Answers to Procedure Step Questions

☐ 4. According to Figure 6-3, the signal at TP11 will be an amplified version of the signal at TP16.

☐ 8. If the green LED is off, the module's input power at the 9-pin connector should be verified. In this way, it can be determined if the problem is with the module or the power input.

☐ 12. Oscilloscope observation of the output waveform shows that the RF output is extremely weak, almost negligible.

☐ 14. The signal at TP12 should be identical to the test signal.

☐ 16. No faulty operation has been observed to this point and step 15 confirms that the CARRIER LEVEL control operates normally.

☐ 18. The results of step 17 confirm proper operation because the signal at TP16 is a correctly modulated AM signal.

☐ 19. The signal at TP 16 is a correctly modulated AM signal while there is no signal (or extremely little) at TP11.

☐ 20. The only logical conclusion based on all the available information is that the RF amplifier located between TP16 and TP11 is defective.

Answers to Review Questions

Answers to Review Questions

EXERCISE 1-1

1. The transmitter, the transmission line, and the receiver.
2. It is based on the use of electrical energy to transmit information. The original information is converted to electric signals and then transmitted directly over wires, or through the air as electromagnetic radio waves. A receiver then recovers the original information by converting the electrical signals to their original form.
3. Amplitude modulation, frequency modulation, phase modulation.
4. Modulation.
5. 3 kHz, because the receiver is supposed to reproduce all the characteristics of the original information signal.

EXERCISE 1-2

1. Amplitude modulation is the process in which message signal information is impressed onto an RF carrier by causing the amplitude of the carrier to vary in accordance with the amplitude of the message signal.

2.

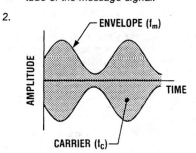

a) AM Waveform

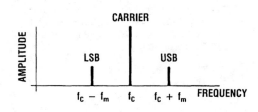

B) AM Spectrum

3. $f_{LSB} = 957\ kHz$, $f_{USB} = 963\ kHz$
4. $f_{LO} = f_C - f_{IF}$, $f_{LO} = f_C + f_{IF}$
5. Frequency domain observations are generally more useful, because they show the frequency components of a signal, as well as the relative amplitudes of the components.

EXERCISE 1-3

1. The frequency contents of the message signal are displaced (translated) to the frequency spectrum position of the carrier signal. This translation action can naturally be reversed using another mixer.
2. Frequency translation allows great reduction in the size of antenna structures. It also permits several different messages to be placed side-by-side in the frequency spectrum – thus allowing the simultaneous operation of many different broadcasting stations.
3. Baseband generally refers to the frequency band occupied by the message signal.
4. LSB: 1499.5 to 1496 kHz, USB: 1500.5 to 1504 kHz
5. The baseband signals must be transmitted using different carrier frequencies, so that the receiver can be tuned to each one individually.

EXERCISE 2-1

1. The square wave can be considered a complex message signal because it contains a great number of frequency components.

2.

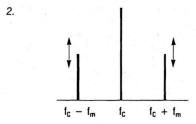

a) Amplitude affects height of spectral lines.

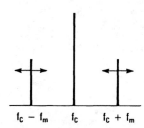

b) Frequency affects position of spectral lines.

3. The difference in height between the peaks and valleys increases.
4. Since the envelope is theoretically identical to the waveform of the modulating signal, an increase in frequency will produce an increase in the number of peaks and valleys.
5. It does not change because it depends only on the amplitude of the message signal.

Answers to Review Questions

EXERCISE 2-2

1. a) $m = 0.20$
    b) $m = 0.33$
    c) $m = 0.75$

2. $m = \dfrac{A_m}{A_c} = \dfrac{.25}{.50} = 0.50$

3. Overmodulation occurs when $m > 1$. It is undesirable since it produces interference with other stations because frequencies outside the allocated bandwidth are produced.
4. This indicates linear overmodulation of the AM signal.
5. 1.00

EXERCISE 2-3

1. $P_T = P_C + P_{SB}$, $\mu = \dfrac{m^2}{2 + m^2}$

2. The maximum value for the modulation index without creating overmodulation and interference is 1. Therefore, $m^2/(2 + m^2) = \frac{1}{3}$.
3. There is a difference of 6 dB between the carrier level and the sidebands. Therefore, the modulation index equals 1 (Figure 2-11).
4. Since $P_C = 0$ dBm, which corresponds to 1 mW, and $P_{SB} = -3$ dBm, corresponding to 0.5 mW, the total power is therefore 1.5 mW. ($P_{LSB} = P_{USB} = -6$ dBm $= 0.25$ mW). The actual power of the signal is 1000 times greater, or $1.5 \times 10^{-3} \times 10^3 = 1.5$ W.
5. $\Delta = 8$ dB, therefore $m = 0.80$ (Figure 2-11).
    $\mu = 0.8^2/(2 + 0.8^2) = .64/2.64 = 24.2\%$
    $P_C = 10$ kW and

    $$\mu = \dfrac{P_{SB}}{P_T} = \dfrac{P_{SB}}{P_C + P_{SB}}$$

    therefore $.242 (10 + P_{SB}) = P_{SB}$, from which $P_{SB} \simeq 3.1$ kW and $P_{LSB} = P_{USB} = 3.1/2 = 1.55$ kW. The total power P_T is therefore $10 + 3.1 = 13.1$ kW.

EXERCISE 3-1

1. Superheterodyne receiver.
2. RF selection, frequency translation from RF to IF, filtering and amplification of the IF signal, detection (demodulation) to recover the transmitted information.
3. 6 kHz
4. Sum and difference frequencies of both input signals are produced in which the difference frequency corresponds to the fixed IF (455 kHz). Frequency translation of the message signal from RF to IF has therefore been accomplished. Further processing by the IF stage allows only the information contained in the IF signal to be passed on to the detector stage for demodulation.

5. The intermediate frequency.

EXERCISE 3-2

1. Since $f_C = f_{LO} + f_{IF}$, f_{IMAGE} is equal to $f_C + 2f_{IF} = 600 + 910 = 1510$ kHz.
2. Since f_{IMAGE} is equal to $f_C + 2f_{IF}$, $f_C = 2500 - 910 = 1590$ kHz.
3. The role of the mixer is to perform frequency-translation from RF to IF so that the message signal can be processed more effectively.
4. The RF stage.
5. Intraband image frequencies can be eliminated by choosing an intermediate frequency high enough so that $f_C + 2f_{IF}$ lies outside the band of operation. However, this does not eliminate image frequencies, since other communications facilities outside the band of operation can exist.

EXERCISE 3-3

1. If the IF stage bandwidth is much less than 10 kHz, there may be unacceptable distortion in the demodulated message signal because a part of its spectral content will be lost.
2. Since the IF stage bandwidth is 6 kHz, the maximum message signal frequency will be limited to 3 kHz. (Remember, AM doubles the bandwidth of the baseband signal). This means that the AM signal frequency content from 3 kHz to 5 kHz will be attenuated by the receiver causing deterioration in the quality of the demodulated signal.
3. The IF stage.
4. The large IF stage gain causes problems because any spurious signals at 455 kHz will be amplified and pass through the IF stage causing interference and distortion.
5. This can be considered normal because the frequency-response characteristics of all practical circuits are seldom perfectly flat throughout the passband. Also, the particular filter or stage is sometimes detuned slightly to one side of the center frequency for which it has been designed.

EXERCISE 3-4

1.

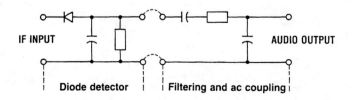

IF INPUT — AUDIO OUTPUT

Diode detector   Filtering and ac coupling

Answers to Review Questions

2. The diode detector rectifies the negative (or positive) alternance of the input signal to "strip off" the message signal information. This signal is then filtered and usually ac coupled to the audio amplifier thus reproducing the original message signal.

3. The 0.6 V drop represents a loss of power and therefore limits the ability of an envelope detector to demodulate weak signals especially when there is no AGC circuit.

4. The AGC circuit helps maintain a constant signal level by controlling the gain of the RF and / or IF stages. Therefore, demodulation is much easier because the AGC provides feedback based on the level of the demodulated signal.

5. The SYNC detector provides better results because it does not consume much of the input signal power and it provides some gain for the output signal. When this is combined with an AGC circuit, large RF signal variations and a modulation index approaching 1 are possible with less distortion in the output. This is not the case for an envelope detector.

EXERCISE 4-1

1.

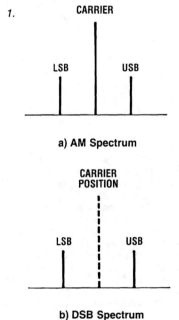

a) AM Spectrum

b) DSB Spectrum

The main difference is shown in (b) above; the carrier is absent in the spectrum of a DSB signal.

2. The major advantage is better power utilization since no RF power is "wasted" in the carrier. According to the definition given in Unit 2, this means that 100% transmission efficiency is obtained with a DSB signal. This is quite an improvement over the 33 1/3% maximum which is possible with an AM signal.

3. There is no advantage in bandwidth gained by using AM instead of DSB modulation, because DSB is mainly AM with the carrier power reduced to minimum. This does not change in any way the frequency spectrum behavior caused by varying the modulating signal frequency.

4. RF power is a DSB signal increases in a greater proportion because sideband power (which represents the message signal power) is the only power contained in the RF signal. In an AM signal, however, total sideband power can only be one-third of the RF power (with 100% modulation). Therefore, variations in the message signal amplitude in an AM signal do not have as much effect on the RF power.

5. Amount of carrier suppression.

EXERCISE 4-2

1. A COSTAS detector.

2. The waveform corresponds to the line traced through alternate lobes of the DSB signal.

3.

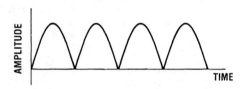

Waveform obtained using an envelope detector

4. The mixer output signal represents the error signal controlling the VCO frequency. Since the operation of a mixer in the time domain is mathematically equivalent to multiplication, the error signal is prevented from indicating a phase error which would cause the VCO frequency to change (see DISCUSSION). In this way carrier frequency synchronization is maintained.

5. The PLL synchronous detector causes the VCO frequency to change because the phase reversal of the carrier signal is interpreted as a phase error, thus producing an error signal causing the VCO frequency to change.

Answers to Review Questions

EXERCISE 5-1

1.

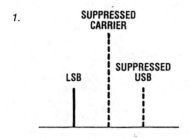

SSB Spectrum (LSB)

As shown in the figure, the carrier and one of the sidebands (USB) are suppressed. An AM signal contains a carrier component and both sidebands, while a DSB spectrum contains both sidebands with the carrier suppressed.

2. The two principal advantages are efficient power utilization (no carrier present) and economic bandwidth use (only one sideband is transmitted).

3. The filter method of generating SSB signals used in the Analog Communications Training System consists essentially in placing one of the message signal sidebands inside the passband of a fixed, narrow-bandwidth IF filter. This is accomplished by mixing the message signal with a BFO signal whose frequency is adjustable over a narrow range. The sideband which has been positioned outside the passband of the IF filter is greatly attenuated by the process, and the selected sideband within the passband is then frequency-translated by another mixing operation (with the VFO) up to the carrier frequency. The reproduced sideband, caused by the second mixing operation (see DISCUSSION), is then removed before transmission of the RF signal.

4. There is not necessarily a problem with the generator if the BFO has been misadjusted to position both sidebands within the passband of the IF filter. If this is not the case, either the IF filter is defective, or effective sideband selection is impossible because of a message signal bandwidth too small for the Beat Frequency Oscillator-IF filter combination to separate into two sidebands.

5. Since voice communications involve frequencies up to 3 kHz, the resulting SSB communications will produce a distorted audio signal on reception. This is because the IF filter bandwidth of 2 kHz is too narrow for the message signal bandwidth. A maximum 2-kHz bandwidth is possible if the message signal is centered in the passband of the IF filter.

EXERCISE 5-2

1. Since the message signal is a 2.5 kHz tone, the mixer output signal will contain two frequency components. One is at 460 kHz, the other at 455 kHz. Because the two components represent the LSB and the USB, reference to Figure 5-5 (c) shows that the LSB is being transmitted since the LSB has been pulled into the passband of the IF filter while the USB has been pushed outside.

2. The BFO frequency must be adjusted at 457.5 kHz (see Question 1).

3. Adjusting the receiver BFO (BFO-RX) at 452.5 kHz causes sideband reversal, since the spectral relationship set up at the transmitter is not conserved. High and low frequency content is interchanged and the demodulated audio signal will be unintelligible.

4. The frequency of the demodulated audio signal will increase.

5. The probable cause is misadjustment of the BFO at the receiver. Sideband reversal seems evident since the sounds from the drum and the violin are opposite to what they should be. When the BFO at the receiver is adjusted for LSB reception of a USB transmission (and vice versa), the result is sideband reversal.

EXERCISE 6-1

1. Troubleshooting is the act of locating and diagnosing malfunctions or breakdowns in equipment by means of systematic checking or analysis.

2. 2, 7, 4, 1, 3, 6, 5 – Trace and analyze the signals along their from path from input to output (or the reverse) using proper test equipment.

3. It is a more difficult method to apply because extensive knowledge of equipment operating principles is necessary. Troubleshooting from output to input means that you must decide whether the output is correct based upon your theoretical knowledge and practical experience. This may be insufficient when working with unknown equipment. When troubleshooting from input to output, you begin with a known signal and you check whether or not the following signal is a correctly transformed version of this known signal.

4. The principal advantage is that a x 10 probe provides 10 times less capacitive loading on the equipment. This may be a significant factor for some RF circuits.

5. The two fundamental rules are: first, observe the symptoms of the problem, and second, relate the problem to specific functional blocks.

Module Front Panels

Module Front Panels

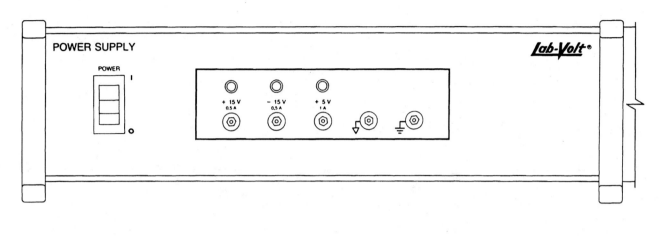

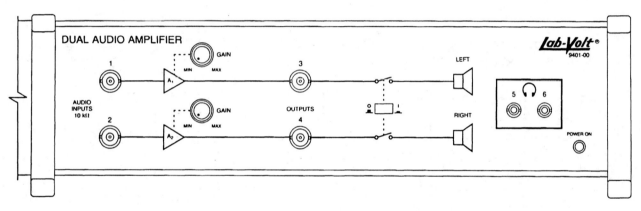

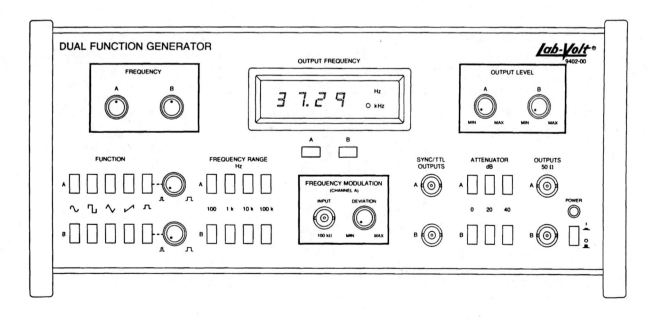

Module Front Panels

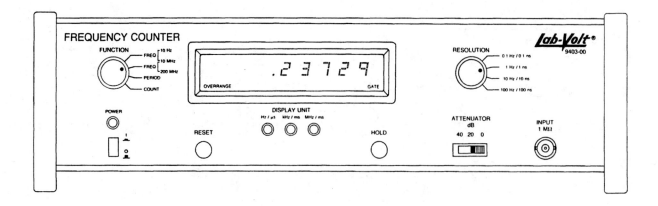

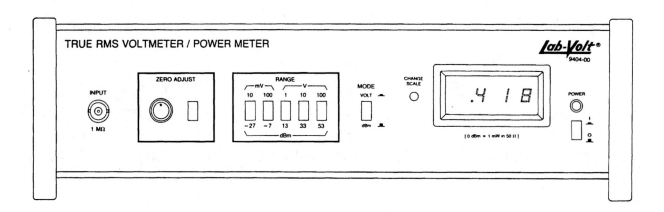

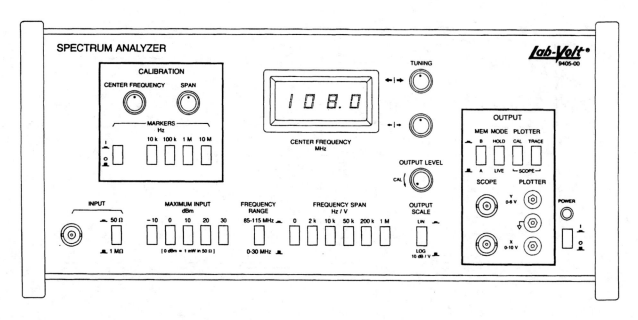

Module Front Panels

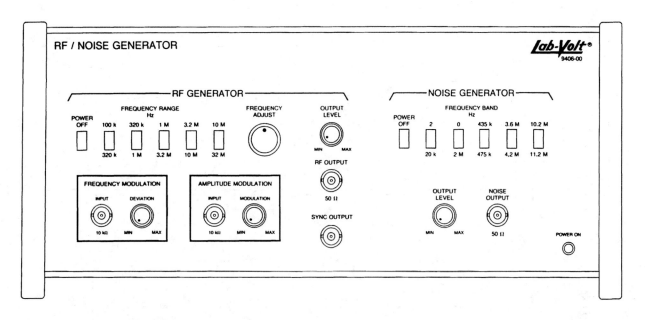

RF / NOISE GENERATOR

Lab-Volt®
9406-00

RF GENERATOR

NOISE GENERATOR

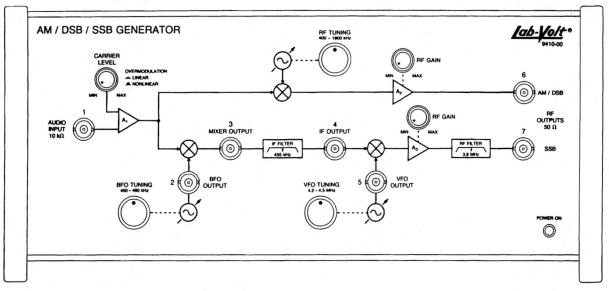

AM / DSB / SSB GENERATOR

Lab-Volt®
9410-00

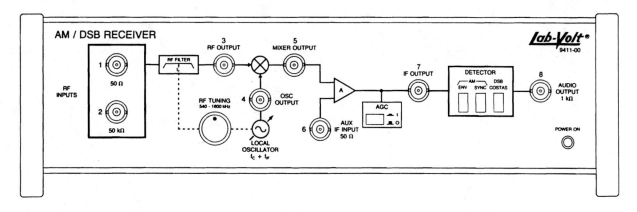

AM / DSB RECEIVER

Lab-Volt®
9411-00

Module Front Panels

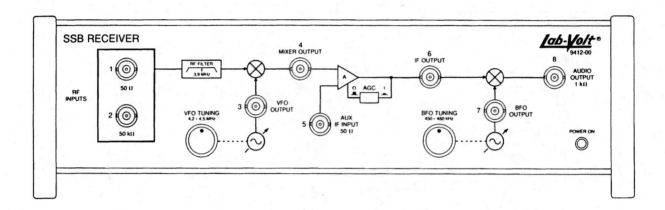

Test Points and Diagrams

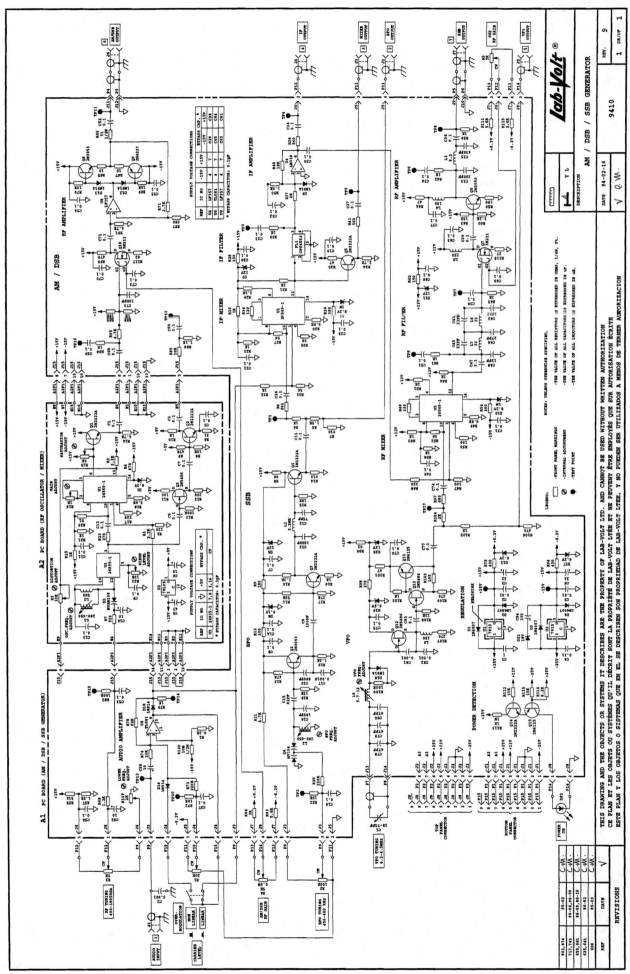

D-2

Test Points and Diagrams

TEST POINT	DESCRIPTION
TP1	BFO Output
TP2	BFO Tuning Control (dc voltage)
TP3	SSB IF Filter Output
TP4	SSB IF Output
TP5	SSB IF Mixer Output
TP6	SSB RF Amplifier Output from the SSB Generator (before output filter)
TP7	SSB RF Filter output
TP8	SSB RF Output
TP9	SSB RF Mixer Output
TP10	Carrier Level Control (dc voltage)
TP11	AM / DSB RF Output
TP12	Audio Input
TP13	VCO Square Wave (carrier frequency)
TP14	Audio Amplifier Output
TP15	RF Tuning Control (dc voltage)
TP16	AM / DSB RF Mixer Output
TP17	VFO Output

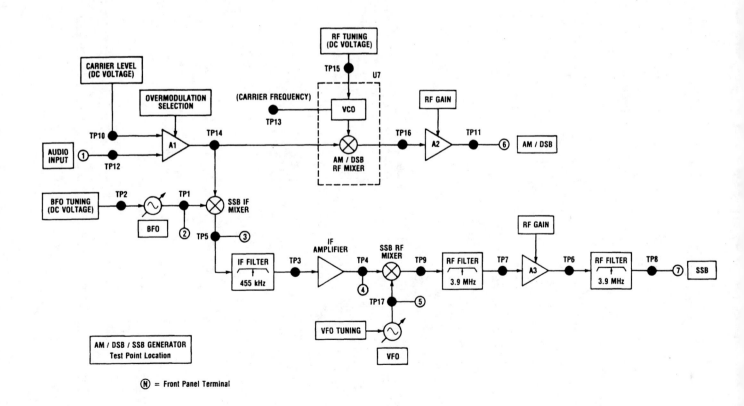

Test Point Locations – AM / DSB / SSB Generator.

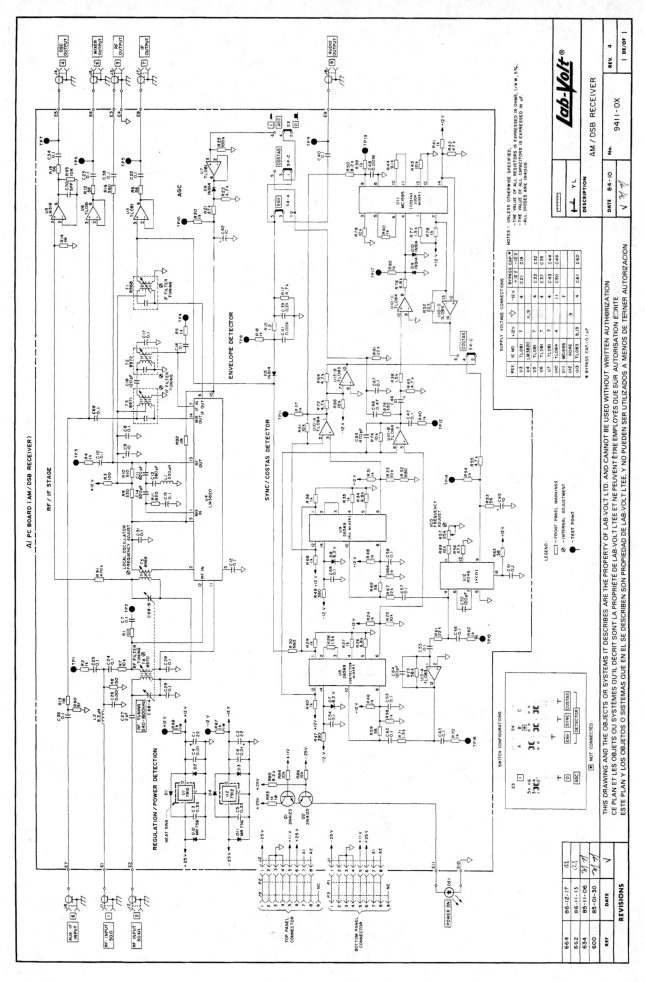

Test Points and Diagrams

TEST POINT	DESCRIPTION
TP1	50 Ω RF Input
TP2	RF Filter Output
TP3	RF Output
TP4	IF Filter Output
TP5	IF Output
TP6	RF Mixer Output
TP7	Local Oscillator Output
TP8	Envelope Detector Output (unfiltered)
TP9	Audio Output
TP10	DC Control Voltage from AGC
TP11	PLL Mixer Output
TP12	Detector Mixer Output (filtered)
TP13	PLL Mixer Output (filtered)
TP14	VCO Input
TP15	VCO Output
TP16	VCO Output (after phase shifter)
TP17	Output of Costas Loop Comparator

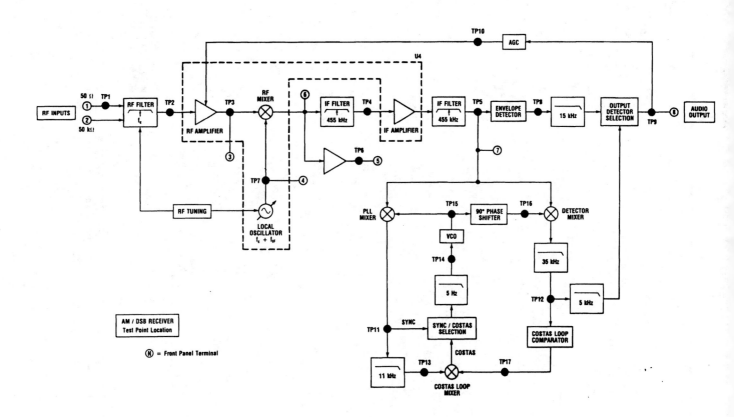

Test Point Locations – AM / DSB Receiver.

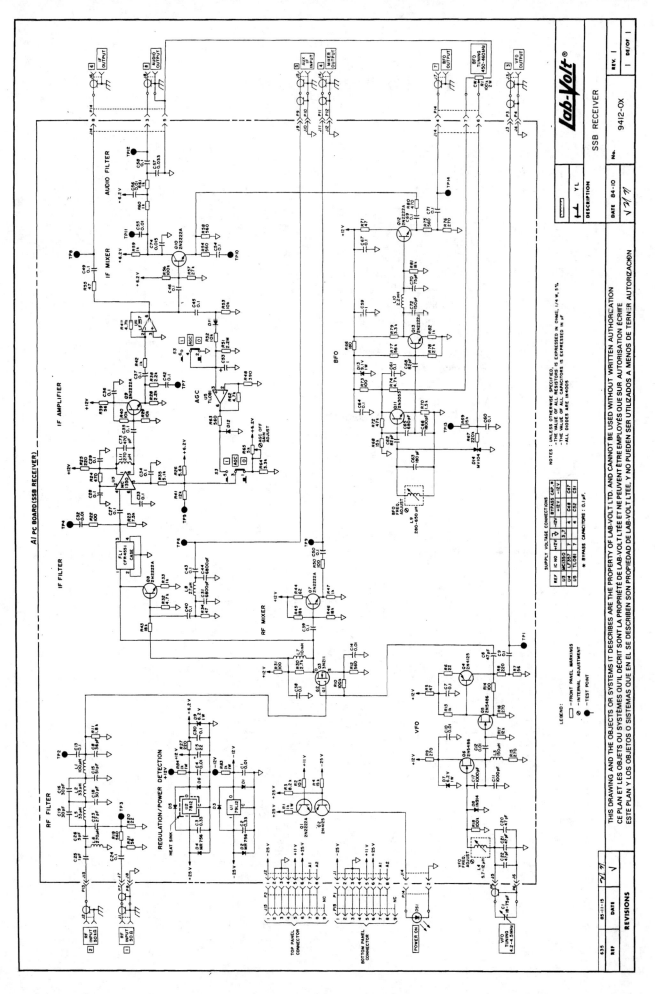

SSB RECEIVER

No. 9412-OX

REV. 1

D-6

Test Points and Diagrams

TEST POINT	DESCRIPTION
TP1	VFO Output
TP2	RF Filter Output
TP3	50 Ω RF Input
TP4	IF Filter Output
TP5	DC Control Voltage from AGC
TP6	Auxiliary IF Input
TP7	IF Signal after First IF Amplifier Stage
TP8	IF Output
TP9	RF Mixer Output
TP10	Emitter of IF Mixer Transistor
TP11	IF Mixer Output
TP12	Audio Output
TP13	BFO Tuning Control (dc voltage)
TP14	BFO Output

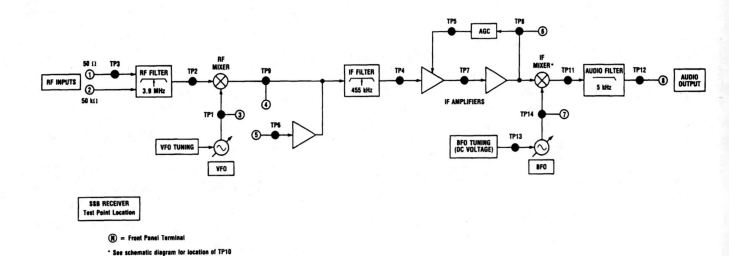

Test Point Locations – SSB Receiver.

TROUBLESHOOTING WORKSHEET – AM / DSB / SSB

Type of Communications   : ☐ AM   ☐ DSB   ☐ SSB

Problem With   : ☐ Transmitter   ☐ Receiver

Name of Module   : _____

Fault Number* (or description)   : _____

Fault Activated By   : _____

Student's Name   : _____

Steps Completed in Troubleshooting Sequence (See Exercise 6-1):

☐ 1   ☐ 2   ☐ 3   ☐ 4   ☐ 5   ☐ 6   ☐ 7

Problem Description and Symptoms †:_____

_____

_____

_____

_____

_____

_____

_____

_____

Defective Functional Block: _____

Instructor's Comments: _____

_____

_____

_____

_____

Notes: _____

_____

_____

_____

*At instructor's discretion.
†Sketch waveforms and spectra on reverse side.

TROUBLESHOOTING WORKSHEET – AM / DSB / SSB WAVEFORMS AND SPECTRA

Notes: _____

_____

_____

Notes: _____

_____

_____

Notes: _____

_____

_____

Notes: _____

_____

_____

Notes: _____

_____

_____

Notes: _____

_____

_____

SET UP AND CALIBRATION OF THE 9405 SPECTRUM ANALYZER MODULE

SET UP AND CALIBRATION OF THE 9405 SPECTRUM ANALYZER MODULE

This procedure assumes the use of a two-channel, dual-trace oscilloscope. If a single-channel oscilloscope having an external sweep input (X-axis) is used, the sensitivity of the input must be 1 V / DIV in order to properly calibrate the Spectrum Analyzer. Also, a 20-30 minute equipment warm-up is suggested for the Spectrum Analyzer module to ensure accurate frequency calibration.

1. Connect the X and Y SCOPE outputs of the Spectrum Analyzer to the respective X and Y inputs on the oscilloscope.

2. Set the oscilloscope sensitivity controls for both channels at 1 V / DIV, and select the X-Y mode of operation.

3. Set the input coupling switches of the oscilloscope to the ground (GND) position, and then use the horizontal and vertical position controls to place the luminous spot at the position shown in Figure E-1.

   Note: *Adjust the oscilloscope's intensity control at a low level, and* **do not leave the luminous spot stationary for long periods of time** *or oscilloscope damage may occur.*

4. Set the input coupling switches for both oscilloscope channels to the DC position. Disconnect any signal that may be connected to the INPUT of the Spectrum Analyzer, and set the Spectrum Analyzer controls to the following positions:

MARKERS	: O
INPUT*	: 50 Ω
MAXIMUM INPUT*	: 0 dBm
FREQUENCY RANGE	: 0-30 MHz or 85-115 MHz
FREQUENCY SPAN	: 1 MHz / V
OUTPUT SCALE	: LOG
OUTPUT LEVEL	: CAL
MEMory*	: A
MODE	: LIVE
PLOTTER	: SCOPE (both switches)

   * Although the suggested setting should be used, this control has no effect on calibration.

5. Use the TUNING controls on the Spectrum Analyzer to locate the 0 Hz (or 85 MHz, for the 85-115 MHz FREQUENCY RANGE) reference line, and position it in the center of the screen. Adjust the intensity and focus controls on the oscilloscope for a well-defined image.

6. Select successively the 200 kHz / V and the 50 kHz / V FREQUENCY SPANs, and readjust the TUNING controls to keep the reference line aligned with the center vertical line of the oscilloscope screen.

7. Adjust the CENTER FREQUENCY control of the CALIBRATION section to obtain 0.0, or 85.0, on the CENTER FREQUENCY display. The center vertical line of the oscilloscope screen now corresponds to the fixed reference point from where frequencies are measured. The Spectrum Analyzer is now sufficiently calibrated for general spectral observations. **If accurate frequency analysis is to be performed, however, continue with the remaining steps in the procedure.**

8. For accurate frequency calibration, the TUNING controls are turned until the CENTER FREQUENCY display indicates the approximate frequency of the INPUT signal to be analyzed. For example, analysis of an AM station at 1520 kHz, using the 10 kHz / V FREQUENCY SPAN, requires that you adjust the TUNING until 1.5 MHz is displayed. The SPAN control of the CALIBRATION section is then used to calibrate the Spectrum Analyzer on the 10 kHz / V FREQUENCY SPAN. For an FM station at 91.6 MHz, adjust until 91.6 MHz is displayed, and then choose the appropriate FREQUENCY SPAN-MARKERS combination (see step 13).

9. Adjust the TUNING controls so that the CENTER FREQUENCY display reads the approximate INPUT signal frequency, and then select the 10 kHz / V FREQUENCY SPAN.

10. Select the 10 kHz MARKERS and place the MARKERS-generator switch of the CALIBRATION section in the on (I) position. Adjust the SPAN and TUN-ING controls so that the 10 kHz MARKERS coincide, as closely as possible, with the vertical graticule lines on the oscilloscope screen.

11. The Spectrum Analyzer is now calibrated on the 10 kHz / V FREQUENCY SPAN to give correct results around the frequency to which it has been set. If other FREQUENCY SPANs are to be used, re-calibration using the appropriate MARKERS must be performed at the selected frequency.

    Note: *For approximate results, calibration at the input signal frequency, using the 100 kHz MARKERS on the 50 kHz / V FREQUENCY SPAN, is sufficient. Note that alignment of the MARKERS with the vertical graticule lines on both sides of the center reference line is not always possible, especially on the 1 MHz / V FREQUENCY SPAN. This depends on the CENTER FREQUENCY-FREQUENCY SPAN-MARKERS combination. In such cases, align only the MARKERS which lie to the right of the center reference line. In any event, the MARKERS displayed on the oscilloscope screen represent precise frequencies, independently of their horizontal spacing, because they are derived from a crystal oscillator.*

12. It is not necessary to calibrate each FREQUENCY SPAN in sequence. For example, if analysis of a 950-kHz signal is to be performed using the 2 kHz / V FREQUENCY SPAN, turn the TUNING controls until you read 1.0 on the calibrated CENTER FREQUENCY display and then calibrate the 2 kHz / V FREQUENCY SPAN using the 10 kHz MARKERS.

13. For calibration on other FREQUENCY SPANs, tune the Spectrum Analyzer to read the approximate frequency of the signal to be analyzed, and select the FREQUENCY SPAN to be used. Select the appropriate MARKERS according to the following table:

FREQUENCY SPAN	MARKERS
1 MHz / V	1 MHz or 10 MHz
200 kHz / V	100 kHz
50 kHz / V	100 kHz
10 kHz / V	10 kHz
2 kHz / V	10 kHz

14. Once calibration is completed, place the MARKERS-generator switch in the off (O) position.

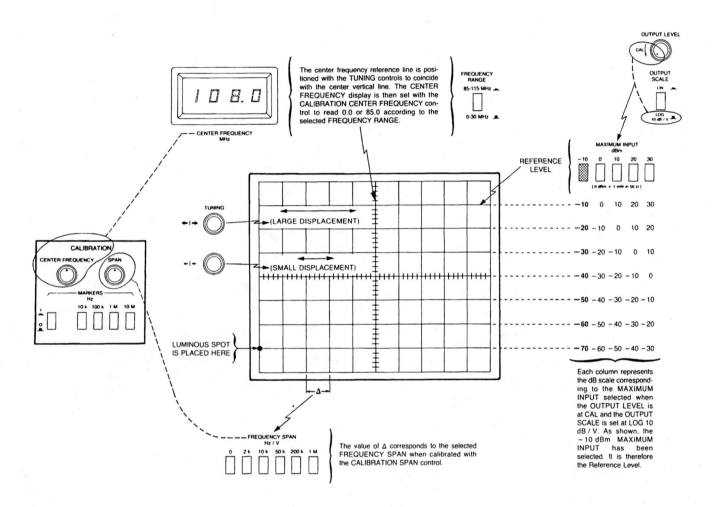

Figure E-1. Spectrum Analyzer controls and definitions.

Equipment Utilization Chart

The following Lab-Volt equipment is required to perform the exercises in this manual:

ANALOG COMMUNICATIONS TRAINING SYSTEM EQUIPMENT

MODEL	DESCRIPTION	LABORATORY EXERCISE																				
		1-1	1-2	1-3	2-1	2-2	2-3	3-1	3-2	3-3	3-4	4-1	4-2	5-1	5-2	6-1	6-2	6-3	6-4	6-5	6-6	6-7
8948	Connection Cables and Accessories	1	1	1	1	1	1	1	1	1	1	1	1	1	1	1	1	1	1	1	1	1
9401	Power Supply / Dual Audio Amplifier	1	1	1	1	1	1	1	1	1	1	1	1	1	1	1	1	1	1	1	1	1
9402	Dual Function Generator	1	1	1	1	1	1		1	1	1	1	1	1	1	1	1	1	1	1	1	1
9403	Frequency Counter	1	1	1	1	1	1	1	1	1	1	1	1	1	1	1	1	1	1	1	1	1
9404	True RMS Voltmeter / Power Meter						1	1	1	1												
9405	Spectrum Analyzer		1	1	1	1	1	1	1	1	1	1		1		1	1	1	1	1	1	1
9406	RF / Noise Generator			1																		
9410	AM / DSB / SSB Generator	1	1	1	1	1	1	1	1	1	1	1	1	1	1	1	1	1	1	1	1	1
9411	AM / DSB Receiver	1	1	1				1	1	1	1	1	1						1		1	
9412	SSB Receiver														1					1		1

Bibliography

Kennedy, George, *Electronic Communication Systems*, Second Edition, New-York, McGraw-Hill Inc., 1977.

Malvino, Albert Paul, *Electronic Principles*, Second Edition, New-York, McGraw-Hill Inc., 1979.

Miller, Gary M., *Modern Electronic Communication*, Second Edition, Englewood Cliffs, New-Jersey, Prentice-Hall Inc., 1983.

Stremler, Ferrel G., *Introduction to Communication Systems*, Second Edition, Reading, Massachusetts, Addison-Wesley, 1982.

ANALOG COMMUNICATIONS –VOLUME 2
AM / DSB / SSB
26867-00
Second Edition: October 1986
Printed: November 2004

We Value Your Opinion!

Please take a few minutes to complete this questionnaire. Your answers and comments will enable us to produce better manuals. Return it to the address on the reverse side of this page or ask your instructor to forward it.

How long are the exercises?

☐ Too long ☐ Adequate ☐ Too short

Do the Discussions cover enough information?

☐ Too little ☐ Acceptable ☐ Too much

How easy to follow are the Procedures?

☐ Too difficult ☐ Adequate ☐ Very easy

How useful is the Procedure Summary?

☐ Of little use ☐ Useful ☐ Very useful

How many hours were required per exercise?

☐ 1 ☐ 2 ☐ 3 or more

PUBLICATION ERRORS AND COMMENTS

Please enclose photocopies of pages where errors were found and indicate the modifications that should be carried out.

If you want to receive the corrected pages, please fill in the identification section.

BACKGROUND INFORMATION

☐ Instructor ☐ Student

☐ High School ☐ Vocational ☐ Technical Institute ☐ University

IDENTIFICATION

NAME _____

ADDRESS _____

_____

PHONE _____ FAX _____